# BigNum Math

Implementing Cryptographic Multiple Precision Arithmetic

Tom St Denis
LibTom Projects

Greg Rose
QUALCOMM Australia

| KEY | SERIAL NUMBER |
| --- | --- |
| 001 | HJIRTCV764 |
| 002 | PO9873D5FG |
| 003 | 829KM8NJH2 |
| 004 | HJ9899923N |
| 005 | CVPLQ6WQ23 |
| 006 | VBP965T5T5 |
| 007 | HJJJ863WD3E |
| 008 | 2987GVTWMK |
| 009 | 629MP5SDJT |
| 010 | IMWQ295T6T |

PUBLISHED BY Syngress Publishing, Inc.
800 Hingham Street
Rockland, MA 02370

BigNum Math: Implementing Cryptographic Multiple Precision Arithmetic

ISBN: 1597491128

Publisher: Andrew Williams          Page Layout and Art: Tom St Denis
Copy Editor: Beth Roberts           Cover Designer: Michael Kavish

Distributed by O'Reilly Media, Inc. in the United States and Canada.

For information on rights, translations, and bulk sales, contact Matt Pedersen, Director
of Sales and Rights, at Syngress Publishing; email matt@syngress.com or fax to
781-681-3585.

Transferred to Digital Printing 2009

# Contents

**Preface**     **xv**

**1 Introduction**     **1**

  1.1   Multiple Precision Arithmetic . . . . . . . . . . . . . . . . . . . . 1

      1.1.1   What Is Multiple Precision Arithmetic? . . . . . . . . . . 1

      1.1.2   The Need for Multiple Precision Arithmetic . . . . . . . . 2

      1.1.3   Benefits of Multiple Precision Arithmetic . . . . . . . . 3

  1.2   Purpose of This Text . . . . . . . . . . . . . . . . . . . . . . . 4

  1.3   Discussion and Notation . . . . . . . . . . . . . . . . . . . . . 5

      1.3.1   Notation . . . . . . . . . . . . . . . . . . . . . . . . . . 5

      1.3.2   Precision Notation . . . . . . . . . . . . . . . . . . . . . 5

      1.3.3   Algorithm Inputs and Outputs . . . . . . . . . . . . . . 6

      1.3.4   Mathematical Expressions . . . . . . . . . . . . . . . . 6

      1.3.5   Work Effort . . . . . . . . . . . . . . . . . . . . . . . . 7

  1.4   Exercises . . . . . . . . . . . . . . . . . . . . . . . . . . . . . 7

  1.5   Introduction to LibTomMath . . . . . . . . . . . . . . . . . . 9

      1.5.1   What Is LibTomMath? . . . . . . . . . . . . . . . . . . 9

      1.5.2   Goals of LibTomMath . . . . . . . . . . . . . . . . . . 9

  1.6   Choice of LibTomMath . . . . . . . . . . . . . . . . . . . . . 10

      1.6.1   Code Base . . . . . . . . . . . . . . . . . . . . . . . . . 10

      1.6.2   API Simplicity . . . . . . . . . . . . . . . . . . . . . . 11

      1.6.3   Optimizations . . . . . . . . . . . . . . . . . . . . . . . 11

      1.6.4   Portability and Stability . . . . . . . . . . . . . . . . . 12

      1.6.5   Choice . . . . . . . . . . . . . . . . . . . . . . . . . . . 12

**2  Getting Started**                                                    **13**

2.1  Library Basics . . . . . . . . . . . . . . . . . .   13

2.2  What Is a Multiple Precision Integer? . . . . . . . . . . . . . .   14

    2.2.1  The mp_int Structure . . . . . . . . . .   15

2.3  Argument Passing . . . . . . . . . . . . . . . . .   17

2.4  Return Values . . . . . . . . . . . . . . . . . . .   18

2.5  Initialization and Clearing . . . . . . . . . . . . . . .   19

    2.5.1  Initializing an mp_int . . . . . . . . . . . . . .   19

    2.5.2  Clearing an mp_int . . . . . . . . . . . . . .   22

2.6  Maintenance Algorithms . . . . . . . . . . . . . .   24

    2.6.1  Augmenting an mp_int's Precision . . . . . .   24

    2.6.2  Initializing Variable Precision mp_ints . . . . . .   27

    2.6.3  Multiple Integer Initializations and Clearings . . . . . .   29

    2.6.4  Clamping Excess Digits . . . . . . . . . .   31

**3  Basic Operations**                                                   **35**

3.1  Introduction . . . . . . . . . . . . . . . . . . . .   35

3.2  Assigning Values to mp_int Structures . . . . . . . . . . .   35

    3.2.1  Copying an mp_int . . . . . . . . . . . . . .   35

    3.2.2  Creating a Clone . . . . . . . . . . . . . .   39

3.3  Zeroing an Integer . . . . . . . . . . . . . . . . .   41

3.4  Sign Manipulation . . . . . . . . . . . . . . . . .   42

    3.4.1  Absolute Value . . . . . . . . . . . . . .   42

    3.4.2  Integer Negation . . . . . . . . . . . . . .   43

3.5  Small Constants . . . . . . . . . . . . . . . . . .   44

    3.5.1  Setting Small Constants . . . . . . . . . . . .   44

    3.5.2  Setting Large Constants . . . . . . . . . . . .   46

3.6  Comparisons . . . . . . . . . . . . . . . . . . . .   47

    3.6.1  Unsigned Comparisons . . . . . . . . . . . .   47

    3.6.2  Signed Comparisons . . . . . . . . . . . . . .   50

**4  Basic Arithmetic**                                                   **53**

4.1  Introduction . . . . . . . . . . . . . . . . . . . .   53

4.2  Addition and Subtraction . . . . . . . . . . . . . .   54

    4.2.1  Low Level Addition . . . . . . . . . . . . . .   54

    4.2.2  Low Level Subtraction . . . . . . . . . . . .   59

    4.2.3  High Level Addition . . . . . . . . . . . . . .   63

    4.2.4  High Level Subtraction . . . . . . . . . . . .   66

|       | 4.3   | Bit and Digit Shifting | 69  |
|       | 4.3.1 | Multiplication by Two | 69  |
|       | 4.3.2 | Division by Two | 72  |
|       | 4.4   | Polynomial Basis Operations | 75  |
|       | 4.4.1 | Multiplication by $x$ | 75  |
|       | 4.4.2 | Division by $x$ | 78  |
|       | 4.5   | Powers of Two | 81  |
|       | 4.5.1 | Multiplication by Power of Two | 82  |
|       | 4.5.2 | Division by Power of Two | 85  |
|       | 4.5.3 | Remainder of Division by Power of Two | 88  |

**5  Multiplication and Squaring** — **91**

|   | 5.1 | The Multipliers | 91 |
|   | 5.2 | Multiplication | 92 |
|   | 5.2.1 | The Baseline Multiplication | 92 |
|   | 5.2.2 | Faster Multiplication by the "Comba" Method | 97 |
|   | 5.2.3 | Even Faster Multiplication | 104 |
|   | 5.2.4 | Polynomial Basis Multiplication | 107 |
|   | 5.2.5 | Karatsuba Multiplication | 109 |
|   | 5.2.6 | Toom-Cook 3-Way Multiplication | 116 |
|   | 5.2.7 | Signed Multiplication | 126 |
|   | 5.3 | Squaring | 128 |
|   | 5.3.1 | The Baseline Squaring Algorithm | 129 |
|   | 5.3.2 | Faster Squaring by the "Comba" Method | 133 |
|   | 5.3.3 | Even Faster Squaring | 137 |
|   | 5.3.4 | Polynomial Basis Squaring | 138 |
|   | 5.3.5 | Karatsuba Squaring | 138 |
|   | 5.3.6 | Toom-Cook Squaring | 143 |
|   | 5.3.7 | High Level Squaring | 144 |

**6  Modular Reduction** — **147**

|   | 6.1 | Basics of Modular Reduction | 147 |
|   | 6.2 | The Barrett Reduction | 148 |
|   | 6.2.1 | Fixed Point Arithmetic | 148 |
|   | 6.2.2 | Choosing a Radix Point | 150 |
|   | 6.2.3 | Trimming the Quotient | 151 |
|   | 6.2.4 | Trimming the Residue | 152 |
|   | 6.2.5 | The Barrett Algorithm | 153 |

|  | 6.2.6 | The Barrett Setup Algorithm | 156 |
| 6.3 | | The Montgomery Reduction | 158 |
|  | 6.3.1 | Digit Based Montgomery Reduction | 160 |
|  | 6.3.2 | Baseline Montgomery Reduction | 162 |
|  | 6.3.3 | Faster "Comba" Montgomery Reduction | 167 |
|  | 6.3.4 | Montgomery Setup | 173 |
| 6.4 | | The Diminished Radix Algorithm | 175 |
|  | 6.4.1 | Choice of Moduli | 177 |
|  | 6.4.2 | Choice of $k$ | 178 |
|  | 6.4.3 | Restricted Diminished Radix Reduction | 178 |
|  | 6.4.4 | Unrestricted Diminished Radix Reduction | 184 |
| 6.5 | | Algorithm Comparison | 189 |

**7 Exponentiation** — **191**

| 7.1 | | Exponentiation Basics | 191 |
|  | 7.1.1 | Single Digit Exponentiation | 193 |
| 7.2 | | $k$-ary Exponentiation | 195 |
|  | 7.2.1 | Optimal Values of $k$ | 196 |
|  | 7.2.2 | Sliding Window Exponentiation | 197 |
| 7.3 | | Modular Exponentiation | 198 |
|  | 7.3.1 | Barrett Modular Exponentiation | 203 |
| 7.4 | | Quick Power of Two | 214 |

**8 Higher Level Algorithms** — **217**

| 8.1 | | Integer Division with Remainder | 217 |
|  | 8.1.1 | Quotient Estimation | 219 |
|  | 8.1.2 | Normalized Integers | 220 |
|  | 8.1.3 | Radix-$\beta$ Division with Remainder | 221 |
| 8.2 | | Single Digit Helpers | 231 |
|  | 8.2.1 | Single Digit Addition and Subtraction | 232 |
|  | 8.2.2 | Single Digit Multiplication | 235 |
|  | 8.2.3 | Single Digit Division | 237 |
|  | 8.2.4 | Single Digit Root Extraction | 241 |
| 8.3 | | Random Number Generation | 245 |
| 8.4 | | Formatted Representations | 247 |
|  | 8.4.1 | Reading Radix-n Input | 247 |
|  | 8.4.2 | Generating Radix-$n$ Output | 252 |

**9  Number Theoretic Algorithms**                                      **255**
   9.1   Greatest Common Divisor . . . . . . . . . . . . . . . . . . 255
         9.1.1   Complete Greatest Common Divisor . . . . . . . . . . . 258
   9.2   Least Common Multiple . . . . . . . . . . . . . . . . . . . 263
   9.3   Jacobi Symbol Computation . . . . . . . . . . . . . . . . 265
         9.3.1   Jacobi Symbol . . . . . . . . . . . . . . . . . . . 266
   9.4   Modular Inverse . . . . . . . . . . . . . . . . . . . . . . 271
         9.4.1   General Case . . . . . . . . . . . . . . . . . . . . 273
   9.5   Primality Tests . . . . . . . . . . . . . . . . . . . . . . . 279
         9.5.1   Trial Division . . . . . . . . . . . . . . . . . . . . 279
         9.5.2   The Fermat Test . . . . . . . . . . . . . . . . . . 282
         9.5.3   The Miller-Rabin Test . . . . . . . . . . . . . . . . 284

**Bibliography**                                                        **289**

**Index**                                                              **291**

# List of Figures

1.1  Typical Data Types for the C Programming Language . . . . . . .  2
1.2  Exercise Scoring System . . . . . . . . . . . . . . . . . . . . . .  8

2.1  Design Flow of the First Few Original LibTomMath Functions. . .  14
2.2  The mp_int Structure . . . . . . . . . . . . . . . . . . . . . . .  16
2.3  LibTomMath Error Codes . . . . . . . . . . . . . . . . . . . . .  18
2.4  Algorithm mp_init . . . . . . . . . . . . . . . . . . . . . . . .  20
2.5  Algorithm mp_clear . . . . . . . . . . . . . . . . . . . . . . . .  22
2.6  Algorithm mp_grow . . . . . . . . . . . . . . . . . . . . . . . .  25
2.7  Algorithm mp_init_size . . . . . . . . . . . . . . . . . . . . . .  27
2.8  Algorithm mp_init_multi . . . . . . . . . . . . . . . . . . . . .  29
2.9  Algorithm mp_clamp . . . . . . . . . . . . . . . . . . . . . . .  31

3.1  Algorithm mp_copy . . . . . . . . . . . . . . . . . . . . . . . .  36
3.2  Algorithm mp_init_copy . . . . . . . . . . . . . . . . . . . . .  40
3.3  Algorithm mp_zero . . . . . . . . . . . . . . . . . . . . . . . .  41
3.4  Algorithm mp_abs . . . . . . . . . . . . . . . . . . . . . . . . .  42
3.5  Algorithm mp_neg . . . . . . . . . . . . . . . . . . . . . . . . .  43
3.6  Algorithm mp_set . . . . . . . . . . . . . . . . . . . . . . . . .  45
3.7  Algorithm mp_set_int . . . . . . . . . . . . . . . . . . . . . . .  46
3.8  Comparison Return Codes . . . . . . . . . . . . . . . . . . . . .  48
3.9  Algorithm mp_cmp_mag . . . . . . . . . . . . . . . . . . . . .  48
3.10 Algorithm mp_cmp . . . . . . . . . . . . . . . . . . . . . . . .  50

4.1  Algorithm s_mp_add . . . . . . . . . . . . . . . . . . . . . . .  55
4.2  Algorithm s_mp_sub . . . . . . . . . . . . . . . . . . . . . . .  60
4.3  Algorithm mp_add . . . . . . . . . . . . . . . . . . . . . . . .  64

4.4    Addition Guide Chart . . . . . . . . . . . . . . . . . . . . . . . .    65
4.5    Algorithm mp_sub . . . . . . . . . . . . . . . . . . . . . . . . . .    67
4.6    Subtraction Guide Chart . . . . . . . . . . . . . . . . . . . . . .    67
4.7    Algorithm mp_mul_2 . . . . . . . . . . . . . . . . . . . . . . . .    70
4.8    Algorithm mp_div_2 . . . . . . . . . . . . . . . . . . . . . . . .    73
4.9    Algorithm mp_lshd . . . . . . . . . . . . . . . . . . . . . . . . .    76
4.10   Sliding Window Movement . . . . . . . . . . . . . . . . . . . . .    77
4.11   Algorithm mp_rshd . . . . . . . . . . . . . . . . . . . . . . . . .    79
4.12   Algorithm mp_mul_2d . . . . . . . . . . . . . . . . . . . . . . .    82
4.13   Algorithm mp_div_2d . . . . . . . . . . . . . . . . . . . . . . .    85
4.14   Algorithm mp_mod_2d . . . . . . . . . . . . . . . . . . . . . . .    88

5.1    Algorithm s_mp_mul_digs . . . . . . . . . . . . . . . . . . . . .    93
5.2    Long-Hand Multiplication Diagram . . . . . . . . . . . . . . . .    94
5.3    Comba Multiplication Diagram . . . . . . . . . . . . . . . . . .    98
5.4    Algorithm Comba Fixup . . . . . . . . . . . . . . . . . . . . . .    98
5.5    Algorithm fast_s_mp_mul_digs . . . . . . . . . . . . . . . . . .    100
5.6    Algorithm fast_mult . . . . . . . . . . . . . . . . . . . . . . . .    105
5.7    Asymptotic Running Time of Polynomial Basis Multiplication . . .    108
5.8    Algorithm mp_karatsuba_mul . . . . . . . . . . . . . . . . . . .    111
5.9    Algorithm mp_toom_mul . . . . . . . . . . . . . . . . . . . . . .    118
5.10   Algorithm mp_mul . . . . . . . . . . . . . . . . . . . . . . . . .    126
5.11   Squaring Optimization Diagram . . . . . . . . . . . . . . . . . .    128
5.12   Algorithm s_mp_sqr . . . . . . . . . . . . . . . . . . . . . . . .    130
5.13   Algorithm fast_s_mp_sqr . . . . . . . . . . . . . . . . . . . . .    134
5.14   Algorithm mp_karatsuba_sqr . . . . . . . . . . . . . . . . . . .    139
5.15   Algorithm mp_sqr . . . . . . . . . . . . . . . . . . . . . . . . .    144

6.1    Algorithm mp_reduce . . . . . . . . . . . . . . . . . . . . . . . .    153
6.2    Algorithm mp_reduce_setup . . . . . . . . . . . . . . . . . . . .    157
6.3    Algorithm Montgomery Reduction . . . . . . . . . . . . . . . . .    158
6.4    Example of Montgomery Reduction (I) . . . . . . . . . . . . . . .    159
6.5    Algorithm Montgomery Reduction (modified I) . . . . . . . . . .    159
6.6    Example of Montgomery Reduction (II) . . . . . . . . . . . . . .    160
6.7    Algorithm Montgomery Reduction (modified II) . . . . . . . . . .    161
6.8    Example of Montgomery Reduction . . . . . . . . . . . . . . . .    161
6.9    Algorithm mp_montgomery_reduce . . . . . . . . . . . . . . . .    163
6.10   Algorithm fast_mp_montgomery_reduce . . . . . . . . . . . . . .    168

6.11 Algorithm mp_montgomery_setup . . . . . . . . . . . . . . . 174
6.12 Algorithm Diminished Radix Reduction . . . . . . . . . . . . 176
6.13 Example Diminished Radix Reduction . . . . . . . . . . . . . 177
6.14 Algorithm mp_dr_reduce . . . . . . . . . . . . . . . . . . . . 179
6.15 Algorithm mp_dr_setup . . . . . . . . . . . . . . . . . . . . 182
6.16 Algorithm mp_dr_is_modulus . . . . . . . . . . . . . . . . . 183
6.17 Algorithm mp_reduce_2k . . . . . . . . . . . . . . . . . . . . 184
6.18 Algorithm mp_reduce_2k_setup . . . . . . . . . . . . . . . . 186
6.19 Algorithm mp_reduce_is_2k . . . . . . . . . . . . . . . . . . 188

7.1  Left to Right Exponentiation . . . . . . . . . . . . . . . . . 192
7.2  Example of Left to Right Exponentiation . . . . . . . . . . . 193
7.3  Algorithm mp_expt_d . . . . . . . . . . . . . . . . . . . . . 194
7.4  $k$-ary Exponentiation . . . . . . . . . . . . . . . . . . . . . 196
7.5  Optimal Values of $k$ for $k$-ary Exponentiation . . . . . . . . 197
7.6  Optimal Values of $k$ for Sliding Window Exponentiation . . . . . 197
7.7  Sliding Window $k$-ary Exponentiation . . . . . . . . . . . . . 198
7.8  Algorithm mp_exptmod . . . . . . . . . . . . . . . . . . . . 199
7.9  Algorithm s_mp_exptmod . . . . . . . . . . . . . . . . . . . 205
7.10 Sliding Window State Diagram . . . . . . . . . . . . . . . . 207
7.11 Algorithm mp_2expt . . . . . . . . . . . . . . . . . . . . . . 214

8.1  Algorithm Radix-$\beta$ Integer Division . . . . . . . . . . . . . . 218
8.2  Algorithm mp_div . . . . . . . . . . . . . . . . . . . . . . . 223
8.3  Algorithm mp_add_d . . . . . . . . . . . . . . . . . . . . . . 232
8.4  Algorithm mp_mul_d . . . . . . . . . . . . . . . . . . . . . . 235
8.5  Algorithm mp_div_d . . . . . . . . . . . . . . . . . . . . . . 238
8.6  Algorithm mp_n_root . . . . . . . . . . . . . . . . . . . . . . 242
8.7  Algorithm mp_rand . . . . . . . . . . . . . . . . . . . . . . . 246
8.8  Lower ASCII Map . . . . . . . . . . . . . . . . . . . . . . . 248
8.9  Algorithm mp_read_radix . . . . . . . . . . . . . . . . . . . 249
8.10 Algorithm mp_toradix . . . . . . . . . . . . . . . . . . . . . 252
8.11 Example of Algorithm mp_toradix. . . . . . . . . . . . . . . 253

9.1  Algorithm Greatest Common Divisor (I) . . . . . . . . . . . 256
9.2  Algorithm Greatest Common Divisor (II) . . . . . . . . . . . 256
9.3  Algorithm Greatest Common Divisor (III) . . . . . . . . . . 257
9.4  Algorithm mp_gcd . . . . . . . . . . . . . . . . . . . . . . . 259

9.5    Algorithm mp_lcm . . . . . . . . . . . . . . . . . . . . . . . 263
9.6    Algorithm mp_jacobi . . . . . . . . . . . . . . . . . . . . . . 268
9.7    Algorithm mp_invmod . . . . . . . . . . . . . . . . . . . . . 274
9.8    Algorithm mp_prime_is_divisible . . . . . . . . . . . . . . . . 280
9.9    Algorithm mp_prime_fermat . . . . . . . . . . . . . . . . . . 283
9.10  Algorithm mp_prime_miller_rabin . . . . . . . . . . . . . . . 285

# Preface

The origins of this book are part of an interesting period of my life. A period that saw me move from a shy and disorganized young adult, into a software developer who has toured various parts of the world, and met countless new friends and colleagues. It all began in December of 2001, nearly five years ago. I started a project that would later become known as LibTomCrypt, and be used by developers throughout industry worldwide.

The LibTomCrypt project was originally started as a way to focus my energies on to something constructive, while also learning new skills. The first year of the project taught me quite a bit about how to organize a product, document and support it and maintain it over time. Around the winter of 2002 I was seeking another project to spread my time with. Realizing that the math performance of LibTomCrypt was lacking, I set out to develop a new math library.

Hence, the LibTomMath project was born. It was originally merely a set of patches against an existing project that quickly grew into a project of its own. Writing the math library from scratch was fundamental to producing a stable and independent product. It also taught me what sort of algorithms are available to do operations such as modular exponentiation. The library became fairly stable and reliable after only a couple of months of development and was immediately put to use.

In the summer of 2003, I was yet again looking for another project to grow into. Realizing that merely implementing the math routines is not enough to truly understand them, I set out to try and explain them myself. In doing so, I eventually mastered the concepts behind the algorithms. This knowledge is what I hope will be passed on to the reader. This text is actually derived from the public domain archives I maintain on my www.libtomcrypt.com Web site.

When I tell people about my LibTom projects (of which there are six) and that I release them as public domain, they are often puzzled. They ask why I did it, and especially why I continue to work on them for free. The best I can explain it is, "Because I can"–which seems odd and perhaps too terse for adult conversation. I often qualify it with "I am able, I am willing," which perhaps explains it better. I am the first to admit there is nothing that special with what I have done. Perhaps others can see that, too, and then we would have a society to be proud of. My LibTom projects are what I am doing to give back to society in the form of tools and knowledge that can help others in their endeavors.

I started writing this book because it was the most logical task to further my goal of open academia. The LibTomMath source code itself was written to be easy to follow and learn from. There are times, however, where pure C source code does not explain the algorithms properly–hence this book. The book literally starts with the foundation of the library and works itself outward to the more complicated algorithms. The use of both pseudo–code and verbatim source code provides a duality of "theory" and "practice" the computer science students of the world shall appreciate. I never deviate too far from relatively straightforward algebra, and I hope this book can be a valuable learning asset.

This book, and indeed much of the LibTom projects, would not exist in its current form if it were not for a plethora of kind people donating their time, resources, and kind words to help support my work. Writing a text of significant length (along with the source code) is a tiresome and lengthy process. Currently, the LibTom project is five years old, composed of literally thousands of users and over 100,000 lines of source code, TEX, and other material. People like Mads Rassmussen and Greg Rose were there at the beginning to encourage me to work well. It is amazing how timely validation from others can boost morale to continue the project. Definitely, my parents were there for me by providing room and board during the many months of work in 2003.

Both Greg and Mads were invaluable sources of support in the early stages of this project. The initial draft of this text, released in August 2003, was the project of several months of dedicated work. Long hours and still going to school were a constant drain of energy that would not have lasted without support.

Of course this book would not be here if it were not for the success of the various LibTom projects. That success is not only the product of my hard work, but also the contribution of hundreds of other people. People like Colin Percival, Sky Schultz, Wayne Scott, J Harper, Dan Kaminsky, Lance James, Simon Johnson, Greg Rose, Clay Culver, Jochen Katz, Zhi Chen, Zed Shaw, Andrew Mann, Matt Johnston, Steven Dake, Richard Amacker, Stefan Arentz, Richard Outerbridge, Martin Carpenter, Craig Schlenter, John Kuhns, Bruce Guenter, Adam Miller, Wesley Shields, John Dirk, Jean–Luc Cooke, Michael Heyman, Nelson Bolyard,

Jim Wigginton, Don Porter, Kevin Kenny, Peter LaDow, Neal Hamilton, David Hulton, Paul Schmidt, Wolfgang Ehrhardt, Johan Lindt, Henrik Goldman, Alex Polushin, Martin Marcel, Brian Gladman, Benjamin Goldberg, Tom Wu, and Pekka Riikonen took their time to contribute ideas, updates, fixes, or encouragement throughout the various project development phases. To my many friends whom I have met through the years, I thank you for the good times and the words of encouragement. I hope I honor your kind gestures with this project.

I'd like to thank the editing team at Syngress for poring over 300 pages of text and correcting it in the short span of a single week. I'd like to thank my friends whom I have not mentioned, who were always available for encouragement and a steady supply of fun. I'd like to thank my friends J Harper, Zed Shaw, and Simon Johnson for reviewing the text before submission. I'd like to thank Lance James of the Secure Science Corporation and the entire crew at Elliptic Semiconductor for sponsoring much of my later development time, for sending me to Toorcon, and introducing me to many of the people whom I know today.

Open Source. Open Academia. Open Minds.

Tom St Denis
Toronto, Canada
May 2006

It's all because I broke my leg. That just happened to be about the same time Tom asked for someone to review the section of the book about Karatsuba multiplication. I was laid up, alone and immobile, and thought, "Why not?" I vaguely knew what Karatsuba multiplication was, but not really, so I thought I could help, learn, and stop myself from watching daytime cable TV, all at once.

At the time of writing this, I've still not met Tom or Mads in meatspace. I've been following Tom's progress since his first splash on the sci.crypt Usenet newsgroup. I watched him go from a clueless newbie, to the cryptographic equivalent of a reformed smoker, to a real contributor to the field, over a period of about two years. I've been impressed with his obvious intelligence, and astounded by his productivity. Of course, he's young enough to be my own child, so he doesn't have my problems with staying awake.

When I reviewed that single section of the book, in its earliest form, I was very pleasantly surprised. So I decided to collaborate more fully, and at least review all of it, and perhaps write some bits, too. There's still a long way to go with it, and I have watched a number of close friends go through the mill of publication, so I think the way to go is longer than Tom thinks it is. Nevertheless, it's a good effort, and I'm pleased to be involved with it.

Greg Rose
Sydney, Australia
June 2003

# Chapter 1

# Introduction

## 1.1 Multiple Precision Arithmetic

### 1.1.1 What Is Multiple Precision Arithmetic?

When we think of long-hand arithmetic such as addition or multiplication, we rarely consider the fact that we instinctively raise or lower the precision of the numbers we are dealing with. For example, in decimal we almost immediately can reason that 7 times 6 is 42. However, 42 has two digits of precision as opposed to the one digit we started with. Further multiplications of say 3 result in a larger precision result 126. In these few examples we have multiple precisions for the numbers we are working with. Despite the various levels of precision, a single subset[1] of algorithms can be designed to accommodate them.

By way of comparison, a fixed or single precision operation would lose precision on various operations. For example, in the decimal system with fixed precision $6 \cdot 7 = 2$.

Essentially, at the heart of computer–based multiple precision arithmetic are the same long-hand algorithms taught in schools to manually add, subtract, multiply, and divide.

---

[1]With the occasional optimization.

## 1.1.2    The Need for Multiple Precision Arithmetic

The most prevalent need for multiple precision arithmetic, often referred to as "bignum" math, is within the implementation of public key cryptography algorithms. Algorithms such as RSA [10] and Diffie-Hellman [11] require integers of significant magnitude to resist known cryptanalytic attacks. For example, at the time of this writing a typical RSA modulus would be at least greater than $10^{309}$. However, modern programming languages such as ISO C [17] and Java [18] only provide intrinsic support for integers that are relatively small and single precision.

| Data Type | Range |
|-----------|-------|
| char | $-128\ldots127$ |
| short | $-32768\ldots32767$ |
| long | $-2147483648\ldots2147483647$ |
| long long | $-9223372036854775808\ldots9223372036854775807$ |

Figure 1.1: Typical Data Types for the C Programming Language

The largest data type guaranteed to be provided by the ISO C programming language[2] can only represent values up to $10^{19}$ as shown in Figure 1.1. On its own, the C language is insufficient to accommodate the magnitude required for the problem at hand. An RSA modulus of magnitude $10^{19}$ could be trivially factored[3] on the average desktop computer, rendering any protocol based on the algorithm insecure. Multiple precision algorithms solve this problem by extending the range of representable integers while using single precision data types.

Most advancements in fast multiple precision arithmetic stem from the need for faster and more efficient cryptographic primitives. Faster modular reduction and exponentiation algorithms such as Barrett's reduction algorithm, which have appeared in various cryptographic journals, can render algorithms such as RSA and Diffie-Hellman more efficient. In fact, several major companies such as RSA Security, Certicom, and Entrust have built entire product lines on the implementation and deployment of efficient algorithms.

However, cryptography is not the only field of study that can benefit from fast multiple precision integer routines. Another auxiliary use of multiple precision integers is high precision floating point data types. The basic IEEE [12] standard

---

[2] As per the ISO C standard. However, each compiler vendor is allowed to augment the precision as they see fit.

[3] A Pollard-Rho factoring would take only $2^{16}$ time.

floating point type is made up of an integer mantissa $q$, an exponent $e$, and a sign bit $s$. Numbers are given in the form $n = q \cdot b^e \cdot -1^s$, where $b = 2$ is the most common base for IEEE. Since IEEE floating point is meant to be implemented in hardware, the precision of the mantissa is often fairly small (*23, 48, and 64 bits*). The mantissa is merely an integer, and a multiple precision integer could be used to create a mantissa of much larger precision than hardware alone can efficiently support. This approach could be useful where scientific applications must minimize the total output error over long calculations.

Yet another use for large integers is within arithmetic on polynomials of large characteristic (i.e., $GF(p)[x]$ for large $p$). In fact, the library discussed within this text has already been used to form a polynomial basis library[4].

## 1.1.3 Benefits of Multiple Precision Arithmetic

The benefit of multiple precision representations over single or fixed precision representations is that no precision is lost while representing the result of an operation that requires excess precision. For example, the product of two $n$-bit integers requires at least $2n$ bits of precision to be represented faithfully. A multiple precision algorithm would augment the precision of the destination to accommodate the result, while a single precision system would truncate excess bits to maintain a fixed level of precision.

It is possible to implement algorithms that require large integers with fixed precision algorithms. For example, elliptic curve cryptography (*ECC*) is often implemented on smartcards by fixing the precision of the integers to the maximum size the system will ever need. Such an approach can lead to vastly simpler algorithms that can accommodate the integers required even if the host platform cannot natively accommodate them[5]. However, as efficient as such an approach may be, the resulting source code is not normally very flexible. It cannot, at run time, accommodate inputs of higher magnitude than the designer anticipated.

Multiple precision algorithms have the most overhead of any style of arithmetic. For the the most part the overhead can be kept to a minimum with careful planning, but overall, it is not well suited for most memory starved platforms. However, multiple precision algorithms do offer the most flexibility in terms of the magnitude of the inputs. That is, the same algorithms based on multiple precision integers can accommodate any reasonable size input without the designer's

---

[4]See http://poly.libtomcrypt.org for more details.

[5]For example, the average smartcard processor has an 8–bit accumulator.

explicit forethought. This leads to lower cost of ownership for the code, as it only has to be written and tested once.

## 1.2   Purpose of This Text

The purpose of this text is to instruct the reader regarding how to implement efficient multiple precision algorithms. That is, to explain a limited subset of the core theory behind the algorithms, and the various "housekeeping" elements that are neglected by authors of other texts on the subject. Several texts [1, 2] give considerably detailed explanations of the theoretical aspects of algorithms and often very little information regarding the practical implementation aspects.

In most cases, how an algorithm is explained and how it is actually implemented are two very different concepts. For example, the Handbook of Applied Cryptography (*HAC*), algorithm 14.7 on page 594, gives a relatively simple algorithm for performing multiple precision integer addition. However, the description lacks any discussion concerning the fact that the two integer inputs may be of differing magnitudes. As a result, the implementation is not as simple as the text would lead people to believe. Similarly, the division routine (*algorithm 14.20, pp. 598*) does not discuss how to handle sign or the dividend's decreasing magnitude in the main loop (*step #3*).

Both texts also do not discuss several key optimal algorithms required, such as "Comba" and Karatsuba multipliers and fast modular inversion, which we consider practical oversights. These optimal algorithms are vital to achieve any form of useful performance in non–trivial applications.

To solve this problem, the focus of this text is on the practical aspects of implementing a multiple precision integer package. As a case study, the "LibTom-Math"[6] package is used to demonstrate algorithms with real implementations[7] that have been field tested and work very well. The LibTomMath library is freely available on the Internet for all uses, and this text discusses a very large portion of the inner workings of the library.

The algorithms presented will always include at least one "pseudo-code" description followed by the actual C source code that implements the algorithm. The pseudo-code can be used to implement the same algorithm in other programming languages as the reader sees fit.

---

[6]Available at `http://math.libtomcrypt.com`
[7]In the ISO C programming language.

This text shall also serve as a walk-through of the creation of multiple precision algorithms from scratch, showing the reader how the algorithms fit together and where to start on various taskings.

## 1.3 Discussion and Notation

### 1.3.1 Notation

A multiple precision integer of $n$-digits shall be denoted as $x = (x_{n-1}, \ldots, x_1, x_0)_\beta$ and represent the integer $x \equiv \sum_{i=0}^{n-1} x_i \beta^i$. The elements of the array $x$ are said to be the radix $\beta$ digits of the integer. For example, $x = (1, 2, 3)_{10}$ would represent the integer $1 \cdot 10^2 + 2 \cdot 10^1 + 3 \cdot 10^0 = 123$.

The term "mp_int" shall refer to a composite structure that contains the digits of the integer it represents, and auxiliary data required to manipulate the data. These additional members are discussed further in section 2.2.1. For the purposes of this text, a "multiple precision integer" and an "mp_int" are assumed synonymous. When an algorithm is specified to accept an mp_int variable, it is assumed the various auxiliary data members are present as well. An expression of the type *variablename.item* implies that it should evaluate to the member named "item" of the variable. For example, a string of characters may have a member "length" that would evaluate to the number of characters in the string. If the string $a$ equals *hello*, then it follows that $a.length = 5$.

For certain discussions, more generic algorithms are presented to help the reader understand the final algorithm used to solve a given problem. When an algorithm is described as accepting an integer input, it is assumed the input is a plain integer with no additional multiple precision members. That is, algorithms that use integers as opposed to mp_ints as inputs do not concern themselves with the housekeeping operations required such as memory management. These algorithms will be used to establish the relevant theory that will subsequently be used to describe a multiple precision algorithm to solve the same problem.

### 1.3.2 Precision Notation

The variable $\beta$ represents the radix of a single digit of a multiple precision integer and must be of the form $q^p$ for $q, p \in \mathbb{Z}^+$. A single precision variable must be able to represent integers in the range $0 \leq x < q\beta$, while a double precision variable must be able to represent integers in the range $0 \leq x < q\beta^2$. The extra radix-

$q$ factor allows additions and subtractions to proceed without truncation of the carry. Since all modern computers are binary, it is assumed that $q$ is two.

Within the source code that will be presented for each algorithm, the data type **mp_digit** will represent a single precision integer type, while the data type **mp_word** will represent a double precision integer type. In several algorithms (notably the Comba routines), temporary results will be stored in arrays of double precision mp_words. For the purposes of this text, $x_j$ will refer to the $j$'th digit of a single precision array, and $\hat{x}_j$ will refer to the $j$'th digit of a double precision array. Whenever an expression is to be assigned to a double precision variable, it is assumed that all single precision variables are promoted to double precision during the evaluation. Expressions that are assigned to a single precision variable are truncated to fit within the precision of a single precision data type.

For example, if $\beta = 10^2$, a single precision data type may represent a value in the range $0 \leq x < 10^3$, while a double precision data type may represent a value in the range $0 \leq x < 10^5$. Let $a = 23$ and $b = 49$ represent two single precision variables. The single precision product shall be written as $c \leftarrow a \cdot b$, while the double precision product shall be written as $\hat{c} \leftarrow a \cdot b$. In this particular case, $\hat{c} = 1127$ and $c = 127$. The most significant digit of the product would not fit in a single precision data type and as a result $c \neq \hat{c}$.

### 1.3.3   Algorithm Inputs and Outputs

Within the algorithm descriptions all variables are assumed scalars of either single or double precision as indicated. The only exception to this rule is when variables have been indicated to be of type mp_int. This distinction is important, as scalars are often used as array indicies and various other counters.

### 1.3.4   Mathematical Expressions

The $\lfloor \ \rfloor$ brackets imply an expression truncated to an integer not greater than the expression itself; for example, $\lfloor 5.7 \rfloor = 5$. Similarly, the $\lceil \ \rceil$ brackets imply an expression rounded to an integer not less than the expression itself; for example, $\lceil 5.1 \rceil = 6$. Typically, when the / division symbol is used, the intention is to perform an integer division with truncation; for example, $5/2 = 2$, which will often be written as $\lfloor 5/2 \rfloor = 2$ for clarity. When an expression is written as a fraction a real value division is implied; for example, $\frac{5}{2} = 2.5$.

The norm of a multiple precision integer, for example $||x||$, will be used to represent the number of digits in the representation of the integer; for example,

$||123|| = 3$ and $||79452|| = 5$.

### 1.3.5 Work Effort

To measure the efficiency of the specified algorithms, a modified big-Oh notation is used. In this system, all single precision operations are considered to have the same cost[8]. That is, a single precision addition, multiplication, and division are assumed to take the same time to complete. While this is generally not true in practice, it will simplify the discussions considerably.

Some algorithms have slight advantages over others, which is why some constants will not be removed in the notation. For example, a normal baseline multiplication (section 5.2.1) requires $O(n^2)$ work, while a baseline squaring (section 5.3) requires $O(\frac{n^2+n}{2})$ work. In standard big-Oh notation, these would both be said to be equivalent to $O(n^2)$. However, in the context of this text, this is not the case, as the magnitude of the inputs will typically be rather small. As a result, small constant factors in the work effort will make an observable difference in algorithm efficiency.

All algorithms presented in this text have a polynomial time work level; that is, of the form $O(n^k)$ for $n, k \in \mathbb{Z}^+$. This will help make useful comparisons in terms of the speed of the algorithms and how various optimizations will help pay off in the long run.

## 1.4 Exercises

Within the more advanced chapters a section is set aside to give the reader some challenging exercises related to the discussion at hand. These exercises are not designed to be prize–winning problems, but instead to be thought provoking. Wherever possible the problems are forward minded, stating problems that will be answered in subsequent chapters. The reader is encouraged to finish the exercises as they appear to get a better understanding of the subject material.

That being said, the problems are designed to affirm knowledge of a particular subject matter. Students in particular are encouraged to verify they can answer the problems correctly before moving on.

Similar to the exercises as described in [1, pp. ix], these exercises are given a scoring system based on the difficulty of the problem. However, unlike [1], the problems do not get nearly as hard. The scoring of these exercises ranges from

---

[8]Except where explicitly noted.

one (the easiest) to five (the hardest). Figure 1.2 summarizes the scoring system used.

| [1] | An easy problem that should only take the reader a manner of minutes to solve. Usually does not involve much computer time to solve. |
| [2] | An easy problem that involves a marginal amount of computer time usage. Usually requires a program to be written to solve the problem. |
| [3] | A moderately hard problem that requires a non-trivial amount of work. Usually involves trivial research and development of new theory from the perspective of a student. |
| [4] | A moderately hard problem that involves a non-trivial amount of work and research, the solution to which will demonstrate a higher mastery of the subject matter. |
| [5] | A hard problem that involves concepts that are difficult for a novice to solve. Solutions to these problems will demonstrate a complete mastery of the given subject. |

Figure 1.2: Exercise Scoring System

Problems at the first level are meant to be simple questions the reader can answer quickly without programming a solution or devising new theory. These problems are quick tests to see if the material is understood. Problems at the second level are also designed to be easy, but will require a program or algorithm to be implemented to arrive at the answer. These two levels are essentially entry level questions.

Problems at the third level are meant to be a bit more difficult than the first two levels. The answer is often fairly obvious, but arriving at an exacting solution requires some thought and skill. These problems will almost always involve devising a new algorithm or implementing a variation of another algorithm previously presented. Readers who can answer these questions will feel comfortable with the concepts behind the topic at hand.

Problems at the fourth level are meant to be similar to those of the level–three questions except they will require additional research to be completed. The reader will most likely not know the answer right away, nor will the text provide the exact details of the answer until a subsequent chapter.

Problems at the fifth level are meant to be the hardest problems relative to all the other problems in the chapter. People who can correctly answer fifth–level problems have a mastery of the subject matter at hand.

Often problems will be tied together. The purpose of this is to start a chain of thought that will be discussed in future chapters. The reader is encouraged to answer the follow-up problems and try to draw the relevance of problems.

# 1.5 Introduction to LibTomMath

## 1.5.1 What Is LibTomMath?

LibTomMath is a free and open source multiple precision integer library written entirely in portable ISO C. By *portable* it is meant that the library does not contain any code that is computer platform dependent or otherwise problematic to use on any given platform.

The library has been successfully tested under numerous operating systems, including Unix[9], Mac OS, Windows, Linux, Palm OS, and on standalone hardware such as the Gameboy Advance. The library is designed to contain enough functionality to be able to develop applications such as public key cryptosystems and still maintain a relatively small footprint.

## 1.5.2 Goals of LibTomMath

Libraries that obtain the most efficiency are rarely written in a high level programming language such as C. However, even though this library is written entirely in ISO C, considerable care has been taken to optimize the algorithm implementations within the library. Specifically, the code has been written to work well with the GNU C Compiler (*GCC*) on both x86 and ARM processors. Wherever possible, highly efficient algorithms, such as Karatsuba multiplication, sliding window exponentiation, and Montgomery reduction have been provided to make the library more efficient.

Even with the nearly optimal and specialized algorithms that have been included, the application programing interface (*API*) has been kept as simple as possible. Often, generic placeholder routines will make use of specialized algorithms automatically without the developer's specific attention. One such example is the generic multiplication algorithm **mp_mul()**, which will automatically use Toom–Cook, Karatsuba, Comba, or baseline multiplication based on the magnitude of the inputs and the configuration of the library.

---

[9]All of these trademarks belong to their respective rightful owners.

Making LibTomMath as efficient as possible is not the only goal of the LibTom-Math project. Ideally, the library should be source compatible with another popular library, which makes it more attractive for developers to use. In this case, the MPI library was used as an API template for all the basic functions. MPI was chosen because it is another library that fits in the same niche as LibTomMath. Even though LibTomMath uses MPI as the template for the function names and argument passing conventions, it has been written from scratch by Tom St Denis.

The project is also meant to act as a learning tool for students, the logic being that no easy-to-follow "bignum" library exists that can be used to teach computer science students how to perform fast and reliable multiple precision integer arithmetic. To this end, the source code has been given quite a few comments and algorithm discussion points.

## 1.6   Choice of LibTomMath

LibTomMath was chosen as the case study of this text not only because the author of both projects is one and the same, but for more worthy reasons. Other libraries such as GMP [13], MPI [14], LIP [16], and OpenSSL [15] have multiple precision integer arithmetic routines but would not be ideal for this text for reasons that will be explained in the following sub-sections.

### 1.6.1   Code Base

The LibTomMath code base is all portable ISO C source code. This means that there are no platform–dependent conditional segments of code littered throughout the source. This clean and uncluttered approach to the library means that a developer can more readily discern the true intent of a given section of source code without trying to keep track of what conditional code will be used.

The code base of LibTomMath is well organized. Each function is in its own separate source code file, which allows the reader to find a given function very quickly. On average there are 76 lines of code per source file, which makes the source very easily to follow. By comparison, MPI and LIP are single file projects making code tracing very hard. GMP has many conditional code segments segments that also hinder tracing.

When compiled with GCC for the x86 processor and optimized for speed, the entire library is approximately 100KiB[10], which is fairly small compared to GMP

---

[10]The notation "KiB" means $2^{10}$ octets, similarly "MiB" means $2^{20}$ octets.

(over 250KiB). LibTomMath is slightly larger than MPI (which compiles to about 50KiB), but is also much faster and more complete than MPI.

## 1.6.2  API Simplicity

LibTomMath is designed after the MPI library and shares the API design. Quite often, programs that use MPI will build with LibTomMath without change. The function names correlate directly to the action they perform. Almost all of the functions share the same parameter passing convention. The learning curve is fairly shallow with the API provided, which is an extremely valuable benefit for the student and developer alike.

The LIP library is an example of a library with an API that is awkward to work with. LIP uses function names that are often "compressed" to illegible shorthand. LibTomMath does not share this characteristic.

The GMP library also does not return error codes. Instead, it uses a POSIX.1 signal system where errors are signaled to the host application. This happens to be the fastest approach, but definitely not the most versatile. In effect, a math error (i.e., invalid input, heap error, etc.) can cause a program to stop functioning, which is definitely undesirable in many situations.

## 1.6.3  Optimizations

While LibTomMath is certainly not the fastest library (GMP often beats LibTom-Math by a factor of two), it does feature a set of optimal algorithms for tasks such as modular reduction, exponentiation, multiplication, and squaring. GMP and LIP also feature such optimizations, while MPI only uses baseline algorithms with no optimizations. GMP lacks a few of the additional modular reduction optimizations that LibTomMath features[11].

LibTomMath is almost always an order of magnitude faster than the MPI library at computationally expensive tasks such as modular exponentiation. In the grand scheme of "bignum" libraries, LibTomMath is faster than the average library and usually slower than the best libraries such as GMP and OpenSSL by only a small factor.

---

[11] At the time of this writing, GMP only had Barrett and Montgomery modular reduction algorithms.

**New Developments**

Since the writing of the original manuscript, a new project, TomsFastMath, has been created. It is directly derived from LibTomMath, with a major focus on multiplication, squaring, and reduction performance. It relaxes the portability requirements to use inline assembly for performance. Readers are encouraged to check out this project at `http://tfm.libtomcrypt.com` to see how far performance can go with the code in this book.

## 1.6.4   Portability and Stability

LibTomMath will build "out of the box" on any platform equipped with a modern version of the GNU C Compiler (*GCC*). This means that without changes the library will build without configuration or setting up any variables. LIP and MPI will build "out of the box" as well but have numerous known bugs. Most notably, the author of MPI has recently stopped working on his library, and LIP has long since been discontinued.

GMP requires a configuration script to run and will not build out of the box. GMP and LibTomMath are still in active development and are very stable across a variety of platforms.

## 1.6.5   Choice

LibTomMath is a relatively compact, well–documented, highly optimized, and portable library, which seems only natural for the case study of this text. Various source files from the LibTomMath project will be included within the text. However, readers are encouraged to download their own copies of the library to actually be able to work with the library.

# Chapter 2

# Getting Started

## 2.1 Library Basics

The trick to writing any useful library of source code is to build a solid foundation and work outward from it. First, a problem along with allowable solution parameters should be identified and analyzed. In this particular case, the inability to accommodate multiple precision integers is the problem. Furthermore, the solution must be written as portable source code that is reasonably efficient across several different computer platforms.

After a foundation is formed, the remainder of the library can be designed and implemented in a hierarchical fashion. That is, to implement the lowest level dependencies first and work toward the most abstract functions last. For example, before implementing a modular exponentiation algorithm, one would implement a modular reduction algorithm. By building outward from a base foundation instead of using a parallel design methodology, you end up with a project that is highly modular. Being highly modular is a desirable property of any project as it often means the resulting product has a small footprint and updates are easy to perform.

Usually, when I start a project I will begin with the header files. I define the data types I think I will need and prototype the initial functions that are not dependent on other functions (within the library). After I implement these base functions, I prototype more dependent functions and implement them. The process repeats until I implement all the functions I require. For example, in the case of LibTomMath, I implemented functions such as mp_init() well before

I implemented mp_mul(), and even further before I implemented mp_exptmod(). As an example as to why this design works, note that the Karatsuba and Toom-Cook multipliers were written *after* the dependent function mp_exptmod() was written. Adding the new multiplication algorithms did not require changes to the mp_exptmod() function itself and lowered the total cost of ownership and development (*so to speak*) for new algorithms. This methodology allows new algorithms to be tested in a complete framework with relative ease (Figure 2.1).

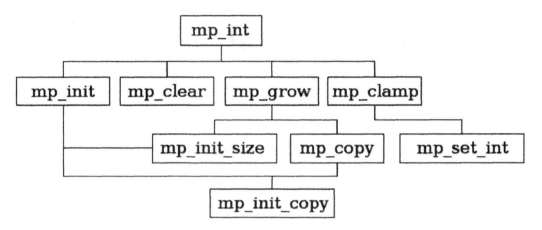

Figure 2.1: Design Flow of the First Few Original LibTomMath Functions.

Only after the majority of the functions were in place did I pursue a less hierarchical approach to auditing and optimizing the source code. For example, one day I may audit the multipliers and the next day the polynomial basis functions.

It only makes sense to begin the text with the preliminary data types and support algorithms required. This chapter discusses the core algorithms of the library that are the dependents for every other algorithm.

## 2.2   What Is a Multiple Precision Integer?

Recall that most programming languages, in particular ISO C [17], only have fixed precision data types that on their own cannot be used to represent values larger than their precision will allow. The purpose of multiple precision algorithms is to use fixed precision data types to create and manipulate multiple precision integers that may represent values that are very large.

In the decimal system, the largest single digit value is 9. However, by concatenating digits together, larger numbers may be represented. Newly prepended digits (*to the left*) are said to be in a different power of ten column. That is, the number 123 can be described as having a 1 in the hundreds column, 2 in the tens column, and 3 in the ones column. Or more formally, $123 = 1 \cdot 10^2 + 2 \cdot 10^1 + 3 \cdot 10^0$. Computer–based multiple precision arithmetic is essentially the same concept. Larger integers are represented by adjoining fixed precision computer words with the exception that a different radix is used.

What most people probably do not think about explicitly are the various other attributes that describe a multiple precision integer. For example, the integer $154_{10}$ has two immediately obvious properties. First, the integer is positive; that is, the sign of this particular integer is positive as opposed to negative. Second, the integer has three digits in its representation. There is an additional property that the integer possesses that does not concern pencil-and-paper arithmetic. The third property is how many digit placeholders are available to hold the integer.

A visual example of this third property is ensuring there is enough space on the paper to write the integer. For example, if one starts writing a large number too far to the right on a piece of paper, he will have to erase it and move left. Similarly, computer algorithms must maintain strict control over memory usage to ensure that the digits of an integer will not exceed the allowed boundaries. These three properties make up what is known as a multiple precision integer, or mp_int for short.

## 2.2.1 The mp_int Structure

The mp_int structure is the ISO C–based manifestation of what represents a multiple precision integer. The ISO C standard does not provide for any such data type, but it does provide for making composite data types known as structures. The following is the structure definition used within LibTomMath.

```
typedef struct {
    int used, alloc, sign;
    mp_digit *dp;
} mp_int;
```

Figure 2.2: The mp_int Structure

The mp_int structure (Figure 2.2) can be broken down as follows.

- The **used** parameter denotes how many digits of the array **dp** contain the digits used to represent a given integer. The **used** count must be positive (or zero) and may not exceed the **alloc** count.

- The **alloc** parameter denotes how many digits are available in the array to use by functions before it has to increase in size. When the **used** count of a result exceeds the **alloc** count, all the algorithms will automatically increase the size of the array to accommodate the precision of the result.

- The pointer **dp** points to a dynamically allocated array of digits that represent the given multiple precision integer. It is padded with (**alloc** − **used**) zero digits. The array is maintained in a least significant digit order. As a pencil and paper analogy the array is organized such that the rightmost digits are stored first starting at the location indexed by zero[1] in the array. For example, if **dp** contains $\{a, b, c, \ldots\}$ where $\mathbf{dp}_0 = a$, $\mathbf{dp}_1 = b$, $\mathbf{dp}_2 = c$, ... then it would represent the integer $a + b\beta + c\beta^2 + \ldots$

- The **sign** parameter denotes the sign as either zero/positive (**MP_ZPOS**) or negative (**MP_NEG**).

**Valid mp_int Structures**

Several rules are placed on the state of an mp_int structure and are assumed to be followed for reasons of efficiency. The only exceptions are when the structure is passed to initialization functions such as mp_init() and mp_init_copy().

1. The value of **alloc** may not be less than one. That is, **dp** always points to a previously allocated array of digits.

---

[1] In C, all arrays begin at the zero index.

2. The value of **used** may not exceed **alloc** and must be greater than or equal to zero.

3. The value of **used** implies the digit at index $(used - 1)$ of the **dp** array is non-zero. That is, leading zero digits in the most significant positions must be trimmed.

   (a) Digits in the **dp** array at and above the **used** location must be zero.

4. The value of **sign** must be **MP_ZPOS** if **used** is zero; this represents the mp_int value of zero.

## 2.3   Argument Passing

A convention of argument passing must be adopted early in the development of any library. Making the function prototypes consistent will help eliminate many headaches in the future as the library grows to significant complexity. In LibTomMath, the multiple precision integer functions accept parameters from left to right as pointers to mp_int structures. That means that the source (input) operands are placed on the left and the destination (output) on the right. Consider the following examples.

```
mp_mul(&a, &b, &c);    /* c = a * b */
mp_add(&a, &b, &a);    /* a = a + b */
mp_sqr(&a, &b);        /* b = a * a */
```

The left to right order is a fairly natural way to implement the functions since it lets the developer read aloud the functions and make sense of them. For example, the first function would read "multiply a and b and store in c."

Certain libraries (*LIP by Lenstra for instance* ) accept parameters the other way around, to mimic the order of assignment expressions. That is, the destination (output) is on the left and arguments (inputs) are on the right. In truth, it is entirely a matter of preference. In the case of LibTomMath the convention from the MPI library has been adopted.

Another very useful design consideration, provided for in LibTomMath, is whether to allow argument sources to also be a destination. For example, the second example (*mp_add*) adds $a$ to $b$ and stores in $a$. This is an important feature to implement since it allows the calling functions to cut down on the number of variables it must maintain. However, to implement this feature, specific care has to be given to ensure the destination is not modified before the source is fully read.

## 2.4   Return Values

A well–implemented application, no matter what its purpose, should trap as many runtime errors  as possible and return them to the caller. By catching runtime errors a library can be guaranteed to prevent undefined behavior. However, the end developer can still manage to cause a library to crash. For example, by passing an invalid pointer an application may fault by dereferencing memory not owned by the application.

In the case of LibTomMath the only errors that are checked for are related to inappropriate inputs (division by zero for instance) and memory allocation errors. It will not check that the mp_int passed to any function is valid, nor will it check pointers for validity. Any function that can cause a runtime error will return an error code as an **int** data type with one of the values in Figure 2.3.

| Value | Meaning |
| --- | --- |
| **MP_OKAY** | The function was successful |
| **MP_VAL** | One of the input value(s) was invalid |
| **MP_MEM** | The function ran out of heap memory |

Figure 2.3: LibTomMath Error Codes

When an error is detected within a function, it should free any memory it allocated, often during the initialization of temporary mp_ints, and return as soon as possible. The goal is to leave the system in the same state it was when the function was called. Error checking with this style of API is fairly simple.

```
int err;
if ((err = mp_add(&a, &b, &c)) != MP_OKAY) {
   printf("Error: %s\n", mp_error_to_string(err));
   exit(EXIT_FAILURE);
}
```

The GMP [13] library uses C style *signals* to flag errors, which is of questionable use. Not all errors are fatal and it was not deemed ideal by the author of

LibTomMath to force developers to have signal handlers for such cases.

## 2.5 Initialization and Clearing

The logical starting point when actually writing multiple precision integer functions is the initialization and clearing of the mp_int structures. These two algorithms will be used by the majority of the higher level algorithms.

Given the basic mp_int structure, an initialization routine must first allocate memory to hold the digits of the integer. Often it is optimal to allocate a sufficiently large pre-set number of digits even though the initial integer will represent zero. If only a single digit were allocated, quite a few subsequent reallocations would occur when operations are performed on the integers. There is a trade-off between how many default digits to allocate and how many reallocations are tolerable. Obviously, allocating an excessive amount of digits initially will waste memory and become unmanageable.

If the memory for the digits has been successfully allocated, the rest of the members of the structure must be initialized. Since the initial state of an mp_int is to represent the zero integer, the allocated digits must be set to zero, the **used** count set to zero, and **sign** set to **MP_ZPOS**.

### 2.5.1 Initializing an mp_int

An mp_int is said to be initialized if it is set to a valid, preferably default, state such that all the members of the structure are set to valid values. The mp_init algorithm will perform such an action (Figure 2.4).

---

Algorithm **mp_init**.
**Input**. An mp_int $a$
**Output**. Allocate memory and initialize $a$ to a known valid mp_int state.

---

1. Allocate memory for **MP_PREC** digits.
2. If the allocation failed, return($MP\_MEM$)
3. for $n$ from 0 to $MP\_PREC - 1$ do
   3.1 $a_n \leftarrow 0$
4. $a.sign \leftarrow MP\_ZPOS$
5. $a.used \leftarrow 0$
6. $a.alloc \leftarrow MP\_PREC$
7. Return($MP\_OKAY$)

---

Figure 2.4: Algorithm mp_init

**Algorithm mp_init.** The purpose of this function is to initialize an mp_int structure so that the rest of the library can properly manipulate it. It is assumed that the input may not have had any of its members previously initialized, which is certainly a valid assumption if the input resides on the stack.

Before any of the members such as **sign**, **used**, or **alloc** are initialized, the memory for the digits is allocated. If this fails, the function returns before setting any of the other members. The **MP_PREC** name represents a constant[2] used to dictate the minimum precision of newly initialized mp_int integers. Ideally, it is at least equal to the smallest precision number you'll be working with.

Allocating a block of digits at first instead of a single digit has the benefit of lowering the number of usually slow heap operations later functions will have to perform in the future. If **MP_PREC** is set correctly, the slack memory and the number of heap operations will be trivial.

Once the allocation has been made, the digits have to be set to zero, and the **used**, **sign**, and **alloc** members initialized. This ensures that the mp_int will always represent the default state of zero regardless of the original condition of the input.

**Remark.** This function introduces the idiosyncrasy that all iterative loops, commonly initiated with the "for" keyword, iterate incrementally when the "to" keyword is placed between two expressions. For example, "for $a$ from $b$ to $c$ do" means that a subsequent expression (or body of expressions) is to be evaluated

---

[2]Defined in the "tommath.h" header file within LibTomMath.

up to $c - b$ times so long as $b \leq c$. In each iteration, the variable $a$ is substituted for a new integer that lies inclusively between $b$ and $c$. If $b > c$ occurred, the loop would not iterate. By contrast, if the "downto" keyword were used in place of "to," the loop would iterate decrementally.

```
File: bn_mp_init.c
018   /* init a new mp_int */
019   int mp_init (mp_int * a)
020   {
021     int i;
022
023     /* allocate memory required and clear it */
024     a->dp = OPT_CAST(mp_digit) XMALLOC (sizeof (mp_digit) * MP_PREC);
025     if (a->dp == NULL) {
026       return MP_MEM;
027     }
028
029     /* set the digits to zero */
030     for (i = 0; i < MP_PREC; i++) {
031         a->dp[i] = 0;
032     }
033
034     /* set the used to zero, allocated digits to the default precision
035      * and sign to positive */
036     a->used  = 0;
037     a->alloc = MP_PREC;
038     a->sign  = MP_ZPOS;
039
040     return MP_OKAY;
041   }
042
```

One immediate observation of this initialization function is that it does not return a pointer to a mp_int structure. It is assumed that the caller has already allocated memory for the mp_int structure, typically on the application stack. The call to mp_init() is used only to initialize the members of the structure to a known default state.

Here we see (line 24) the memory allocation is performed first. This allows us to exit cleanly and quickly if there is an error. If the allocation fails, the routine will return **MP_MEM** to the caller to indicate there was a memory error. The function XMALLOC is what actually allocates the memory. Technically,

XMALLOC is not a function but a macro defined in *tommath.h*. By default, XMALLOC will evaluate to malloc(), which is the C library's built-in memory allocation routine.

To assure the mp_int is in a known state, the digits must be set to zero. On most platforms this could have been accomplished by using calloc() instead of malloc(). However, to correctly initialize an integer type to a given value in a portable fashion, you have to actually assign the value. The for loop (line 30) performs this required operation.

After the memory has been successfully initialized, the remainder of the members are initialized (lines 34 through 35) to their respective default states. At this point, the algorithm has succeeded and a success code is returned to the calling function. If this function returns **MP_OKAY**, it is safe to assume the mp_int structure has been properly initialized and is safe to use with other functions within the library.

### 2.5.2   Clearing an mp_int

When an mp_int is no longer required by the application, the memory allocated for its digits must be returned to the application's memory pool with the mp_clear algorithm (Figure 2.5).

---

Algorithm **mp_clear**.
**Input**. An mp_int $a$
**Output**. The memory for $a$ shall be deallocated.

---

1. If $a$ has been previously freed, then return($MP\_OKAY$).
2. for $n$ from 0 to $a.used - 1$ do
   2.1 $a_n \leftarrow 0$
3. Free the memory allocated for the digits of $a$.
4. $a.used \leftarrow 0$
5. $a.alloc \leftarrow 0$
6. $a.sign \leftarrow MP\_ZPOS$
7. Return($MP\_OKAY$).

---

Figure 2.5: Algorithm mp_clear

**Algorithm mp_clear.** This algorithm accomplishes two goals. First, it clears the digits and the other mp_int members. This ensures that if a developer accidentally re-uses a cleared structure it is less likely to cause problems. The second goal is to free the allocated memory.

The logic behind the algorithm is extended by marking cleared mp_int structures so that subsequent calls to this algorithm will not try to free the memory multiple times. Cleared mp_ints are detectable by having a pre-defined invalid digit pointer **dp** setting.

Once an mp_int has been cleared, the mp_int structure is no longer in a valid state for any other algorithm with the exception of algorithms mp_init, mp_init_copy, mp_init_size, and mp_clear.

```
File: bn_mp_clear.c
018    /* clear one (frees)  */
019    void
020    mp_clear (mp_int * a)
021    {
022      int i;
023
024      /* only do anything if a hasn't been freed previously */
025      if (a->dp != NULL) {
026        /* first zero the digits */
027        for (i = 0; i < a->used; i++) {
028            a->dp[i] = 0;
029        }
030
031        /* free ram */
032        XFREE(a->dp);
033
034        /* reset members to make debugging easier */
035        a->dp    = NULL;
036        a->alloc = a->used = 0;
037        a->sign  = MP_ZPOS;
038      }
039    }
040
```

The algorithm only operates on the mp_int if it hasn't been previously cleared. The if statement (line 25) checks to see if the **dp** member is not **NULL**. If the mp_int is a valid mp_int, then **dp** cannot be **NULL**, in which case the if statement will evaluate to true.

The digits of the mp_int are cleared by the for loop (line 27), which assigns a zero to every digit. Similar to mp_init(), the digits are assigned zero instead of using block memory operations (such as memset()) since this is more portable.

The digits are deallocated off the heap via the XFREE macro. Similar to XMALLOC, the XFREE macro actually evaluates to a standard C library function; in this case, free(). Since free() only deallocates the memory, the pointer still has to be reset to **NULL** manually (line 35).

Now that the digits have been cleared and deallocated, the other members are set to their final values (lines 36 and 37).

## 2.6  Maintenance Algorithms

The previous sections described how to initialize and clear an mp_int structure. To further support operations that are to be performed on mp_int structures (such as addition and multiplication), the dependent algorithms must be able to augment the precision of an mp_int and initialize mp_ints with differing initial conditions.

These algorithms complete the set of low–level algorithms required to work with mp_int structures in the higher level algorithms such as addition, multiplication, and modular exponentiation.

### 2.6.1  Augmenting an mp_int's Precision

When you are storing a value in an mp_int structure, a sufficient number of digits must be available to accommodate the entire result of an operation without loss of precision. Quite often, the size of the array given by the **alloc** member is large enough to simply increase the **used** digit count. However, when the size of the array is too small it must be re-sized appropriately to accommodate the result. The mp_grow algorithm provides this functionality (Figure 2.6).

---

Algorithm **mp_grow**.
**Input**. An mp_int $a$ and an integer $b$.
**Output**. $a$ is expanded to accommodate $b$ digits.

---

1. if $a.alloc \geq b$, then return($MP\_OKAY$)
2. $u \leftarrow b \pmod{MP\_PREC}$
3. $v \leftarrow b + 2 \cdot MP\_PREC - u$
4. Reallocate the array of digits $a$ to size $v$
5. If the allocation failed, then return($MP\_MEM$).
6. for n from a.alloc to $v - 1$ do
    6.1 $a_n \leftarrow 0$
7. $a.alloc \leftarrow v$
8. Return($MP\_OKAY$)

---

Figure 2.6: Algorithm mp_grow

**Algorithm mp_grow.** It is ideal to prevent reallocations from being performed if they are not required (step one). This is useful to prevent mp_ints from growing excessively in code that erroneously calls mp_grow.

The requested digit count is padded up to the next multiple of **MP_PREC** plus an additional **MP_PREC** (steps two and three). This helps prevent many trivial reallocations that would grow an mp_int by trivially small values.

It is assumed that the reallocation (step four) leaves the lower *a.alloc* digits of the mp_int intact. This is much akin to how the *realloc* function from the standard C library works. Since the newly allocated digits are assumed to contain undefined values, they are initially set to zero.

```
File: bn_mp_grow.c
018    /* grow as required */
019    int mp_grow (mp_int * a, int size)
020    {
021      int       i;
022      mp_digit *tmp;
023
024      /* if the alloc size is smaller alloc more ram */
025      if (a->alloc < size) {
026        /* ensure there are always at least MP_PREC digits extra on top */
027        size += (MP_PREC * 2) - (size % MP_PREC);
028
```

```
029        /* reallocate the array a->dp
030         *
031         * We store the return in a temporary variable
032         * in case the operation failed we don't want
033         * to overwrite the dp member of a.
034         */
035        tmp = OPT_CAST(mp_digit) XREALLOC (a->dp, sizeof (mp_digit) * size);
036        if (tmp == NULL) {
037           /* reallocation failed but "a" is still valid [can be freed] */
038           return MP_MEM;
039        }
040
041        /* reallocation succeeded so set a->dp */
042        a->dp = tmp;
043
044        /* zero excess digits */
045        i       = a->alloc;
046        a->alloc = size;
047        for (; i < a->alloc; i++) {
048           a->dp[i] = 0;
049        }
050     }
051     return MP_OKAY;
052  }
053
```

A quick optimization is to first determine if a memory reallocation is required at all. The if statement (line 24) checks if the **alloc** member of the mp_int is smaller than the requested digit count. If the count is not larger than **alloc** the function skips the reallocation part, thus saving time.

When a reallocation is performed, it is turned into an optimal request to save time in the future. The requested digit count is padded upwards to 2nd multiple of **MP_PREC** larger than **alloc** (line 25). The XREALLOC function is used to reallocate the memory. As per the other functions, XREALLOC is actually a macro that evaluates to realloc by default. The realloc function leaves the base of the allocation intact, which means the first **alloc** digits of the mp_int are the same as before the reallocation. All that is left is to clear the newly allocated digits and return.

Note that the reallocation result is actually stored in a temporary pointer *tmp*. This is to allow this function to return an error with a valid pointer. Earlier releases of the library stored the result of XREALLOC into the mp_int $a$. That would result in a memory leak if XREALLOC ever failed.

## 2.6.2 Initializing Variable Precision mp_ints

Occasionally, the number of digits required will be known in advance of an initialization, based on, for example, the size of input mp_ints to a given algorithm. The purpose of algorithm mp_init_size is similar to mp_init except that it will allocate *at least* a specified number of digits (Function 2.7).

---

Algorithm **mp_init_size**.
**Input**. An mp_int $a$ and the requested number of digits $b$.
**Output**. $a$ is initialized to hold at least $b$ digits.

---

1. $u \leftarrow b \pmod{MP\_PREC}$
2. $v \leftarrow b + 2 \cdot MP\_PREC - u$
3. Allocate $v$ digits.
4. for $n$ from 0 to $v - 1$ do
   4.1 $a_n \leftarrow 0$
5. $a.sign \leftarrow MP\_ZPOS$
6. $a.used \leftarrow 0$
7. $a.alloc \leftarrow v$
8. Return($MP\_OKAY$)

---

Figure 2.7: Algorithm mp_init_size

**Algorithm mp_init_size.** This algorithm will initialize an mp_int structure $a$ like algorithm mp_init, with the exception that the number of digits allocated can be controlled by the second input argument $b$. The input size is padded upwards so it is a multiple of **MP_PREC** plus an additional **MP_PREC** digits. This padding is used to prevent trivial allocations from becoming a bottleneck in the rest of the algorithms (Figure 2.7).

Like algorithm mp_init, the mp_int structure is initialized to a default state representing the integer zero. This particular algorithm is useful if it is known ahead of time the approximate size of the input. If the approximation is correct, no further memory reallocations are required to work with the mp_int.

```
File: bn_mp_init_size.c
018    /* init an mp_init for a given size */
```

```
019    int mp_init_size (mp_int * a, int size)
020    {
021      int x;
022
023      /* pad size so there are always extra digits */
024      size += (MP_PREC * 2) - (size % MP_PREC);
025
026      /* alloc mem */
027      a->dp = OPT_CAST(mp_digit) XMALLOC (sizeof (mp_digit) * size);
028      if (a->dp == NULL) {
029        return MP_MEM;
030      }
031
032      /* set the members */
033      a->used  = 0;
034      a->alloc = size;
035      a->sign  = MP_ZPOS;
036
037      /* zero the digits */
038      for (x = 0; x < size; x++) {
039          a->dp[x] = 0;
040      }
041
042      return MP_OKAY;
043    }
044
```

The number of digits $b$ requested is padded (line 24) by first augmenting it to the next multiple of **MP_PREC** and then adding **MP_PREC** to the result. If the memory can be successfully allocated, the mp_int is placed in a default state representing the integer zero. Otherwise, the error code **MP_MEM** will be returned (line 29).

The digits are allocated and set to zero at the same time with the calloc() function (line 27). The **used** count is set to zero, the **alloc** count is set to the padded digit count and the **sign** flag is set to **MP_ZPOS** to achieve a default valid mp_int state (lines 33, 34, and 35). If the function returns successfully, then it is correct to assume that the mp_int structure is in a valid state for the remainder of the functions to work with.

### 2.6.3 Multiple Integer Initializations and Clearings

Occasionally, a function will require a series of mp_int data types to be made available simultaneously. The purpose of algorithm mp_init_multi (Figure 2.8) is to initialize a variable length array of mp_int structures in a single statement. It is essentially a shortcut to multiple initializations.

---

Algorithm **mp_init_multi**.
**Input**. Variable length array $V_k$ of mp_int variables of length $k$.
**Output**. The array is initialized such that each mp_int of $V_k$ is ready to use.

---

1. for $n$ from 0 to $k - 1$ do
   1.1. Initialize the mp_int $V_n$ (*mp_init*)
   1.2. If initialization failed then do
      1.2.1. for $j$ from 0 to $n$ do
         1.2.1.1. Free the mp_int $V_j$ (*mp_clear*)
      1.2.2. Return(*MP_MEM*)
2. Return(*MP_OKAY*)

---

Figure 2.8: Algorithm mp_init_multi

**Algorithm mp_init_multi.** The algorithm will initialize the array of mp_int variables one at a time. If a runtime error has been detected (*step 1.2*), all of the previously initialized variables are cleared. The goal is an "all or nothing" initialization, which allows for quick recovery from runtime errors (Figure 2.8).

```
File: bn_mp_init_multi.c
017    #include <stdarg.h>
018
019    int mp_init_multi(mp_int *mp, ...)
020    {
021        mp_err res = MP_OKAY;      /* Assume ok until proven otherwise */
022        int n = 0;                 /* Number of ok inits */
023        mp_int* cur_arg = mp;
024        va_list args;
025
026        va_start(args, mp);        /* init args to next argument from caller */
027        while (cur_arg != NULL) {
028            if (mp_init(cur_arg) != MP_OKAY) {
```

```
029             /* Oops - error! Back-track and mp_clear what we already
030                 succeeded in init-ing, then return error.
031             */
032             va_list clean_args;
033
034             /* end the current list */
035             va_end(args);
036
037             /* now start cleaning up */
038             cur_arg = mp;
039             va_start(clean_args, mp);
040             while (n--) {
041                 mp_clear(cur_arg);
042                 cur_arg = va_arg(clean_args, mp_int*);
043             }
044             va_end(clean_args);
045             res = MP_MEM;
046             break;
047         }
048         n++;
049         cur_arg = va_arg(args, mp_int*);
050     }
051     va_end(args);
052     return res;                    /* Assumed ok, if error flagged above. */
053 }
054
055
```

This function initializes a variable length list of mp_int structure pointers. However, instead of having the mp_int structures in an actual C array, they are simply passed as arguments to the function. This function makes use of the "..." argument syntax of the C programming language. The list is terminated with a final **NULL** argument appended on the right.

The function uses the "stdarg.h" *va* functions to step in a portable fashion through the arguments to the function. A count $n$ of successfully initialized mp_int structures is maintained (line 48) such that if a failure does occur, the algorithm can backtrack and free the previously initialized structures (lines 28 to 47).

### 2.6.4    Clamping Excess Digits

When a function anticipates a result will be $n$ digits, it is simpler to assume this is true within the body of the function instead of checking during the computation. For example, a multiplication of a $i$ digit number by a $j$ digit produces a result of at most $i + j$ digits. It is entirely possible that the result is $i + j - 1$, though, with no final carry into the last position. However, suppose the destination had to be first expanded (*via mp_grow*) to accommodate $i + j - 1$ digits than further expanded to accommodate the final carry. That would be a considerable waste of time since heap operations are relatively slow.

The ideal solution is to always assume the result is $i + j$ and fix up the **used** count after the function terminates. This way, a single heap operation (*at most*) is required. However, if the result was not checked there would be an excess high order zero digit.

For example, suppose the product of two integers was $x_n = (0x_{n-1}x_{n-2}...x_0)_\beta$. The leading zero digit will not contribute to the precision of the result. In fact, through subsequent operations more leading zero digits would accumulate to the point the size of the integer would be prohibitive. As a result, even though the precision is very low the representation is excessively large.

The mp_clamp algorithm is designed to solve this very problem. It will trim high-order zeros by decrementing the **used** count until a non-zero most significant digit is found. Also in this system, zero is considered a positive number, which means that if the **used** count is decremented to zero, the sign must be set to **MP_ZPOS**.

---

Algorithm **mp_clamp**.
**Input**. An mp_int $a$
**Output**. Any excess leading zero digits of $a$ are removed

1. while $a.used > 0$ and $a_{a.used-1} = 0$ do
     1.1 $a.used \leftarrow a.used - 1$
2. if $a.used = 0$ then do
     2.1 $a.sign \leftarrow MP\_ZPOS$

---

Figure 2.9: Algorithm mp_clamp

**Algorithm mp_clamp.** As can be expected, this algorithm is very simple.

The loop in step one is expected to iterate only once or twice at the most. For example, this will happen in cases where there is not a carry to fill the last position. Step two fixes the sign for when all of the digits are zero to ensure that the mp_int is valid at all times (Figure 2.9).

```
File: bn_mp_clamp.c
018    /* trim unused digits
019     *
020     * This is used to ensure that leading zero digits are
021     * trimed and the leading "used" digit will be non-zero
022     * Typically very fast.  Also fixes the sign if there
023     * are no more leading digits
024     */
025    void
026    mp_clamp (mp_int * a)
027    {
028      /* decrease used while the most significant digit is
029       * zero.
030       */
031      while (a->used > 0 && a->dp[a->used - 1] == 0) {
032        --(a->used);
033      }
034
035      /* reset the sign flag if used == 0 */
036      if (a->used == 0) {
037        a->sign = MP_ZPOS;
038      }
039    }
040
```

Note on line 31 how to test for the **used** count is made on the left of the && operator. In the C programming language, the terms to && are evaluated left to right with a boolean short-circuit if any condition fails. This is important since if the **used** is zero, the test on the right would fetch below the array. That is obviously undesirable. The parenthesis on line 32 is used to make sure the **used** count is decremented and not the pointer "a".

# Exercises

[1] Discuss the relevance of the **used** member of the mp_int structure.

[1] Discuss the consequences of not using padding when performing allocations.

[2] Estimate an ideal value for **MP_PREC** when performing 1024-bit RSA encryption when $\beta = 2^{28}$.

[1] Discuss the relevance of the algorithm mp_clamp. What does it prevent?

[1] Give an example of when the algorithm mp_init_copy might be useful.

# Chapter 3

# Basic Operations

## 3.1 Introduction

In the previous chapter, a series of low–level algorithms was established that dealt with initializing and maintaining mp_int structures. This chapter will discuss another set of seemingly non-algebraic algorithms that will form the low–level basis of the entire library. While these algorithms are relatively trivial, it is important to understand how they work before proceeding since these algorithms will be used almost intrinsically in the following chapters.

The algorithms in this chapter deal primarily with more "programmer" related tasks such as creating copies of mp_int structures, assigning small values to mp_int structures and comparisons of the values mp_int structures represent.

## 3.2 Assigning Values to mp_int Structures

### 3.2.1 Copying an mp_int

Assigning the value that a given mp_int structure represents to another mp_int structure shall be known as making a copy for the purposes of this text. The copy of the mp_int will be a separate entity that represents the same value as the mp_int it was copied from. The mp_copy algorithm provides this functionality (Figure 3.1).

35

---

Algorithm **mp_copy**.
**Input**. An mp_int $a$ and $b$.
**Output**. Store a copy of $a$ in $b$.

---

1. If $b.alloc < a.used$ then grow $b$ to $a.used$ digits. ($mp\_grow$)
2. for $n$ from 0 to $a.used - 1$ do
   2.1 $b_n \leftarrow a_n$
3. for $n$ from $a.used$ to $b.used - 1$ do
   3.1 $b_n \leftarrow 0$
4. $b.used \leftarrow a.used$
5. $b.sign \leftarrow a.sign$
6. return($MP\_OKAY$)

---

Figure 3.1: Algorithm mp_copy

**Algorithm mp_copy.** This algorithm copies the mp_int $a$ such that upon successful termination of the algorithm, the mp_int $b$ will represent the same integer as the mp_int $a$. The mp_int $b$ shall be a complete and distinct copy of the mp_int $a$, meaning that the mp_int $a$ can be modified and it shall not affect the value of the mp_int $b$.

If $b$ does not have enough room for the digits of $a$, it must first have its precision augmented via the mp_grow algorithm. The digits of $a$ are copied over the digits of $b$, and any excess digits of $b$ are set to zero (steps two and three). The **used** and **sign** members of $a$ are finally copied over the respective members of $b$.

**Remark.** This algorithm also introduces a new idiosyncrasy that will be used throughout the rest of the text. The error return codes of other algorithms are not explicitly checked in the pseudo-code presented. For example, in step one of the mp_copy algorithm, the return of mp_grow is not explicitly checked to ensure it succeeded. Text space is limited so it is assumed that if an algorithm fails it will clear all temporarily allocated mp_ints and return the error code itself. However, the C code presented will demonstrate all of the error handling logic required to implement the pseudo-code.

```
File: bn_mp_copy.c
018    /* copy, b = a */
019    int
020    mp_copy (mp_int * a, mp_int * b)
021    {
```

```
022     int     res, n;
023
024     /* if dst == src do nothing */
025     if (a == b) {
026       return MP_OKAY;
027     }
028
029     /* grow dest */
030     if (b->alloc < a->used) {
031       if ((res = mp_grow (b, a->used)) != MP_OKAY) {
032         return res;
033       }
034     }
035
036     /* zero b and copy the parameters over */
037     {
038       register mp_digit *tmpa, *tmpb;
039
040       /* pointer aliases */
041
042       /* source */
043       tmpa = a->dp;
044
045       /* destination */
046       tmpb = b->dp;
047
048       /* copy all the digits */
049       for (n = 0; n < a->used; n++) {
050         *tmpb++ = *tmpa++;
051       }
052
053       /* clear high digits */
054       for (; n < b->used; n++) {
055         *tmpb++ = 0;
056       }
057     }
058
059     /* copy used count and sign */
060     b->used = a->used;
061     b->sign = a->sign;
062     return MP_OKAY;
```

```
063     }
064
```

Occasionally, a dependent algorithm may copy an mp_int effectively into itself such as when the input and output mp_int structures passed to a function are one and the same. For this case, it is optimal to return immediately without copying digits (line 25).

The mp_int $b$ must have enough digits to accommodate the used digits of the mp_int $a$. If $b.alloc$ is less than $a.used$, the algorithm mp_grow is used to augment the precision of $b$ (lines 30 to 33). To simplify the inner loop that copies the digits from $a$ to $b$, two aliases $tmpa$ and $tmpb$ point directly at the digits of the mp_ints $a$ and $b$, respectively. These aliases (lines 43 and 46) allow the compiler to access the digits without first dereferencing the mp_int pointers and then subsequently the pointer to the digits.

After the aliases are established, the digits from $a$ are copied into $b$ (lines 49 to 51) and then the excess digits of $b$ are set to zero (lines 54 to 56). Both "for" loops make use of the pointer aliases, and in fact the alias for $b$ is carried through into the second "for" loop to clear the excess digits. This optimization allows the alias to stay in a machine register fairly easy between the two loops.

**Remarks.** The use of pointer aliases is an implementation methodology first introduced in this function that will be used considerably in other functions. Technically, a pointer alias is simply a shorthand alias used to lower the number of pointer dereferencing operations required to access data. For example, a for loop may resemble

```
for (x = 0; x < 100; x++) {
    a->num[4]->dp[x] = 0;
}
```

This could be re-written using aliases as

```
mp_digit *tmpa;
a = a->num[4]->dp;
for (x = 0; x < 100; x++) {
    *a++ = 0;
}
```

In this case, an alias is used to access the array of digits within an mp_int structure directly. It may seem that a pointer alias is strictly not required, as a compiler may optimize out the redundant pointer operations. However, there are two dominant reasons to use aliases.

The first reason is that most compilers will not effectively optimize pointer arithmetic. For example, some optimizations may work for the Microsoft Visual C++ compiler (MSVC) and not for the GNU C Compiler (GCC). Moreover, some optimizations may work for GCC and not MSVC. As such it is ideal to find a common ground for as many compilers as possible. Pointer aliases optimize the code considerably before the compiler even reads the source code, which means the end compiled code stands a better chance of being faster.

The second reason is that pointer aliases often can make an algorithm simpler to read. Consider the first "for" loop of the function mp_copy() re-written to not use pointer aliases.

```
/* copy all the digits */
for (n = 0; n < a->used; n++) {
   b->dp[n] = a->dp[n];
}
```

Whether this code is harder to read depends strongly on the individual. However, it is quantifiably slightly more complicated, as there are four variables within the statement instead of just two.

**Nested Statements**

Another commonly used technique in the source routines is that certain sections of code are nested. This is used in particular with the pointer aliases to highlight code phases. For example, a Comba multiplier (discussed in Chapter 6) will typically have three different phases. First, the temporaries are initialized, then the columns calculated, and finally the carries are propagated. In this example, the middle column production phase will typically be nested as it uses temporary variables and aliases the most.

The nesting also simplifies the source code, as variables that are nested are only valid for their scope. As a result, the various temporary variables required do not propagate into other sections of code.

## 3.2.2 Creating a Clone

Another common operation is to make a local temporary copy of an mp_int argument. To initialize an mp_int and then copy another existing mp_int into the newly initialized mp_int will be known as creating a clone. This is useful within functions that need to modify an argument but do not wish to modify the original copy. The mp_init_copy algorithm has been designed to help perform this task (Figure 3.2).

---

Algorithm **mp_init_copy**.
**Input**. An mp_int $a$ and $b$
**Output**. $a$ is initialized to be a copy of $b$.

---

1. Init $a$. (*mp_init*)
2. Copy $b$ to $a$. (*mp_copy*)
3. Return the status of the copy operation.

---

Figure 3.2: Algorithm mp_init_copy

**Algorithm mp_init_copy.** This algorithm will initialize an mp_int variable and copy another previously initialized mp_int variable into it. As such, this algorithm will perform two operations in one step.

```
File: bn_mp_init_copy.c
018   /* creates "a" then copies b into it */
019   int mp_init_copy (mp_int * a, mp_int * b)
020   {
021     int      res;
022
023     if ((res = mp_init (a)) != MP_OKAY) {
024       return res;
025     }
026     return mp_copy (b, a);
027   }
028
```

This will initialize **a** and make it a verbatim copy of the contents of **b**. Note that **a** will have its own memory allocated, which means that **b** may be cleared after the call and **a** will be left intact.

## 3.3  Zeroing an Integer

Resetting an mp_int to the default state is a common step in many algorithms. The mp_zero algorithm will be used to perform this task (Figure 3.3).

---
Algorithm **mp_zero**.
**Input**. An mp_int $a$
**Output**. Zero the contents of $a$

---
1. $a.used \leftarrow 0$
2. $a.sign \leftarrow$ MP_ZPOS
3. for $n$ from 0 to $a.alloc - 1$ do
   3.1 $a_n \leftarrow 0$

---

Figure 3.3: Algorithm mp_zero

**Algorithm mp_zero.** This algorithm simply resets a mp_int to the default state.

```
File: bn_mp_zero.c
018    /* set to zero */
019    void mp_zero (mp_int * a)
020    {
021      int        n;
022      mp_digit *tmp;
023
024      a->sign = MP_ZPOS;
025      a->used = 0;
026
027      tmp = a->dp;
028      for (n = 0; n < a->alloc; n++) {
029          *tmp++ = 0;
030      }
031    }
032
```

After the function is completed, all of the digits are zeroed, the **used** count is zeroed, and the **sign** variable is set to **MP_ZPOS**.

## 3.4   Sign Manipulation

### 3.4.1   Absolute Value

With the mp_int representation of an integer, calculating the absolute value is trivial. The mp_abs algorithm will compute the absolute value of an mp_int (Figure 3.4).

---

Algorithm **mp_abs**.
**Input**. An mp_int $a$
**Output**. Computes $b = |a|$

---

1. Copy $a$ to $b$. (*mp_copy*)
2. If the copy failed return(*MP_MEM*).
3. $b.sign \leftarrow MP\_ZPOS$
4. Return(*MP_OKAY*)

---

Figure 3.4: Algorithm mp_abs

**Algorithm mp_abs.** This algorithm computes the absolute of an mp_int input. First, it copies $a$ over $b$. This is an example of an algorithm where the check in mp_copy that determines if the source and destination are equal proves useful. This allows, for instance, the developer to pass the same mp_int as the source and destination to this function without additional logic to handle it.

```
File: bn_mp_abs.c
018    /* b = |a| */
019     *
020     * Simple function copies the input and fixes the sign to positive
021     */
022    int
023    mp_abs (mp_int * a, mp_int * b)
024    {
025      int     res;
026
027      /* copy a to b */
028      if (a != b) {
029         if ((res = mp_copy (a, b)) != MP_OKAY) {
030            return res;
```

```
031          }
032       }
033
034       /* force the sign of b to positive */
035       b->sign = MP_ZPOS;
036
037       return MP_OKAY;
038    }
039
```

This fairly trivial algorithm first eliminates non–required duplications (line 28) and then sets the **sign** flag to **MP_ZPOS**.

### 3.4.2  Integer Negation

With the mp_int representation of an integer, calculating the negation is also trivial. The mp_neg algorithm will compute the negative of an mp_int input (Figure 3.5).

---

Algorithm **mp_neg**.
**Input**. An mp_int $a$
**Output**. Computes $b = -a$

---

1. Copy $a$ to $b$. (*mp_copy*)
2. If the copy failed return($MP\_MEM$).
3. If $a.used = 0$ then return($MP\_OKAY$).
4. If $a.sign = MP\_ZPOS$ then do
   4.1 $b.sign = MP\_NEG$.
5. else do
   5.1 $b.sign = MP\_ZPOS$.
6. Return($MP\_OKAY$)

---

Figure 3.5: Algorithm mp_neg

**Algorithm mp_neg.**  This algorithm computes the negation of an input. First, it copies $a$ over $b$. If $a$ has no used digits, then the algorithm returns immediately. Otherwise, it flips the sign flag and stores the result in $b$. Note that if $a$ had no digits, then it must be positive by definition. Had step three been omitted, the algorithm would return zero as negative.

```
File: bn_mp_neg.c
018   /* b = -a */
019   int mp_neg (mp_int * a, mp_int * b)
020   {
021     int    res;
022     if (a != b) {
023        if ((res = mp_copy (a, b)) != MP_OKAY) {
024           return res;
025        }
026     }
027
028     if (mp_iszero(b) != MP_YES) {
029        b->sign = (a->sign == MP_ZPOS) ? MP_NEG : MP_ZPOS;
030     } else {
031        b->sign = MP_ZPOS;
032     }
033
034     return MP_OKAY;
035   }
036
```

Like mp_abs(), this function avoids non–required duplications (line 22) and then sets the sign. We have to make sure that only non–zero values get a **sign** of **MP_NEG**. If the mp_int is zero, the **sign** is hard–coded to **MP_ZPOS**.

# 3.5  Small Constants

## 3.5.1  Setting Small Constants

Often, a mp_int must be set to a relatively small value such as 1 or 2. For these cases, the mp_set algorithm is useful (Figure 3.6).

---

Algorithm **mp_set**.
**Input**. An mp_int $a$ and a digit $b$
**Output**. Make $a$ equivalent to $b$

---

1. Zero $a$ (*mp_zero*).
2. $a_0 \leftarrow b \pmod{\beta}$
3. $a.used \leftarrow \begin{cases} 1 & \text{if } a_0 > 0 \\ 0 & \text{if } a_0 = 0 \end{cases}$

---

Figure 3.6: Algorithm mp_set

**Algorithm mp_set.** This algorithm sets a mp_int to a small single digit value. Step number 1 ensures that the integer is reset to the default state. The single digit is set (*modulo $\beta$*) and the **used** count is adjusted accordingly.

```
File: bn_mp_set.c
018    /* set to a digit */
019    void mp_set (mp_int * a, mp_digit b)
020    {
021      mp_zero (a);
022      a->dp[0] = b & MP_MASK;
023      a->used  = (a->dp[0] != 0) ? 1 : 0;
024    }
025
```

First, we zero (line 21) the mp_int to make sure the other members are initialized for a small positive constant. mp_zero() ensures that the **sign** is positive and the **used** count is zero. Next, we set the digit and reduce it modulo $\beta$ (line 22). After this step, we have to check if the resulting digit is zero or not. If it is not, we set the **used** count to one, otherwise to zero.

We can quickly reduce modulo $\beta$ since it is of the form $2^k$, and a quick binary AND operation with $2^k - 1$ will perform the same operation.

One important limitation of this function is that it will only set one digit. The size of a digit is not fixed, meaning source that uses this function should take that into account. Only trivially small constants can be set using this function.

## 3.5.2   Setting Large Constants

To overcome the limitations of the mp_set algorithm, the mp_set_int algorithm is ideal. It accepts a "long" data type as input and will always treat it as a 32-bit integer (Figure 3.7).

---

Algorithm **mp_set_int**.
**Input**. An mp_int $a$ and a "long" integer $b$
**Output**. Make $a$ equivalent to $b$

---

1. Zero $a$ ($mp\_zero$)
2. for $n$ from 0 to 7 do
   2.1 $a \leftarrow a \cdot 16$ ($mp\_mul2d$)
   2.2 $u \leftarrow \lfloor b/2^{4(7-n)} \rfloor$ (mod 16)
   2.3 $a_0 \leftarrow a_0 + u$
   2.4 $a.used \leftarrow a.used + 1$
3. Clamp excess used digits ($mp\_clamp$)

---

Figure 3.7: Algorithm mp_set_int

**Algorithm mp_set_int.** The algorithm performs eight iterations of a simple loop where in each iteration, four bits from the source are added to the mp_int. Step 2.1 will multiply the current result by sixteen, making room for four more bits in the less significant positions. In step 2.2, the next four bits from the source are extracted and are added to the mp_int. The **used** digit count is incremented to reflect the addition. The **used** digit counter is incremented since if any of the leading digits were zero, the mp_int would have zero digits used and the newly added four bits would be ignored.

Excess zero digits are trimmed in steps 2.1 and 3 by using higher level algorithms mp_mul2d and mp_clamp.

```
File: bn_mp_set_int.c
018    /* set a 32-bit const */
019    int mp_set_int (mp_int * a, unsigned long b)
020    {
021      int     x, res;
022
023      mp_zero (a);
024
```

```
025     /* set four bits at a time */
026     for (x = 0; x < 8; x++) {
027       /* shift the number up four bits */
028       if ((res = mp_mul_2d (a, 4, a)) != MP_OKAY) {
029         return res;
030       }
031
032       /* OR in the top four bits of the source */
033       a->dp[0] |= (b >> 28) & 15;
034
035       /* shift the source up to the next four bits */
036       b <<= 4;
037
038       /* ensure that digits are not clamped off */
039       a->used += 1;
040     }
041     mp_clamp (a);
042     return MP_OKAY;
043   }
044
```

This function sets four bits of the number at a time to handle all practical **DIGIT_BIT** sizes. The addition on line 39 ensures that the newly added in bits are added to the number of digits. While it may not seem obvious as to why the digit counter does not grow exceedingly large, it is because of the shift on line 28 and the call to mp_clamp() on line 41. Both functions will clamp excess leading digits, which keeps the number of used digits low.

## 3.6 Comparisons

### 3.6.1 Unsigned Comparisons

Comparing a multiple precision integer is performed with the same algorithm used to compare two decimal numbers. For example, to compare $1,234$ to $1,264$, the digits are extracted by their positions. That is, we compare $1 \cdot 10^3 + 2 \cdot 10^2 + 3 \cdot 10^1 + 4 \cdot 10^0$ to $1 \cdot 10^3 + 2 \cdot 10^2 + 6 \cdot 10^1 + 4 \cdot 10^0$ by comparing single digits at a time, starting with the highest magnitude positions. If any leading digit of one integer is greater than a digit in the same position of another integer, then obviously it must be greater.

The first comparison routine that will be developed is the unsigned magnitude compare, which will perform a comparison based on the digits of two mp_int variables alone. It will ignore the sign of the two inputs. Such a function is useful when an absolute comparison is required or if the signs are known to agree in advance.

To facilitate working with the results of the comparison functions, three constants are required (Figure 3.8).

| Constant | Meaning |
|----------|---------|
| **MP_GT** | Greater Than |
| **MP_EQ** | Equal To |
| **MP_LT** | Less Than |

Figure 3.8: Comparison Return Codes

---

Algorithm **mp_cmp_mag**.
**Input**. Two mp_ints $a$ and $b$.
**Output**. Unsigned comparison results ($a$ to the left of $b$).

1. If $a.used > b.used$ then return($MP\_GT$)
2. If $a.used < b.used$ then return($MP\_LT$)
3. for n from $a.used - 1$ to 0 do
    3.1 if $a_n > b_n$ then return($MP\_GT$)
    3.2 if $a_n < b_n$ then return($MP\_LT$)
4. Return($MP\_EQ$)

---

Figure 3.9: Algorithm mp_cmp_mag

**Algorithm mp_cmp_mag.** By saying "$a$ to the left of $b$," it is meant that the comparison is with respect to $a$. That is, if $a$ is greater than $b$ it will return **MP_GT** and similar with respect to when $a = b$ and $a < b$. The first two steps compare the number of digits used in both $a$ and $b$. Obviously, if the digit counts differ there would be an imaginary zero digit in the smaller number where the leading digit of the larger number is. If both have the same number of digits, the actual digits themselves must be compared starting at the leading digit (Figure 3.9).

By step three, both inputs must have the same number of digits so, it is safe to
start from either $a.used - 1$ or $b.used - 1$ and count down to the zero'th digit. If
after all of the digits have been compared and no difference is found, the algorithm
returns **MP_EQ**.

```
File: bn_mp_cmp_mag.c
018    /* compare magnitude of two ints (unsigned) */
019    int mp_cmp_mag (mp_int * a, mp_int * b)
020    {
021      int      n;
022      mp_digit *tmpa, *tmpb;
023
024      /* compare based on # of non-zero digits */
025      if (a->used > b->used) {
026        return MP_GT;
027      }
028
029      if (a->used < b->used) {
030        return MP_LT;
031      }
032
033      /* alias for a */
034      tmpa = a->dp + (a->used - 1);
035
036      /* alias for b */
037      tmpb = b->dp + (a->used - 1);
038
039      /* compare based on digits  */
040      for (n = 0; n < a->used; ++n, --tmpa, --tmpb) {
041        if (*tmpa > *tmpb) {
042          return MP_GT;
043        }
044
045        if (*tmpa < *tmpb) {
046          return MP_LT;
047        }
048      }
049      return MP_EQ;
050    }
051
```

The two if statements (lines 25 and 29) compare the number of digits in the two inputs. These two are performed before all the digits are compared, since it is a very cheap test to perform and can potentially save considerable time. The implementation given is also not valid without those two statements. *b.alloc* may be smaller than *a.used*, meaning that undefined values will be read from *b* past the end of the array of digits.

## 3.6.2   Signed Comparisons

Comparing with sign comparisons is also fairly critical in several routines (*division, for example*). Based on an unsigned magnitude comparison, a trivial signed comparison algorithm can be written.

---

Algorithm **mp_cmp**.
**Input**. Two mp_ints $a$ and $b$
**Output**. Signed Comparison Results ($a$ to the left of $b$)

---

1. if $a.sign = MP\_NEG$ and $b.sign = MP\_ZPOS$ then return($MP\_LT$)
2. if $a.sign = MP\_ZPOS$ and $b.sign = MP\_NEG$ then return($MP\_GT$)
3. if $a.sign = MP\_NEG$ then
   3.1 Return the unsigned comparison of $b$ and $a$ (*mp_cmp_mag*)
4 Otherwise
   4.1 Return the unsigned comparison of $a$ and $b$

---

Figure 3.10: Algorithm mp_cmp

**Algorithm mp_cmp.** The first two steps compare the signs of the two inputs. If the signs do not agree, then it can return right away with the appropriate comparison code. When the signs are equal, the digits of the inputs must be compared to determine the correct result. In step three, the unsigned comparison flips the order of the arguments since they are both negative. For instance, if $-a > -b$ then $|a| < |b|$. Step four will compare the two when they are both positive (Figure 3.10).

```
File: bn_mp_cmp.c
018    /* compare two ints (signed)*/
019    int
020    mp_cmp (mp_int * a, mp_int * b)
021    {
022      /* compare based on sign */
023      if (a->sign != b->sign) {
024         if (a->sign == MP_NEG) {
025            return MP_LT;
026         } else {
027            return MP_GT;
028         }
029      }
030
031      /* compare digits */
032      if (a->sign == MP_NEG) {
033         /* if negative compare opposite direction */
034         return mp_cmp_mag(b, a);
035      } else {
036         return mp_cmp_mag(a, b);
037      }
038    }
039
```

The two if statements (lines 23 and 24) perform the initial sign comparison. If the signs are not equal, then whichever has the positive sign is larger. The inputs are compared (line 32) based on magnitudes. If the signs were both negative, then the unsigned comparison is performed in the opposite direction (line 34). Otherwise, the signs are assumed to be positive and a forward direction unsigned comparison is performed.

# Exercises

[2]   Modify algorithm mp_set_int to accept as input a variable length array of bits.

[3]   Give the probability that algorithm mp_cmp_mag will have to compare $k$ digits of two random digits (of equal magnitude) before a difference is found.

[1]   Suggest a simple method to speed up the implementation of mp_cmp_mag based on the observations made in the previous problem.

# Chapter 4

# Basic Arithmetic

## 4.1 Introduction

At this point, algorithms for initialization, clearing, zeroing, copying, comparing, and setting small constants have been established. The next logical set of algorithms to develop are addition, subtraction, and digit shifting algorithms. These algorithms make use of the lower level algorithms and are the crucial building block for the multiplication algorithms. It is very important that these algorithms are highly optimized. On their own they are simple $O(n)$ algorithms but they can be called from higher level algorithms, which easily places them at $O(n^2)$ or even $O(n^3)$ work levels.

All of the algorithms within this chapter make use of the logical bit shift operations denoted by $<<$ and $>>$ for left and right logical shifts, respectively. A logical shift is analogous to sliding the decimal point of radix-10 representations. For example, the real number 0.9345 is equivalent to 93.45%, which is found by sliding the decimal two places to the right (*multiplying by* $\beta^2 = 10^2$). Algebraically, a binary logical shift is equivalent to a division or multiplication by a power of two. For example, $a << k = a \cdot 2^k$ while $a >> k = \lfloor a/2^k \rfloor$.

One significant difference between a logical shift and the way decimals are shifted is that digits below the zero'th position are removed from the number. For example, consider $1101_2 >> 1$; using decimal notation this would produce $110.1_2$. However, with a logical shift the result is $110_2$.

## 4.2   Addition and Subtraction

In common twos complement fixed precision arithmetic negative numbers are easily represented by subtraction from the modulus. For example, with 32-bit integers, $a-b$ (mod $2^{32}$) is the same as $a+(2^{32}-b)$ (mod $2^{32}$) since $2^{32} \equiv 0$ (mod $2^{32}$). As a result, subtraction can be performed with a trivial series of logical operations and an addition.

However, in multiple precision arithmetic, negative numbers are not represented in the same way. Instead, a sign flag is used to keep track of the sign of the integer. As a result, signed addition and subtraction are actually implemented as conditional usage of lower level addition or subtraction algorithms with the sign fixed up appropriately.

The lower level algorithms will add or subtract integers without regard to the sign flag. That is, they will add or subtract the magnitude of the integers, respectively.

### 4.2.1   Low Level Addition

An unsigned addition of multiple precision integers is performed with the same long-hand algorithm used to add decimal numbers; that is, to add the trailing digits first and propagate the resulting carry upward. Since this is a lower level algorithm, the name will have a "s_" prefix. Historically, that convention stems from the MPI library, where "s_" stood for static functions that were hidden from the developer entirely.

---

Algorithm **s_mp_add**.
**Input**. Two mp_ints $a$ and $b$
**Output**. The unsigned addition $c = |a| + |b|$.

---

1. if $a.used > b.used$ then
   1.1 $min \leftarrow b.used$
   1.2 $max \leftarrow a.used$
   1.3 $x \leftarrow a$
2. else
   2.1 $min \leftarrow a.used$
   2.2 $max \leftarrow b.used$
   2.3 $x \leftarrow b$
3. If $c.alloc < max + 1$ then grow $c$ to hold at least $max + 1$ digits (*mp_grow*)
4. $oldused \leftarrow c.used$
5. $c.used \leftarrow max + 1$
6. $u \leftarrow 0$
7. for $n$ from 0 to $min - 1$ do
   7.1 $c_n \leftarrow a_n + b_n + u$
   7.2 $u \leftarrow c_n >> lg(\beta)$
   7.3 $c_n \leftarrow c_n \pmod{\beta}$
8. if $min \neq max$ then do
   8.1 for $n$ from $min$ to $max - 1$ do
      8.1.1 $c_n \leftarrow x_n + u$
      8.1.2 $u \leftarrow c_n >> lg(\beta)$
      8.1.3 $c_n \leftarrow c_n \pmod{\beta}$
9. $c_{max} \leftarrow u$
10. if $olduse > max$ then
   10.1 for $n$ from $max + 1$ to $oldused - 1$ do
      10.1.1 $c_n \leftarrow 0$
11. Clamp excess digits in $c$. (*mp_clamp*)
12. Return(*MP_OKAY*)

---

Figure 4.1: Algorithm s_mp_add

**Algorithm s_mp_add.** This algorithm is loosely based on algorithm 14.7 of HAC [2, pp. 594], but has been extended to allow the inputs to have different magnitudes. Coincidentally, the description of algorithm A in Knuth [1, pp. 266] shares the same deficiency as the algorithm from [2]. Even the MIX pseudo machine code presented by Knuth [1, pp. 266–267] is incapable of handling inputs of different magnitudes (Figure 4.1).

The first thing that has to be accomplished is to sort out which of the two inputs is the largest. The addition logic will simply add all of the smallest input to the largest input and store that first part of the result in the destination. Then, it will apply a simpler addition loop to excess digits of the larger input.

The first two steps will handle sorting the inputs such that *min* and *max* hold the digit counts of the two inputs. The variable $x$ will be an mp_int alias for the largest input or the second input $b$ if they have the same number of digits. After the inputs are sorted, the destination $c$ is grown as required to accommodate the sum of the two inputs. The original **used** count of $c$ is copied and set to the new used count.

At this point, the first addition loop will go through as many digit positions as both inputs have. The carry variable $\mu$ is set to zero outside the loop. Inside the loop an "addition" step requires three statements to produce one digit of the summand. The first two digits from $a$ and $b$ are added together along with the carry $\mu$. The carry of this step is extracted and stored in $\mu$, and finally the digit of the result $c_n$ is truncated within the range $0 \leq c_n < \beta$.

Now all of the digit positions that both inputs have in common have been exhausted. If $min \neq max$, then $x$ is an alias for one of the inputs that has more digits. A simplified addition loop is then used to essentially copy the remaining digits and the carry to the destination.

The final carry is stored in $c_{max}$, and digits above $max$ up to *oldused* are zeroed, which completes the addition.

```
File: bn_s_mp_add.c
018    /* low level addition, based on HAC pp.594, Algorithm 14.7 */
019    int
020    s_mp_add (mp_int * a, mp_int * b, mp_int * c)
021    {
022      mp_int *x;
023      int      olduse, res, min, max;
024
025      /* find sizes, we let |a| <= |b| which means we have to sort
026       * them.  "x" will point to the input with the most digits
027       */
028      if (a->used > b->used) {
029        min = b->used;
030        max = a->used;
031        x = a;
032      } else {
033        min = a->used;
```

```
034        max = b->used;
035        x = b;
036    }
037
038    /* init result */
039    if (c->alloc < max + 1) {
040      if ((res = mp_grow (c, max + 1)) != MP_OKAY) {
041        return res;
042      }
043    }
044
045    /* get old used digit count and set new one */
046    olduse = c->used;
047    c->used = max + 1;
048
049    {
050      register mp_digit u, *tmpa, *tmpb, *tmpc;
051      register int i;
052
053      /* alias for digit pointers */
054
055      /* first input */
056      tmpa = a->dp;
057
058      /* second input */
059      tmpb = b->dp;
060
061      /* destination */
062      tmpc = c->dp;
063
064      /* zero the carry */
065      u = 0;
066      for (i = 0; i < min; i++) {
067        /* Compute the sum at one digit, T[i] = A[i] + B[i] + U */
068        *tmpc = *tmpa++ + *tmpb++ + u;
069
070        /* U = carry bit of T[i] */
071        u = *tmpc >> ((mp_digit)DIGIT_BIT);
072
073        /* take away carry bit from T[i] */
074        *tmpc++ &= MP_MASK;
```

```
075        }
076
077        /* now copy higher words if any, that is in A+B
078         * if A or B has more digits add those in
079         */
080        if (min != max) {
081          for (; i < max; i++) {
082            /* T[i] = X[i] + U */
083            *tmpc = x->dp[i] + u;
084
085            /* U = carry bit of T[i] */
086            u = *tmpc >> ((mp_digit)DIGIT_BIT);
087
088            /* take away carry bit from T[i] */
089            *tmpc++ &= MP_MASK;
090          }
091        }
092
093        /* add carry */
094        *tmpc++ = u;
095
096        /* clear digits above oldused */
097        for (i = c->used; i < olduse; i++) {
098          *tmpc++ = 0;
099        }
100      }
101
102      mp_clamp (c);
103      return MP_OKAY;
104    }
105
```

We first sort (lines 28 to 36) the inputs based on magnitude and determine the *min* and *max* variables. Note that $x$ is a pointer to an mp_int assigned to the largest input, in effect it is a local alias. Next, we grow the destination (38 to 42) to ensure it can accommodate the result of the addition.

Similar to the implementation of mp_copy, this function uses the braced code and local aliases coding style. The three aliases on lines 56, 59 and 62 represent the two inputs and destination variables, respectively. These aliases are used to ensure the compiler does not have to dereference $a$, $b$, or $c$ (respectively) to access the digits of the respective mp_int.

The initial carry $u$ will be cleared (line 65); note that $u$ is of type mp_digit, which ensures type compatibility within the implementation. The initial addition (lines 66 to 75) adds digits from both inputs until the smallest input runs out of digits. Similarly, the conditional addition loop (lines 81 to 90) adds the remaining digits from the larger of the two inputs. The addition is finished with the final carry being stored in *tmpc* (line 94). Note the "++" operator within the same expression. After line 94, *tmpc* will point to the *c.used*'th digit of the mp_int $c$. This is useful for the next loop (lines 97 to 99), which sets any old upper digits to zero.

## 4.2.2 Low Level Subtraction

The low level unsigned subtraction algorithm is very similar to the low level unsigned addition algorithm. The principal difference is that the unsigned subtraction algorithm requires the result to be positive. That is, when computing $a - b$, the condition $|a| \geq |b|$ must be met for this algorithm to function properly. Keep in mind this low level algorithm is not meant to be used in higher level algorithms directly. This algorithm as will be shown can be used to create functional signed addition and subtraction algorithms.

For this algorithm, a new variable is required to make the description simpler. Recall from section 1.3.1 that a mp_digit must be able to represent the range $0 \leq x < 2\beta$ for the algorithms to work correctly. However, it is allowable that a mp_digit represent a larger range of values. For this algorithm, we will assume that the variable $\gamma$ represents the number of bits available in a mp_digit (*this implies* $2^\gamma > \beta$).

For example, the default for LibTomMath is to use a "unsigned long" for the mp_digit "type" while $\beta = 2^{28}$. In ISO C, an "unsigned long" data type must be able to represent $0 \leq x < 2^{32}$, meaning that in this case $\gamma \geq 32$.

---

Algorithm **s_mp_sub**.
**Input**. Two mp_ints $a$ and $b$ ($|a| \geq |b|$)
**Output**. The unsigned subtraction $c = |a| - |b|$.

---

1. $min \leftarrow b.used$
2. $max \leftarrow a.used$
3. If $c.alloc < max$ then grow $c$ to hold at least $max$ digits. ($mp\_grow$)
4. $oldused \leftarrow c.used$
5. $c.used \leftarrow max$
6. $u \leftarrow 0$
7. for $n$ from 0 to $min - 1$ do
   7.1 $c_n \leftarrow a_n - b_n - u$
   7.2 $u \leftarrow c_n >> (\gamma - 1)$
   7.3 $c_n \leftarrow c_n \pmod{\beta}$
8. if $min < max$ then do
   8.1 for $n$ from $min$ to $max - 1$ do
     8.1.1 $c_n \leftarrow a_n - u$
     8.1.2 $u \leftarrow c_n >> (\gamma - 1)$
     8.1.3 $c_n \leftarrow c_n \pmod{\beta}$
9. if $oldused > max$ then do
   9.1 for $n$ from $max$ to $oldused - 1$ do
     9.1.1 $c_n \leftarrow 0$
10. Clamp excess digits of $c$. ($mp\_clamp$).
11. Return($MP\_OKAY$).

---

Figure 4.2: Algorithm s_mp_sub

**Algorithm s_mp_sub.** This algorithm performs the unsigned subtraction of two mp_int variables under the restriction that the result must be positive. That is, when passing variables $a$ and $b$ the condition that $|a| \geq |b|$ must be met for the algorithm to function correctly. This algorithm is loosely based on algorithm 14.9 [2, pp. 595] and is similar to algorithm S in [1, pp. 267] as well. As was the case of the algorithm s_mp_add both other references lack discussion concerning various practical details such as when the inputs differ in magnitude (Figure 4.2).

The initial sorting of the inputs is trivial in this algorithm since $a$ is guaranteed to have at least the same magnitude of $b$. Steps 1 and 2 set the $min$ and $max$ variables. Unlike the addition routine there is guaranteed to be no carry, which means that the result can be at most $max$ digits in length as opposed to $max + 1$. Similar to the addition algorithm, the **used** count of $c$ is copied locally and set to the maximal count for the operation.

The subtraction loop that begins on step 7 is essentially the same as the addition loop of algorithm s_mp_add, except single precision subtraction is used instead. Note the use of the $\gamma$ variable to extract the carry (*also known as the borrow*) within the subtraction loops. Under the assumption that two's complement single precision arithmetic is used, this will successfully extract the desired carry.

For example, consider subtracting $0101_2$ from $0100_2$, where $\gamma = 4$ and $\beta = 2$. The least significant bit will force a carry upwards to the third bit, which will be set to zero after the borrow. After the very first bit has been subtracted, $4 - 1 \equiv 0011_2$ will remain, When the third bit of $0101_2$ is subtracted from the result it will cause another carry. In this case, though, the carry will be forced to propagate all the way to the most significant bit.

Recall that $\beta < 2^\gamma$. This means that if a carry does occur just before the $lg(\beta)$'th bit it will propagate all the way to the most significant bit. Thus, the high order bits of the mp_digit that are not part of the actual digit will either be all zero, or all one. All that is needed is a single zero or one bit for the carry. Therefore, a single logical shift right by $\gamma - 1$ positions is sufficient to extract the carry. This method of carry extraction may seem awkward, but the reason for it becomes apparent when the implementation is discussed.

If $b$ has a smaller magnitude than $a$, then step 9 will force the carry and copy operation to propagate through the larger input $a$ into $c$. Step 10 will ensure that any leading digits of $c$ above the *max*'th position are zeroed.

```
File: bn_s_mp_sub.c
018    /* low level subtraction (assumes |a| > |b|), HAC pp.595 Algorithm 14.9 */
019    int
020    s_mp_sub (mp_int * a, mp_int * b, mp_int * c)
021    {
022      int       olduse, res, min, max;
023
024      /* find sizes */
025      min = b->used;
026      max = a->used;
027
028      /* init result */
029      if (c->alloc < max) {
030        if ((res = mp_grow (c, max)) != MP_OKAY) {
031          return res;
```

```
032        }
033     }
034     olduse = c->used;
035     c->used = max;
036
037     {
038       register mp_digit u, *tmpa, *tmpb, *tmpc;
039       register int i;
040
041       /* alias for digit pointers */
042       tmpa = a->dp;
043       tmpb = b->dp;
044       tmpc = c->dp;
045
046       /* set carry to zero */
047       u = 0;
048       for (i = 0; i < min; i++) {
049         /* T[i] = A[i] - B[i] - U */
050         *tmpc = *tmpa++ - *tmpb++ - u;
051
052         /* U = carry bit of T[i]
053          * Note this saves performing an AND operation since
054          * if a carry does occur it will propagate all the way to the
055          * MSB.  As a result a single shift is enough to get the carry
056          */
057         u = *tmpc >> ((mp_digit)(CHAR_BIT * sizeof (mp_digit) - 1));
058
059         /* Clear carry from T[i] */
060         *tmpc++ &= MP_MASK;
061       }
062
063       /* now copy higher words if any, e.g. if A has more digits than B  */
064       for (; i < max; i++) {
065         /* T[i] = A[i] - U */
066         *tmpc = *tmpa++ - u;
067
068         /* U = carry bit of T[i] */
069         u = *tmpc >> ((mp_digit)(CHAR_BIT * sizeof (mp_digit) - 1));
070
071         /* Clear carry from T[i] */
072         *tmpc++ &= MP_MASK;
```

```
073          }
074
075          /* clear digits above used (we may not have grown result above) */
076          for (i = c->used; i < olduse; i++) {
077             *tmpc++ = 0;
078          }
079       }
080
081       mp_clamp (c);
082       return MP_OKAY;
083    }
084
085
```

Like low level addition we "sort" the inputs, except in this case, the sorting is hard coded (lines 25 and 26). In reality, the *min* and *max* variables are only aliases and are only used to make the source code easier to read. Again, the pointer alias optimization is used within this algorithm. The aliases *tmpa*, *tmpb*, and *tmpc* are initialized (lines 42, 43 and 44) for $a$, $b$, and $c$, respectively.

The first subtraction loop (lines 47 through 61) subtracts digits from both inputs until the smaller of the two has been exhausted. As remarked earlier, there is an implementation reason for using the "awkward" method of extracting the carry (line 57). The traditional method for extracting the carry would be to shift by $lg(\beta)$ positions and logically AND the least significant bit. The AND operation is required because all of the bits above the $lg(\beta)$'th bit will be set to one after a carry occurs from subtraction. This carry extraction requires two relatively cheap operations to extract the carry. The other method is to simply shift the most significant bit to the least significant bit, thus extracting the carry with a single cheap operation. This optimization only works on twos complement machines, which is a safe assumption to make.

If $a$ has a larger magnitude than $b$, an additional loop (lines 64 through 73) is required to propagate the carry through $a$ and copy the result to $c$.

## 4.2.3   High Level Addition

Now that both lower level addition and subtraction algorithms have been established, an effective high level signed addition algorithm can be established. This high level addition algorithm will be what other algorithms and developers will use to perform addition of mp_int data types.

Recall from section 5.2 that an mp_int represents an integer with an unsigned mantissa (*the array of digits*) and a **sign** flag. A high level addition is actually performed as a series of eight separate cases that can be optimized down to three unique cases.

---

Algorithm **mp_add**.
**Input**. Two mp_ints $a$ and $b$
**Output**. The signed addition $c = a + b$.

---

1. if $a.sign = b.sign$ then do
   1.1 $c.sign \leftarrow a.sign$
   1.2 $c \leftarrow |a| + |b|$ ($s\_mp\_add$)
2. else do
   2.1 if $|a| < |b|$ then do ($mp\_cmp\_mag$)
      2.1.1 $c.sign \leftarrow b.sign$
      2.1.2 $c \leftarrow |b| - |a|$ ($s\_mp\_sub$)
   2.2 else do
      2.2.1 $c.sign \leftarrow a.sign$
      2.2.2 $c \leftarrow |a| - |b|$
3. Return($MP\_OKAY$).

---

Figure 4.3: Algorithm mp_add

**Algorithm mp_add.** This algorithm performs the signed addition of two mp_int variables. There is no reference algorithm to draw upon from either [1] or [2] since they both only provide unsigned operations. The algorithm is fairly straightforward but restricted, since subtraction can only produce positive results (Figure 4.3).

Figure 4.4 lists the eight possible input combinations and is sorted to show that only three specific cases need to be handled. The return code of the unsigned operations at steps 1.2, 2.1.2, and 2.2.2 are forwarded to step 3 to check for errors. This simplifies the description of the algorithm considerably and best follows how the implementation actually was achieved.

Also note how the **sign** is set before the unsigned addition or subtraction is performed. Recall from the descriptions of algorithms s_mp_add and s_mp_sub that the mp_clamp function is used at the end to trim excess digits. The mp_clamp algorithm will set the **sign** to **MP_ZPOS** when the **used** digit count reaches zero.

| Sign of $a$ | Sign of $b$ | $|a| > |b|$ | Unsigned Operation | Result Sign Flag |
|:---:|:---:|:---:|:---:|:---:|
| + | + | Yes | $c = a + b$ | $a.sign$ |
| + | + | No | $c = a + b$ | $a.sign$ |
| − | − | Yes | $c = a + b$ | $a.sign$ |
| − | − | No | $c = a + b$ | $a.sign$ |
| | | | | |
| + | − | No | $c = b - a$ | $b.sign$ |
| − | + | No | $c = b - a$ | $b.sign$ |
| | | | | |
| + | − | Yes | $c = a - b$ | $a.sign$ |
| − | + | Yes | $c = a - b$ | $a.sign$ |

Figure 4.4: Addition Guide Chart

For example, consider performing $-a + a$ with algorithm mp_add. By the description of the algorithm the sign is set to **MP_NEG**, which would produce a result of $-0$. However, since the sign is set first, then the unsigned addition is performed, the subsequent usage of algorithm mp_clamp within algorithm s_mp_add will force $-0$ to become 0.

```
File: bn_mp_add.c
018    /* high level addition (handles signs) */
019    int mp_add (mp_int * a, mp_int * b, mp_int * c)
020    {
021      int     sa, sb, res;
022
023      /* get sign of both inputs */
024      sa = a->sign;
025      sb = b->sign;
026
027      /* handle two cases, not four */
028      if (sa == sb) {
029        /* both positive or both negative */
030        /* add their magnitudes, copy the sign */
031        c->sign = sa;
032        res = s_mp_add (a, b, c);
033      } else {
034        /* one positive, the other negative */
035        /* subtract the one with the greater magnitude from */
```

```
036          /* the one of the lesser magnitude.  The result gets */
037          /* the sign of the one with the greater magnitude. */
038          if (mp_cmp_mag (a, b) == MP_LT) {
039            c->sign = sb;
040            res = s_mp_sub (b, a, c);
041          } else {
042            c->sign = sa;
043            res = s_mp_sub (a, b, c);
044          }
045       }
046    return res;
047  }
048
049
```

The source code follows the algorithm fairly closely. The most notable new source code addition is the usage of the *res* integer variable, which is used to pass the result of the unsigned operations forward. Unlike in the algorithm, the variable *res* is merely returned as is without explicitly checking it and returning the constant **MP_OKAY**. The observation is this algorithm will succeed or fail only if the lower level functions do so. Returning their return code is sufficient.

## 4.2.4   High Level Subtraction

The high level signed subtraction algorithm is essentially the same as the high level signed addition algorithm.

---

Algorithm **mp_sub**.
**Input**. Two mp_ints $a$ and $b$
**Output**. The signed subtraction $c = a - b$.

---

1. if $a.sign \neq b.sign$ then do
  1.1 $c.sign \leftarrow a.sign$
  1.2 $c \leftarrow |a| + |b|$ ($s\_mp\_add$)
2. else do
  2.1 if $|a| \geq |b|$ then do ($mp\_cmp\_mag$)
    2.1.1 $c.sign \leftarrow a.sign$
    2.1.2 $c \leftarrow |a| - |b|$ ($s\_mp\_sub$)
  2.2 else do
    2.2.1 $c.sign \leftarrow \begin{cases} MP\_ZPOS & \text{if } a.sign = MP\_NEG \\ MP\_NEG & \text{otherwise} \end{cases}$
    2.2.2 $c \leftarrow |b| - |a|$
3. Return($MP\_OKAY$).

---

Figure 4.5: Algorithm mp_sub

**Algorithm mp_sub.** This algorithm performs the signed subtraction of two inputs (Figure 4.5). Similar to algorithm mp_add there is no reference in either [1] or [2]. Also this algorithm is restricted by algorithm s_mp_sub. Figure 4.6 lists the eight possible inputs and the operations required.

| Sign of $a$ | Sign of $b$ | $|a| \geq |b|$ | Unsigned Operation | Result Sign Flag |
|:---:|:---:|:---:|:---:|:---:|
| + | − | Yes | $c = a + b$ | $a.sign$ |
| + | − | No | $c = a + b$ | $a.sign$ |
| − | + | Yes | $c = a + b$ | $a.sign$ |
| − | + | No | $c = a + b$ | $a.sign$ |
| | | | | |
| + | + | Yes | $c = a - b$ | $a.sign$ |
| − | − | Yes | $c = a - b$ | $a.sign$ |
| | | | | |
| + | + | No | $c = b - a$ | opposite of $a.sign$ |
| − | − | No | $c = b - a$ | opposite of $a.sign$ |

Figure 4.6: Subtraction Guide Chart

Similar to the case of algorithm mp_add, the **sign** is set first before the unsigned addition or subtraction, to prevent the algorithm from producing $-a - -a = -0$ as a result.

```
File: bn_mp_sub.c
018    /* high level subtraction (handles signs) */
019    int
020    mp_sub (mp_int * a, mp_int * b, mp_int * c)
021    {
022      int     sa, sb, res;
023
024      sa = a->sign;
025      sb = b->sign;
026
027      if (sa != sb) {
028        /* subtract a negative from a positive, OR */
029        /* subtract a positive from a negative. */
030        /* In either case, ADD their magnitudes, */
031        /* and use the sign of the first number. */
032        c->sign = sa;
033        res = s_mp_add (a, b, c);
034      } else {
035        /* subtract a positive from a positive, OR */
036        /* subtract a negative from a negative. */
037        /* First, take the difference between their */
038        /* magnitudes, then... */
039        if (mp_cmp_mag (a, b) != MP_LT) {
040          /* Copy the sign from the first */
041          c->sign = sa;
042          /* The first has a larger or equal magnitude */
043          res = s_mp_sub (a, b, c);
044        } else {
045          /* The result has the *opposite* sign from */
046          /* the first number. */
047          c->sign = (sa == MP_ZPOS) ? MP_NEG : MP_ZPOS;
048          /* The second has a larger magnitude */
049          res = s_mp_sub (b, a, c);
050        }
051      }
052      return res;
053    }
```

Much like the implementation of algorithm mp_add, the variable *res* is used to catch the return code of the unsigned addition or subtraction operations and forward it to the end of the function. On line 39, the "not equal to" **MP_LT** expression is used to emulate a "greater than or equal to" comparison.

## 4.3 Bit and Digit Shifting

It is quite common to think of a multiple precision integer as a polynomial in $x$; that is, $y = f(\beta)$ where $f(x) = \sum_{i=0}^{n-1} a_i x^i$. This notation arises within discussion of Montgomery and Diminished Radix Reduction, and Karatsuba multiplication and squaring.

To facilitate operations on polynomials in $x$ as above, a series of simple "digit" algorithms have to be established. That is to shift the digits left or right and to shift individual bits of the digits left and right. It is important to note that not all "shift" operations are on radix-$\beta$ digits.

### 4.3.1 Multiplication by Two

In a binary system where the radix is a power of two, multiplication by two arises often in other algorithms and is a fairly efficient operation to perform. A single precision logical shift left is sufficient to multiply a single digit by two.

---

Algorithm **mp_mul_2**.
**Input**. One mp_int $a$
**Output**. $b = 2a$.

---

1. If $b.alloc < a.used + 1$ then grow $b$ to hold $a.used + 1$ digits. (*mp_grow*)
2. $oldused \leftarrow b.used$
3. $b.used \leftarrow a.used$
4. $r \leftarrow 0$
5. for $n$ from 0 to $a.used - 1$ do
   5.1 $rr \leftarrow a_n >> (lg(\beta) - 1)$
   5.2 $b_n \leftarrow (a_n << 1) + r \pmod{\beta}$
   5.3 $r \leftarrow rr$
6. If $r \neq 0$ then do
   6.1 $b_{n+1} \leftarrow r$
   6.2 $b.used \leftarrow b.used + 1$
7. If $b.used < oldused - 1$ then do
   7.1 for $n$ from $b.used$ to $oldused - 1$ do
      7.1.1 $b_n \leftarrow 0$
8. $b.sign \leftarrow a.sign$
9. Return($MP\_OKAY$).

---

Figure 4.7: Algorithm mp_mul_2

**Algorithm mp_mul_2.** This algorithm will quickly multiply a mp_int by two provided $\beta$ is a power of two. Neither [1] nor [2] describes such an algorithm despite the fact it arises often in other algorithms. The algorithm is set up much like the lower level algorithm s_mp_add since it is for all intents and purposes equivalent to the operation $b = |a| + |a|$ (Figure 4.7).

Steps 1 and 2 grow the input as required to accommodate the maximum number of **used** digits in the result. The initial **used** count is set to $a.used$ at step 4. Only if there is a final carry will the **used** count require adjustment.

Step 6 is an optimization implementation of the addition loop for this specific case. That is, since the two values being added together are the same, there is no need to perform two reads from the digits of $a$. Step 6.1 performs a single precision shift on the current digit $a_n$ to obtain what will be the carry for the next iteration. Step 6.2 calculates the $n$'th digit of the result as single precision shift of $a_n$ plus the previous carry. Recall from Chapter 5 that $a_n << 1$ is equivalent to $a_n \cdot 2$. An iteration of the addition loop is finished with forwarding the carry to the next iteration.

Step 7 takes care of any final carry by setting the *a.used*'th digit of the result to the carry and augmenting the **used** count of *b*. Step 8 clears any leading digits of *b* in case it originally had a larger magnitude than *a*.

```
File: bn_mp_mul_2.c
018   /* b = a*2 */
019   int mp_mul_2(mp_int * a, mp_int * b)
020   {
021     int     x, res, oldused;
022
023     /* grow to accommodate result */
024     if (b->alloc < a->used + 1) {
025       if ((res = mp_grow (b, a->used + 1)) != MP_OKAY) {
026         return res;
027       }
028     }
029
030     oldused = b->used;
031     b->used = a->used;
032
033     {
034       register mp_digit r, rr, *tmpa, *tmpb;
035
036       /* alias for source */
037       tmpa = a->dp;
038
039       /* alias for dest */
040       tmpb = b->dp;
041
042       /* carry */
043       r = 0;
044       for (x = 0; x < a->used; x++) {
045
046         /* get what will be the *next* carry bit from the
047          * MSB of the current digit
048          */
049         rr = *tmpa >> ((mp_digit)(DIGIT_BIT - 1));
050
051         /* now shift up this digit, add in the carry [from the previous] */
052         *tmpb++ = ((*tmpa++ << ((mp_digit)1)) | r) & MP_MASK;
053
```

```
054            /* copy the carry that would be from the source
055             * digit into the next iteration
056             */
057            r = rr;
058        }
059
060        /* new leading digit? */
061        if (r != 0) {
062            /* add a MSB which is always 1 at this point */
063            *tmpb = 1;
064            ++(b->used);
065        }
066
067        /* now zero any excess digits on the destination
068         * that we didn't write to
069         */
070        tmpb = b->dp + b->used;
071        for (x = b->used; x < oldused; x++) {
072            *tmpb++ = 0;
073        }
074    }
075    b->sign = a->sign;
076    return MP_OKAY;
077 }
078
```

This implementation is essentially an optimized implementation of s_mp_add for the case of doubling an input. The only noteworthy difference is the use of the logical shift operator on line 52 to perform a single precision doubling.

## 4.3.2   Division by Two

A division by two can just as easily be accomplished with a logical shift right, as multiplication by two can be with a logical shift left.

---

Algorithm **mp_div_2**.
**Input**. One mp_int $a$
**Output**. $b = a/2$.

---

1. If $b.alloc < a.used$ then grow $b$ to hold $a.used$ digits. ($mp\_grow$)
2. If the reallocation failed return($MP\_MEM$).
3. $oldused \leftarrow b.used$
4. $b.used \leftarrow a.used$
5. $r \leftarrow 0$
6. for $n$ from $b.used - 1$ to 0 do
   6.1 $rr \leftarrow a_n \pmod 2$
   6.2 $b_n \leftarrow (a_n >> 1) + (r << (lg(\beta) - 1)) \pmod \beta$
   6.3 $r \leftarrow rr$
7. If $b.used < oldused - 1$ then do
   7.1 for $n$ from $b.used$ to $oldused - 1$ do
      7.1.1 $b_n \leftarrow 0$
8. $b.sign \leftarrow a.sign$
9. Clamp excess digits of $b$. ($mp\_clamp$)
10. Return($MP\_OKAY$).

---

Figure 4.8: Algorithm mp_div_2

**Algorithm mp_div_2.** This algorithm will divide an mp_int by two using logical shifts to the right. Like mp_mul_2, it uses a modified low level addition core as the basis of the algorithm. Unlike mp_mul_2, the shift operations work from the leading digit to the trailing digit. The algorithm could be written to work from the trailing digit to the leading digit; however, it would have to stop one short of $a.used - 1$ digits to prevent reading past the end of the array of digits (Figure 4.8).

Essentially, the loop at step 6 is similar to that of mp_mul_2, except the logical shifts go in the opposite direction and the carry is at the least significant bit, not the most significant bit.

```
File: bn_mp_div_2.c
018    /* b = a/2 */
019    int mp_div_2(mp_int * a, mp_int * b)
020    {
021      int       x, res, oldused;
022
023      /* copy */
```

```
024    if (b->alloc < a->used) {
025      if ((res = mp_grow (b, a->used)) != MP_OKAY) {
026        return res;
027      }
028    }
029
030    oldused = b->used;
031    b->used = a->used;
032    {
033      register mp_digit r, rr, *tmpa, *tmpb;
034
035      /* source alias */
036      tmpa = a->dp + b->used - 1;
037
038      /* dest alias */
039      tmpb = b->dp + b->used - 1;
040
041      /* carry */
042      r = 0;
043      for (x = b->used - 1; x >= 0; x--) {
044        /* get the carry for the next iteration */
045        rr = *tmpa & 1;
046
047        /* shift the current digit, add in carry and store */
048        *tmpb-- = (*tmpa-- >> 1) | (r << (DIGIT_BIT - 1));
049
050        /* forward carry to next iteration */
051        r = rr;
052      }
053
054      /* zero excess digits */
055      tmpb = b->dp + b->used;
056      for (x = b->used; x < oldused; x++) {
057        *tmpb++ = 0;
058      }
059    }
060    b->sign = a->sign;
061    mp_clamp (b);
062    return MP_OKAY;
063  }
064
```

## 4.4 Polynomial Basis Operations

Recall from section 4.3 that any integer can be represented as a polynomial in $x$ as $y = f(\beta)$. Such a representation is also known as the polynomial basis [3, pp. 48]. Given such a notation, a multiplication or division by $x$ amounts to shifting whole digits a single place. The need for such operations arises in several other higher level algorithms such as Barrett and Montgomery reduction, integer division, and Karatsuba multiplication.

Converting from an array of digits to polynomial basis is very simple. Consider the integer $y \equiv (a_2, a_1, a_0)_\beta$ and recall that $y = \sum_{i=0}^{2} a_i \beta^i$. Simply replace $\beta$ with $x$ and the expression is in polynomial basis. For example, $f(x) = 8x + 9$ is the polynomial basis representation for 89 using radix ten. That is, $f(10) = 8(10) + 9 = 89$.

### 4.4.1 Multiplication by $x$

Given a polynomial in $x$ such as $f(x) = a_n x^n + a_{n-1} x^{n-1} + ... + a_0$, multiplying by $x$ amounts to shifting the coefficients up one degree. In this case, $f(x) \cdot x = a_n x^{n+1} + a_{n-1} x^n + ... + a_0 x$. From a scalar basis point of view, multiplying by $x$ is equivalent to multiplying by the integer $\beta$.

---

Algorithm **mp_lshd**.
**Input**. One mp_int $a$ and an integer $b$
**Output**. $a \leftarrow a \cdot \beta^b$ (equivalent to multiplication by $x^b$).

---

1. If $b \leq 0$ then return($MP\_OKAY$).
2. If $a.alloc < a.used + b$ then grow $a$ to at least $a.used + b$ digits. ($mp\_grow$).
3. If the reallocation failed return($MP\_MEM$).
4. $a.used \leftarrow a.used + b$
5. $i \leftarrow a.used - 1$
6. $j \leftarrow a.used - 1 - b$
7. for $n$ from $a.used - 1$ to $b$ do
   7.1 $a_i \leftarrow a_j$
   7.2 $i \leftarrow i - 1$
   7.3 $j \leftarrow j - 1$
8. for $n$ from 0 to $b - 1$ do
   8.1 $a_n \leftarrow 0$
9. Return($MP\_OKAY$).

---

Figure 4.9: Algorithm mp_lshd

**Algorithm mp_lshd.** This algorithm multiplies an mp_int by the $b$'th power of $x$. This is equivalent to multiplying by $\beta^b$. The algorithm differs from the other algorithms presented so far as it performs the operation in place instead of storing the result in a separate location. The motivation behind this change is the way this function is typically used. Algorithms such as mp_add store the result in an optionally different third mp_int because the original inputs are often still required. Algorithm mp_lshd (*and similarly algorithm mp_rshd*) is typically used on values where the original value is no longer required. The algorithm will return success immediately if $b \leq 0$, since the rest of algorithm is only valid when $b > 0$ (Figure 4.9).

First, the destination $a$ is grown as required to accommodate the result. The counters $i$ and $j$ are used to form a *sliding window* over the digits of $a$ of length $b$ (Figure 4.10). The head of the sliding window is at $i$ (*the leading digit*) and the tail at $j$ (*the trailing digit*). The loop in step 7 copies the digit from the tail to the head. In each iteration, the window is moved down one digit. The last loop in step 8 sets the lower $b$ digits to zero.

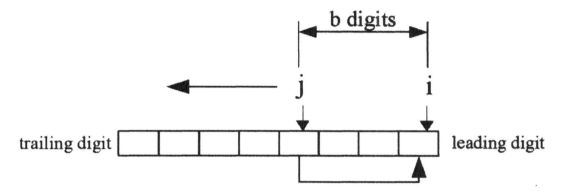

Figure 4.10: Sliding Window Movement

```
File: bn_mp_lshd.c
018    /* shift left a certain amount of digits */
019    int mp_lshd (mp_int * a, int b)
020    {
021      int      x, res;
022
023      /* if its less than zero return */
024      if (b <= 0) {
025        return MP_OKAY;
026      }
027
028      /* grow to fit the new digits */
029      if (a->alloc < a->used + b) {
030        if ((res = mp_grow (a, a->used + b)) != MP_OKAY) {
031          return res;
032        }
033      }
034
035      {
036        register mp_digit *top, *bottom;
037
038        /* increment the used by the shift amount then copy upwards */
039        a->used += b;
040
041        /* top */
```

```
042        top = a->dp + a->used - 1;
043
044        /* base */
045        bottom = a->dp + a->used - 1 - b;
046
047        /* much like mp_rshd this is implemented using a sliding window
048         * except the window goes the otherway around.  Copying from
049         * the bottom to the top.  see bn_mp_rshd.c for more info.
050         */
051        for (x = a->used - 1; x >= b; x--) {
052          *top-- = *bottom--;
053        }
054
055        /* zero the lower digits */
056        top = a->dp;
057        for (x = 0; x < b; x++) {
058          *top++ = 0;
059        }
060      }
061    return MP_OKAY;
062  }
063
```

The if statement (line 24) ensures that the $b$ variable is greater than zero since we do not interpret negative shift counts properly. The **used** count is incremented by $b$ before the copy loop begins. This eliminates the need for an additional variable in the for loop. The variable *top* (line 42) is an alias for the leading digit, while *bottom* (line 45) is an alias for the trailing edge. The aliases form a window of exactly $b$ digits over the input.

## 4.4.2   Division by $x$

Division by powers of $x$ is easily achieved by shifting the digits right and removing any that will end up to the right of the zero'th digit.

---

Algorithm **mp_rshd**.
**Input**. One mp_int $a$ and an integer $b$
**Output**. $a \leftarrow a/\beta^b$ (Divide by $x^b$).

---

1. If $b \leq 0$ then return.
2. If $a.used \leq b$ then do
   2.1 Zero $a$. ($mp\_zero$).
   2.2 Return.
3. $i \leftarrow 0$
4. $j \leftarrow b$
5. for $n$ from 0 to $a.used - b - 1$ do
   5.1 $a_i \leftarrow a_j$
   5.2 $i \leftarrow i + 1$
   5.3 $j \leftarrow j + 1$
6. for $n$ from $a.used - b$ to $a.used - 1$ do
   6.1 $a_n \leftarrow 0$
7. $a.used \leftarrow a.used - b$
8. Return.

---

Figure 4.11: Algorithm mp_rshd

**Algorithm mp_rshd.** This algorithm divides the input in place by the $b$'th power of $x$. It is analogous to dividing by a $\beta^b$ but much quicker since it does not require single precision division. This algorithm does not actually return an error code as it cannot fail (Figure 4.11).

If the input $b$ is less than one, the algorithm quickly returns without performing any work. If the **used** count is less than or equal to the shift count $b$ then it will simply zero the input and return.

After the trivial cases of inputs have been handled, the sliding window is set up. Much like the case of algorithm mp_lshd, a sliding window that is $b$ digits wide is used to copy the digits. Unlike mp_lshd, the window slides in the opposite direction from the trailing to the leading digit. In addition, the digits are copied from the leading to the trailing edge.

Once the window copy is complete, the upper digits must be zeroed and the **used** count decremented.

File: bn_mp_rshd.c
```
018   /* shift right a certain amount of digits */
019   void mp_rshd (mp_int * a, int b)
```

```
020   {
021     int     x;
022
023     /* if b <= 0 then ignore it */
024     if (b <= 0) {
025       return;
026     }
027
028     /* if b > used then simply zero it and return */
029     if (a->used <= b) {
030       mp_zero (a);
031       return;
032     }
033
034     {
035       register mp_digit *bottom, *top;
036
037       /* shift the digits down */
038
039       /* bottom */
040       bottom = a->dp;
041
042       /* top [offset into digits] */
043       top = a->dp + b;
044
045       /* this is implemented as a sliding window where
046        * the window is b-digits long and digits from
047        * the top of the window are copied to the bottom
048        *
049        * e.g.
050
051        b-2 | b-1 | b0 | b1 | b2 | ... | bb |   ---->
052                   /\                   |     ---->
053                     \-------------------/     ---->
054        */
055       for (x = 0; x < (a->used - b); x++) {
056         *bottom++ = *top++;
057       }
058
059       /* zero the top digits */
060       for (; x < a->used; x++) {
```

```
061              *bottom++ = 0;
062         }
063      }
064
065      /* remove excess digits */
066      a->used -= b;
067   }
068
```

The only noteworthy element of this routine is the lack of a return type since it cannot fail. Like mp_lshd(), we form a sliding window except we copy in the other direction. After the window (line 60), we then zero the upper digits of the input to make sure the result is correct.

## 4.5   Powers of Two

Now that algorithms for moving single bits and whole digits exist, algorithms for moving the "in between" distances are required. For example, to quickly multiply by $2^k$ for any $k$ without using a full multiplier algorithm would prove useful. Instead of performing single shifts $k$ times to achieve a multiplication by $2^{\pm k}$, a mixture of whole digit shifting and partial digit shifting is employed.

## 4.5.1   Multiplication by Power of Two

---

Algorithm **mp_mul_2d**.
**Input**. One mp_int $a$ and an integer $b$
**Output**. $c \leftarrow a \cdot 2^b$.

---

1. $c \leftarrow a$. (*mp_copy*)
2. If $c.alloc < c.used + \lfloor b/lg(\beta) \rfloor + 2$ then grow $c$ accordingly.
3. If the reallocation failed return(*MP_MEM*).
4. If $b \geq lg(\beta)$ then
    4.1 $c \leftarrow c \cdot \beta^{\lfloor b/lg(\beta) \rfloor}$ (*mp_lshd*).
    4.2 If step 4.1 failed return(*MP_MEM*).
5. $d \leftarrow b \pmod{lg(\beta)}$
6. If $d \neq 0$ then do
    6.1 $mask \leftarrow 2^d$
    6.2 $r \leftarrow 0$
    6.3 for $n$ from 0 to $c.used - 1$ do
        6.3.1 $rr \leftarrow c_n >> (lg(\beta) - d) \pmod{mask}$
        6.3.2 $c_n \leftarrow (c_n << d) + r \pmod{\beta}$
        6.3.3 $r \leftarrow rr$
    6.4 If $r > 0$ then do
        6.4.1 $c_{c.used} \leftarrow r$
        6.4.2 $c.used \leftarrow c.used + 1$
7. Return(*MP_OKAY*).

---

Figure 4.12: Algorithm mp_mul_2d

**Algorithm mp_mul_2d.** This algorithm multiplies $a$ by $2^b$ and stores the result in $c$. The algorithm uses algorithm mp_lshd and a derivative of algorithm mp_mul_2 to quickly compute the product (Figure 4.12).

First, the algorithm will multiply $a$ by $x^{\lfloor b/lg(\beta) \rfloor}$, which will ensure that the remainder multiplicand is less than $\beta$. For example, if $b = 37$ and $\beta = 2^{28}$, then this step will multiply by $x$ leaving a multiplication by $2^{37-28} = 2^9$ left.

After the digits have been shifted appropriately, at most $lg(\beta) - 1$ shifts are left to perform. Step 5 calculates the number of remaining shifts required. If it is non-zero, a modified shift loop is used to calculate the remaining product. Essentially, the loop is a generic version of algorithm mp_mul_2 designed to handle any shift count in the range $1 \leq x < lg(\beta)$. The *mask* variable is used to extract the upper $d$ bits to form the carry for the next iteration.

This algorithm is loosely measured as a $O(2n)$ algorithm, which means that if the input is $n$-digits, it takes $2n$ "time" to complete. It is possible to optimize this algorithm down to a $O(n)$ algorithm at a cost of making the algorithm slightly harder to follow.

```
File: bn_mp_mul_2d.c
018    /* shift left by a certain bit count */
019    int mp_mul_2d (mp_int * a, int b, mp_int * c)
020    {
021      mp_digit d;
022      int      res;
023
024      /* copy */
025      if (a != c) {
026         if ((res = mp_copy (a, c)) != MP_OKAY) {
027            return res;
028         }
029      }
030
031      if (c->alloc < (int)(c->used + b/DIGIT_BIT + 1)) {
032         if ((res = mp_grow (c, c->used + b / DIGIT_BIT + 1)) != MP_OKAY) {
033            return res;
034         }
035      }
036
037      /* shift by as many digits in the bit count */
038      if (b >= (int)DIGIT_BIT) {
039        if ((res = mp_lshd (c, b / DIGIT_BIT)) != MP_OKAY) {
040           return res;
041        }
042      }
043
044      /* shift any bit count < DIGIT_BIT */
045      d = (mp_digit) (b % DIGIT_BIT);
046      if (d != 0) {
047        register mp_digit *tmpc, shift, mask, r, rr;
048        register int x;
049
050        /* bitmask for carries */
051        mask = (((mp_digit)1) << d) - 1;
052
```

```
053         /* shift for msbs */
054         shift = DIGIT_BIT - d;
055
056         /* alias */
057         tmpc = c->dp;
058
059         /* carry */
060         r    = 0;
061         for (x = 0; x < c->used; x++) {
062           /* get the higher bits of the current word */
063           rr = (*tmpc >> shift) & mask;
064
065           /* shift the current word and OR in the carry */
066           *tmpc = ((*tmpc << d) | r) & MP_MASK;
067           ++tmpc;
068
069           /* set the carry to the carry bits of the current word */
070           r = rr;
071         }
072
073         /* set final carry */
074         if (r != 0) {
075             c->dp[(c->used)++] = r;
076         }
077       }
078     mp_clamp (c);
079     return MP_OKAY;
080   }
081
```

The shifting is performed in place, which means the first step (line 25) is to copy the input to the destination. We avoid calling mp_copy() by making sure the mp_ints are different. The destination then has to be grown (line 32) to accommodate the result.

If the shift count $b$ is larger than $lg(\beta)$, then a call to mp_lshd() is used to handle all the multiples of $lg(\beta)$, leaving only a remaining shift of $lg(\beta) - 1$ or fewer bits left. Inside the actual shift loop (lines 61 to 71) we make use of pre–computed values $shift$ and $mask$ to extract the carry bit(s) to pass into the next iteration of the loop. The $r$ and $rr$ variables form a chain between consecutive iterations to propagate the carry.

## 4.5.2 Division by Power of Two

---
Algorithm **mp_div_2d**.
**Input**. One mp_int $a$ and an integer $b$
**Output**. $c \leftarrow \lfloor a/2^b \rfloor, d \leftarrow a \pmod{2^b}$.

---

1. If $b \leq 0$ then do
   1.1 $c \leftarrow a$ (*mp_copy*)
   1.2 $d \leftarrow 0$ (*mp_zero*)
   1.3 Return($MP\_OKAY$).
2. $c \leftarrow a$
3. $d \leftarrow a \pmod{2^b}$ (*mp_mod_2d*)
4. If $b \geq lg(\beta)$ then do
   4.1 $c \leftarrow \lfloor c/\beta^{\lfloor b/lg(\beta) \rfloor} \rfloor$ (*mp_rshd*).
5. $k \leftarrow b \pmod{lg(\beta)}$
6. If $k \neq 0$ then do
   6.1 $mask \leftarrow 2^k$
   6.2 $r \leftarrow 0$
   6.3 for $n$ from $c.used - 1$ to 0 do
      6.3.1 $rr \leftarrow c_n \pmod{mask}$
      6.3.2 $c_n \leftarrow (c_n >> k) + (r << (lg(\beta) - k))$
      6.3.3 $r \leftarrow rr$
7. Clamp excess digits of $c$. (*mp_clamp*)
8. Return($MP\_OKAY$).

---

Figure 4.13: Algorithm mp_div_2d

**Algorithm mp_div_2d.** This algorithm will divide an input $a$ by $2^b$ and produce the quotient and remainder. The algorithm is designed much like algorithm mp_mul_2d by first using whole digit shifts then single precision shifts. This algorithm will also produce the remainder of the division by using algorithm mp_mod_2d (Figure 4.13).

```
File: bn_mp_div_2d.c
018   /* shift right by a certain bit count
019      (store quotient in c, optional remainder in d) */
020   int mp_div_2d (mp_int * a, int b, mp_int * c, mp_int * d)
021   {
022     mp_digit D, r, rr;
```

```
023    int    x, res;
024    mp_int  t;
025
026
027    /* if the shift count is <= 0 then we do no work */
028    if (b <= 0) {
029      res = mp_copy (a, c);
030      if (d != NULL) {
031        mp_zero (d);
032      }
033      return res;
034    }
035
036    if ((res = mp_init (&t)) != MP_OKAY) {
037      return res;
038    }
039
040    /* get the remainder */
041    if (d != NULL) {
042      if ((res = mp_mod_2d (a, b, &t)) != MP_OKAY) {
043        mp_clear (&t);
044        return res;
045      }
046    }
047
048    /* copy */
049    if ((res = mp_copy (a, c)) != MP_OKAY) {
050      mp_clear (&t);
051      return res;
052    }
053
054    /* shift by as many digits in the bit count */
055    if (b >= (int)DIGIT_BIT) {
056      mp_rshd (c, b / DIGIT_BIT);
057    }
058
059    /* shift any bit count < DIGIT_BIT */
060    D = (mp_digit) (b % DIGIT_BIT);
061    if (D != 0) {
062      register mp_digit *tmpc, mask, shift;
063
```

```
064        /* mask */
065        mask = (((mp_digit)1) << D) - 1;
066
067        /* shift for lsb */
068        shift = DIGIT_BIT - D;
069
070        /* alias */
071        tmpc = c->dp + (c->used - 1);
072
073        /* carry */
074        r = 0;
075        for (x = c->used - 1; x >= 0; x--) {
076          /* get the lower  bits of this word in a temp */
077          rr = *tmpc & mask;
078
079          /* shift the current word and
080              mix in the carry bits from the previous word */
081          *tmpc = (*tmpc >> D) | (r << shift);
082          --tmpc;
083
084          /* set the carry to the carry bits of the current word found above */
085          r = rr;
086        }
087      }
088    mp_clamp (c);
089    if (d != NULL) {
090      mp_exch (&t, d);
091    }
092    mp_clear (&t);
093    return MP_OKAY;
094  }
095
```

The implementation of algorithm mp_div_2d is slightly different than the algorithm specifies. The remainder $d$ may be optionally ignored by passing **NULL** as the pointer to the mp_int variable. The temporary mp_int variable $t$ is used to hold the result of the remainder operation until the end. This allows $d$ and $a$ to represent the same mp_int without modifying $a$ before the quotient is obtained.

The remainder of the source code is essentially the same as the source code for mp_mul_2d. The only significant difference is the direction of the shifts.

### 4.5.3   Remainder of Division by Power of Two

The last algorithm in the series of polynomial basis power of two algorithms is calculating the remainder of division by $2^b$. This algorithm benefits from the fact that in twos complement arithmetic, $a \pmod{2^b}$ is the same as $a$ AND $2^b - 1$.

---

Algorithm **mp_mod_2d**.
**Input**. One mp_int $a$ and an integer $b$
**Output**. $c \leftarrow a \pmod{2^b}$.

---

1. If $b \leq 0$ then do
   1.1 $c \leftarrow 0$ (*mp_zero*)
   1.2 Return($MP\_OKAY$).
2. If $b > a.used \cdot lg(\beta)$ then do
   2.1 $c \leftarrow a$ (*mp_copy*)
   2.2 Return the result of step 2.1.
3. $c \leftarrow a$
4. If step 3 failed return($MP\_MEM$).
5. for $n$ from $\lceil b/lg(\beta) \rceil$ to $c.used$ do
   5.1 $c_n \leftarrow 0$
6. $k \leftarrow b \pmod{lg(\beta)}$
7. $c_{\lfloor b/lg(\beta) \rfloor} \leftarrow c_{\lfloor b/lg(\beta) \rfloor} \pmod{2^k}$.
8. Clamp excess digits of $c$. (*mp_clamp*)
9. Return($MP\_OKAY$).

---

Figure 4.14: Algorithm mp_mod_2d

**Algorithm mp_mod_2d.** This algorithm will quickly calculate the value of $a \pmod{2^b}$. First, if $b$ is less than or equal to zero the result is set to zero. If $b$ is greater than the number of bits in $a$, then it simply copies $a$ to $c$ and returns. Otherwise, $a$ is copied to $b$, leading digits are removed and the remaining leading digit is trimmed to the exact bit count (Figure 4.14).

```
File: bn_mp_mod_2d.c
018    /* calc a value mod 2**b */
019    int
020    mp_mod_2d (mp_int * a, int b, mp_int * c)
021    {
022      int     x, res;
023
```

```
024     /* if b is <= 0 then zero the int */
025     if (b <= 0) {
026       mp_zero (c);
027       return MP_OKAY;
028     }
029
030     /* if the modulus is larger than the value than return */
031     if (b >= (int) (a->used * DIGIT_BIT)) {
032       res = mp_copy (a, c);
033       return res;
034     }
035
036     /* copy */
037     if ((res = mp_copy (a, c)) != MP_OKAY) {
038       return res;
039     }
040
041     /* zero digits above the last digit of the modulus */
042     for (x = (b / DIGIT_BIT) + ((b % DIGIT_BIT) == 0 ? 0 : 1);
043          x < c->used; x++) {
044       c->dp[x] = 0;
045     }
046     /* clear the digit that is not completely outside/inside the modulus */
047     c->dp[b / DIGIT_BIT] &=
048       (mp_digit) (((((mp_digit) 1) << (((mp_digit) b) % DIGIT_BIT)) -
049                    ((mp_digit) 1));
050     mp_clamp (c);
051     return MP_OKAY;
052   }
053
```

We first avoid cases of $b \leq 0$ by simply mp_zero()'ing the destination in such cases. Next, if $2^b$ is larger than the input, we just mp_copy() the input and return right away. After this point we know we must actually perform some work to produce the remainder.

Recalling that reducing modulo $2^k$ and a binary "and" with $2^k - 1$ are numerically equivalent we can quickly reduce the number. First, we zero any digits above the last digit in $2^b$ (line 42). Next, we reduce the leading digit of both (line 47) and then mp_clamp().

# Exercises

[3]  Devise an algorithm that performs $a \cdot 2^b$ for generic values of $b$ in $O(n)$ time.

[3]  Devise an efficient algorithm to multiply by small low hamming weight values such as 3, 5, and 9. Extend it to handle all values up to 64 with a hamming weight less than three.

[2]  Modify the preceding algorithm to handle values of the form $2^k - 1$.

[3]  Using only algorithms mp_mul_2, mp_div_2, and mp_add, create an algorithm to multiply two integers in roughly $O(2n^2)$ time for any $n$-bit input. Note that the time of addition is ignored in the calculation.

[5]  Improve the previous algorithm to have a working time of at most $O\left(2^{(k-1)}n + \left(\frac{2n^2}{k}\right)\right)$ for an appropriate choice of $k$. Again, ignore the cost of addition.

[2]  Devise a chart to find optimal values of $k$ for the previous problem for $n = 64 \ldots 1024$ in steps of 64.

[2]  Using only algorithms mp_abs and mp_sub, devise another method for calculating the result of a signed comparison.

# Chapter 5

# Multiplication and Squaring

## 5.1 The Multipliers

For most number theoretic problems, including certain public key cryptographic algorithms, the "multipliers" form the most important subset of algorithms of any multiple precision integer package. The set of multiplier algorithms include integer multiplication, squaring, and modular reduction, where in each of the algorithms single precision multiplication is the dominant operation performed. This chapter discusses integer multiplication and squaring, leaving modular reductions for the subsequent chapter.

The importance of the multiplier algorithms is for the most part driven by the fact that certain popular public key algorithms are based on modular exponentiation; that is, computing $d \equiv a^b \pmod{c}$ for some arbitrary choice of $a$, $b$, $c$, and $d$. During a modular exponentiation the majority[1] of the processor time is spent performing single precision multiplications.

For centuries, general–purpose multiplication has required a lengthy $O(n^2)$ process, whereby each digit of one multiplicand has to be multiplied against every digit of the other multiplicand. Traditional long-hand multiplication is based on this process; while the techniques can differ, the overall algorithm used is essentially the same. Only "recently" have faster algorithms been studied. First Karatsuba multiplication was discovered in 1962. This algorithm can multiply two

---

[1] Roughly speaking, a modular exponentiation will spend about 40% of the time performing modular reductions, 35% of the time performing squaring, and 25% of the time performing multiplications.

numbers with considerably fewer single precision multiplications when compared to the long-hand approach. This technique led to the discovery of polynomial basis algorithms [19] and subsequently Fourier Transform based solutions.

## 5.2 Multiplication

### 5.2.1 The Baseline Multiplication

Computing the product of two integers in software can be achieved using a trivial adaptation of the standard $O(n^2)$ long-hand multiplication algorithm that schoolchildren are taught. The algorithm is considered an $O(n^2)$ algorithm, since for two $n$-digit inputs $n^2$ single precision multiplications are required. More specifically, for an $m$ and $n$ digit input $m \cdot n$ single precision multiplications are required. To simplify most discussions, it will be assumed that the inputs have a comparable number of digits.

The "baseline multiplication" algorithm is designed to act as the "catch-all" algorithm, only to be used when the faster algorithms cannot be used. This algorithm does not use any particularly interesting optimizations and should ideally be avoided if possible. One important facet of this algorithm is that it has been modified to only produce a certain amount of output digits as resolution. The importance of this modification will become evident during the discussion of Barrett modular reduction. Recall that for an $n$ and $m$ digit input the product will be at most $n + m$ digits. Therefore, this algorithm can be reduced to a full multiplier by having it produce $n + m$ digits of the product.

Recall from section 4.2.2 the definition of $\gamma$ as the number of bits in the type **mp_digit**. We shall now extend the variable set to include $\alpha$, which shall represent the number of bits in the type **mp_word**. This implies that $2^\alpha > 2 \cdot \beta^2$. The constant $\delta = 2^{\alpha - 2lg(\beta)}$ will represent the maximal weight of any column in a product (see 6.2 for more information).

---

Algorithm **s_mp_mul_digs**.
**Input**. mp_int $a$, mp_int $b$ and an integer *digs*
**Output**. $c \leftarrow |a| \cdot |b| \pmod{\beta^{digs}}$.

---

1. If $\min(a.used, b.used) < \delta$ then do
   1.1 Calculate $c = |a| \cdot |b|$ by the Comba method (*see algorithm 5.5*).
   1.2 Return the result of step 1.1

Allocate and initialize a temporary mp_int.
2. Init $t$ to be of size *digs*
3. If step 2 failed return(*MP_MEM*).
4. $t.used \leftarrow digs$

Compute the product.
5. for $ix$ from 0 to $a.used - 1$ do
   5.1 $u \leftarrow 0$
   5.2 $pb \leftarrow \min(b.used, digs - ix)$
   5.3 If $pb < 1$ then goto step 6.
   5.4 for $iy$ from 0 to $pb - 1$ do
       5.4.1 $\hat{r} \leftarrow t_{iy+ix} + a_{ix} \cdot b_{iy} + u$
       5.4.2 $t_{iy+ix} \leftarrow \hat{r} \pmod{\beta}$
       5.4.3 $u \leftarrow \lfloor \hat{r}/\beta \rfloor$
   5.5 if $ix + pb < digs$ then do
       5.5.1 $t_{ix+pb} \leftarrow u$
6. Clamp excess digits of $t$.
7. Swap $c$ with $t$
8. Clear $t$
9. Return(*MP_OKAY*).

---

Figure 5.1: Algorithm s_mp_mul_digs

**Algorithm s_mp_mul_digs.** This algorithm computes the unsigned product of two inputs $a$ and $b$, limited to an output precision of *digs* digits. While it may seem a bit awkward to modify the function from its simple $O(n^2)$ description, the usefulness of partial multipliers will arise in a subsequent algorithm. The algorithm is loosely based on algorithm 14.12 from [2, pp. 595] and is similar to Algorithm M of Knuth [1, pp. 268]. Algorithm s_mp_mul_digs differs from these cited references since it can produce a variable output precision regardless of the precision of the inputs (Figure 5.1).

The first thing this algorithm checks for is whether a Comba multiplier can be used instead. If the minimum digit count of either input is less than $\delta$, then the Comba method may be used instead. After the Comba method is ruled out, the baseline algorithm begins. A temporary mp_int variable $t$ is used to hold the intermediate result of the product. This allows the algorithm to be used to compute products when either $a = c$ or $b = c$ without overwriting the inputs.

All of step 5 is the infamous $O(n^2)$ multiplication loop slightly modified to only produce up to *digs* digits of output. The *pb* variable is given the count of digits to read from $b$ inside the nested loop. If $pb \leq 1$, then no more output digits can be produced and the algorithm will exit the loop. The best way to think of the loops are as a series of $pb \times 1$ multiplications. That is, in each pass of the innermost loop, $a_{ix}$ is multiplied against $b$ and the result is added (*with an appropriate shift*) to $t$.

For example, consider multiplying 576 by 241. That is equivalent to computing $10^0(1)(576) + 10^1(4)(576) + 10^2(2)(576)$, which is best visualized in Figure 5.2.

| | | | 5 | 7 | 6 | |
|---|---|---|---|---|---|---|
| × | | | 2 | 4 | 1 | |
| | | | 5 | 7 | 6 | $10^0(1)(576)$ |
| | 2 | 3 | 6 | 1 | 6 | $10^1(4)(576) + 10^0(1)(576)$ |
| 1 | 3 | 8 | 8 | 1 | 6 | $10^2(2)(576) + 10^1(4)(576) + 10^0(1)(576)$ |

Figure 5.2: Long-Hand Multiplication Diagram

Each row of the product is added to the result after being shifted to the left (*multiplied by a power of the radix*) by the appropriate count. That is, in pass $ix$ of the inner loop the product is added starting at the $ix$'th digit of the result.

Step 5.4.1 introduces the hat symbol (*e.g.*, $\hat{r}$), which represents a double precision variable. The multiplication on that step is assumed to be a double wide output single precision multiplication. That is, two single precision variables are multiplied to produce a double precision result. The step is somewhat optimized from a long-hand multiplication algorithm because the carry from the addition in step 5.4.1 is propagated through the nested loop. If the carry were not propagated immediately, it would overflow the single precision digit $t_{ix+iy}$ and the result would be lost.

At step 5.5 the nested loop is finished and any carry that was left over should be forwarded. The carry does not have to be added to the $ix + pb$'th digit since that digit is assumed to be zero at this point. However, if $ix + pb \geq digs$, the carry is not set, as it would make the result exceed the precision requested.

```
File: bn_s_mp_mul_digs.c
018   /* multiplies |a| * |b| and only computes up to digs digits of result
019    * HAC pp. 595, Algorithm 14.12  Modified so you can control how
020    * many digits of output are created.
021    */
022   int s_mp_mul_digs (mp_int * a, mp_int * b, mp_int * c, int digs)
023   {
024     mp_int   t;
025     int      res, pa, pb, ix, iy;
026     mp_digit u;
027     mp_word r;
028     mp_digit tmpx, *tmpt, *tmpy;
029
030     /* can we use the fast multiplier? */
031     if (((digs) < MP_WARRAY) &&
032         MIN (a->used, b->used) <
033             (1 << ((CHAR_BIT * sizeof (mp_word)) - (2 * DIGIT_BIT)))) {
034       return fast_s_mp_mul_digs (a, b, c, digs);
035     }
036
037     if ((res = mp_init_size (&t, digs)) != MP_OKAY) {
038       return res;
039     }
040     t.used = digs;
041
042     /* compute the digits of the product directly */
043     pa = a->used;
044     for (ix = 0; ix < pa; ix++) {
045       /* set the carry to zero */
046       u = 0;
047
048       /* limit ourselves to making digs digits of output */
049       pb = MIN (b->used, digs - ix);
050
051       /* setup some aliases */
052       /* copy of the digit from a used within the nested loop */
053       tmpx = a->dp[ix];
054
```

```
055        /* an alias for the destination shifted ix places */
056        tmpt = t.dp + ix;
057
058        /* an alias for the digits of b */
059        tmpy = b->dp;
060
061        /* compute the columns of the output and propagate the carry */
062        for (iy = 0; iy < pb; iy++) {
063          /* compute the column as a mp_word */
064          r      = ((mp_word)*tmpt) +
065                   ((mp_word)tmpx) * ((mp_word)*tmpy++) +
066                   ((mp_word) u);
067
068          /* the new column is the lower part of the result */
069          *tmpt++ = (mp_digit) (r & ((mp_word) MP_MASK));
070
071          /* get the carry word from the result */
072          u      = (mp_digit) (r >> ((mp_word) DIGIT_BIT));
073        }
074        /* set carry if it is placed below digs */
075        if (ix + iy < digs) {
076          *tmpt = u;
077        }
078      }
079
080    mp_clamp (&t);
081    mp_exch (&t, c);
082
083    mp_clear (&t);
084    return MP_OKAY;
085  }
086
```

First, we determine (line 31) if the Comba method can be used since it is faster. The conditions for using the Comba routine are that $\min(a.used, b.used) < \delta$ and the number of digits of output is less than **MP_WARRAY**. This new constant is used to control the stack usage in the Comba routines. By default it is set to $\delta$, but can be reduced when memory is at a premium.

If we cannot use the Comba method we proceed to set up the baseline routine. We allocate the the destination mp_int $t$ (line 37) to the exact size of the output to avoid further reallocations. At this point, we now begin the $O(n^2)$ loop.

This implementation of multiplication has the caveat that it can be trimmed to only produce a variable number of digits as output. In each iteration of the outer loop the *pb* variable is set (line 49) to the maximum number of inner loop iterations.

Inside the inner loop we calculate $\hat{r}$ as the mp_word product of the two mp_digits and the addition of the carry from the previous iteration. A particularly important observation is that most modern optimizing C compilers (GCC for instance) can recognize that an $N \times N \rightarrow 2N$ multiplication is all that is required for the product. In x86 terms, for example, this means using the MUL instruction.

Each digit of the product is stored in turn (line 69) and the carry propagated (line 72) to the next iteration.

## 5.2.2 Faster Multiplication by the "Comba" Method

One of the huge drawbacks of the "baseline" algorithms is that at the $O(n^2)$ level the carry must be computed and propagated upwards. This makes the nested loop very sequential and hard to unroll and implement in parallel. The "Comba" [4] method is named after little known (*in cryptographic venues*) Paul G. Comba, who described a method of implementing fast multipliers that do not require nested carry fix-up operations. As an interesting aside it seems that Paul Barrett describes a similar technique in his 1986 paper [6] written five years before.

At the heart of the Comba technique is again the long-hand algorithm, except in this case a slight twist is placed on how the columns of the result are produced. In the standard long-hand algorithm, rows of products are produced and then added together to form the result. In the baseline algorithm, the columns are added together after each iteration to get the result instantaneously.

In the Comba algorithm, the columns of the result are produced entirely independently of each other; that is, at the $O(n^2)$ level a simple multiplication and addition step is performed. The carries of the columns are propagated after the nested loop to reduce the amount of work required. Succinctly, the first step of the algorithm is to compute the product vector $\vec{x}$ as follows:

$$\vec{x}_n = \sum_{i+j=n} a_i b_j, \forall n \in \{0, 1, 2, \ldots, i+j\} \tag{5.1}$$

where $\vec{x}_n$ is the $n'th$ column of the output vector. Consider Figure 5.3, which computes the vector $\vec{x}$ for the multiplication of 576 and 241.

| | | 5 | 7 | 6 | First Input |
|---|---|---|---|---|---|
| × | | 2 | 4 | 1 | Second Input |
| | | $1 \cdot 5 = 5$ | $1 \cdot 7 = 7$ | $1 \cdot 6 = 6$ | First pass |
| | $4 \cdot 5 = 20$ | $4 \cdot 7 + 5 = 33$ | $4 \cdot 6 + 7 = 31$ | 6 | Second pass |
| $2 \cdot 5 = 10$ | $2 \cdot 7 + 20 = 34$ | $2 \cdot 6 + 33 = 45$ | 31 | 6 | Third pass |
| 10 | 34 | 45 | 31 | 6 | Final Result |

Figure 5.3: Comba Multiplication Diagram

At this point the vector $x = \langle 10, 34, 45, 31, 6 \rangle$ is the result of the first step of the Comba multiplier. Now the columns must be fixed by propagating the carry upwards. The resultant vector will have one extra dimension over the input vector, which is congruent to adding a leading zero digit (Figure 5.4).

---

Algorithm **Comba Fixup**.
**Input**. Vector $\vec{x}$ of dimension $k$
**Output**. Vector $\vec{x}$ such that the carries have been propagated.

1. for $n$ from 0 to $k - 1$ do
   1.1 $\vec{x}_{n+1} \leftarrow \vec{x}_{n+1} + \lfloor \vec{x}_n / \beta \rfloor$
   1.2 $\vec{x}_n \leftarrow \vec{x}_n \pmod{\beta}$
2. Return($\vec{x}$).

---

Figure 5.4: Algorithm Comba Fixup

With that algorithm and $k = 5$ and $\beta = 10$ the $\vec{x} = \langle 1, 3, 8, 8, 1, 6 \rangle$ vector is produced. In this case, $241 \cdot 576$ is in fact $138816$ and the procedure succeeded. If the algorithm is correct and, as will be demonstrated shortly, more efficient than the baseline algorithm, why not simply always use this algorithm?

**Column Weight.**

At the nested $O(n^2)$ level the Comba method adds the product of two single precision variables to each column of the output independently. A serious obstacle is if the carry is lost, due to lack of precision before the algorithm has a chance to fix the carries. For example, in the multiplication of two three-digit numbers, the third column of output will be the sum of three single precision multiplications. If the precision of the accumulator for the output digits is less than $3 \cdot (\beta - 1)^2$, then an overflow can occur and the carry information will be lost. For any $m$ and $n$ digit inputs the maximum weight of any column is $\min(m, n)$, which is fairly obvious.

The maximum number of terms in any column of a product is known as the "column weight" and strictly governs when the algorithm can be used. Recall that a double precision type has $\alpha$ bits of resolution and a single precision digit has $lg(\beta)$ bits of precision. Given these two quantities we must not violate:

$$k \cdot (\beta - 1)^2 < 2^\alpha \tag{5.2}$$

which reduces to

$$k \cdot (\beta^2 - 2\beta + 1) < 2^\alpha \tag{5.3}$$

Let $\rho = lg(\beta)$ represent the number of bits in a single precision digit. By further re-arrangement of the equation the final solution is found.

$$k < \frac{2^\alpha}{(2^{2\rho} - 2^{\rho+1} + 1)} \tag{5.4}$$

The defaults for LibTomMath are $\beta = 2^{28}$ and $\alpha = 2^{64}$, which means that $k$ is bounded by $k < 257$. In this configuration, the smaller input may not have more than 256 digits if the Comba method is to be used. This is quite satisfactory for most applications, since 256 digits would allow for numbers in the range of $0 \leq x < 2^{7168}$, which is much larger than most public key cryptographic algorithms require.

---

Algorithm **fast_s_mp_mul_digs**.
**Input**. mp_int $a$, mp_int $b$ and an integer $digs$
**Output**. $c \leftarrow |a| \cdot |b| \pmod{\beta^{digs}}$.

---

Place an array of **MP_WARRAY** single precision digits named $W$ on the stack.
1. If $c.alloc < digs$ then grow $c$ to $digs$ digits. ($mp\_grow$)
2. If step 1 failed return($MP\_MEM$).

3. $pa \leftarrow \text{MIN}(digs, a.used + b.used)$

4. $\_\hat{W} \leftarrow 0$
5. for $ix$ from 0 to $pa - 1$ do
    5.1 $ty \leftarrow \text{MIN}(b.used - 1, ix)$
    5.2 $tx \leftarrow ix - ty$
    5.3 $iy \leftarrow \text{MIN}(a.used - tx, ty + 1)$
    5.4 for $iz$ from 0 to $iy - 1$ do
        5.4.1 $\_\hat{W} \leftarrow \_\hat{W} + a_{tx+iy}b_{ty-iy}$
    5.5 $W_{ix} \leftarrow \_\hat{W} \pmod{\beta}$
    5.6 $\_\hat{W} \leftarrow \lfloor \_\hat{W}/\beta \rfloor$

6. $oldused \leftarrow c.used$
7. $c.used \leftarrow digs$
8. for $ix$ from 0 to $pa$ do
    8.1 $c_{ix} \leftarrow W_{ix}$
9. for $ix$ from $pa + 1$ to $oldused - 1$ do
    9.1 $c_{ix} \leftarrow 0$

10. Clamp $c$.
11. Return MP_OKAY.

---

Figure 5.5: Algorithm fast_s_mp_mul_digs

**Algorithm fast_s_mp_mul_digs.** This algorithm performs the unsigned multiplication of $a$ and $b$ using the Comba method limited to $digs$ digits of precision (Figure 5.5).

The outer loop of this algorithm is more complicated than that of the baseline multiplier. This is because on the inside of the loop we want to produce one column per pass. This allows the accumulator $\_\hat{W}$ to be placed in CPU registers and reduce the memory bandwidth to two **mp_digit** reads per iteration.

The *ty* variable is set to the minimum count of *ix*, or the number of digits in *b*. That way, if *a* has more digits than *b*, this will be limited to $b.used - 1$. The *tx* variable is set to the distance past *b.used* the variable *ix* is. This is used for the immediately subsequent statement where we find *iy*.

The variable *iy* is the minimum digits we can read from either *a* or *b* before running out. Computing one column at a time means we have to scan one integer upwards and the other downwards. *a* starts at *tx* and *b* starts at *ty*. In each pass we are producing the *ix*'th output column and we note that $tx + ty = ix$. As we move *tx* upwards, we have to move *ty* downwards so the equality remains valid. The *iy* variable is the number of iterations until $tx \geq a.used$ or $ty < 0$ occurs.

After every inner pass we store the lower half of the accumulator into $W_{ix}$ and then propagate the carry of the accumulator into the next round by dividing $\_\hat{W}$ by $\beta$.

To measure the benefits of the Comba method over the baseline method, consider the number of operations that are required. If the cost in terms of time of a multiply and addition is *p* and the cost of a carry propagation is *q*, then a baseline multiplication would require $O\left((p + q)n^2\right)$ time to multiply two *n*-digit numbers. The Comba method requires only $O(pn^2 + qn)$ time; however, in practice the speed increase is actually much more. With $O(n)$ space the algorithm can be reduced to $O(pn + qn)$ time by implementing the *n* multiply and addition operations in the nested loop in parallel.

```
File: bn_fast_s_mp_mul_digs.c
018   /* Fast (comba) multiplier
019    *
020    * This is the fast column-array [comba] multiplier.  It is
021    * designed to compute the columns of the product first
022    * then handle the carries afterwards.  This has the effect
023    * of making the nested loops that compute the columns very
024    * simple and schedulable on super-scalar processors.
025    *
026    * This has been modified to produce a variable number of
027    * digits of output so if say only a half-product is required
028    * you don't have to compute the upper half (a feature
029    * required for fast Barrett reduction).
030    *
031    * Based on Algorithm 14.12 on pp.595 of HAC.
032    *
033    */
034   int fast_s_mp_mul_digs (mp_int * a, mp_int * b, mp_int * c, int digs)
```

```
035    {
036      int      olduse, res, pa, ix, iz;
037      mp_digit W[MP_WARRAY];
038      register mp_word  _W;
039
040      /* grow the destination as required */
041      if (c->alloc < digs) {
042        if ((res = mp_grow (c, digs)) != MP_OKAY) {
043          return res;
044        }
045      }
046
047      /* number of output digits to produce */
048      pa = MIN(digs, a->used + b->used);
049
050      /* clear the carry */
051      _W = 0;
052      for (ix = 0; ix < pa; ix++) {
053          int      tx, ty;
054          int      iy;
055          mp_digit *tmpx, *tmpy;
056
057          /* get offsets into the two bignums */
058          ty = MIN(b->used-1, ix);
059          tx = ix - ty;
060
061          /* setup temp aliases */
062          tmpx = a->dp + tx;
063          tmpy = b->dp + ty;
064
065          /* this is the number of times the loop will iterate, essentially
066             while (tx++ < a->used && ty-- >= 0) { ... }
067           */
068          iy = MIN(a->used-tx, ty+1);
069
070          /* execute loop */
071          for (iz = 0; iz < iy; ++iz) {
072              _W += ((mp_word)*tmpx++)*((mp_word)*tmpy--);
073          }
074
075          /* store term */
```

```
076              W[ix] = ((mp_digit)_W) & MP_MASK;
077
078              /* make next carry */
079              _W = _W >> ((mp_word)DIGIT_BIT);
080          }
081
082      /* setup dest */
083      olduse  = c->used;
084      c->used = pa;
085
086      {
087        register mp_digit *tmpc;
088        tmpc = c->dp;
089        for (ix = 0; ix < pa+1; ix++) {
090          /* now extract the previous digit [below the carry] */
091          *tmpc++ = W[ix];
092        }
093
094        /* clear unused digits [that existed in the old copy of c] */
095        for (; ix < olduse; ix++) {
096          *tmpc++ = 0;
097        }
098      }
099      mp_clamp (c);
100      return MP_OKAY;
101    }
102
```

As per the pseudo–code we first calculate $pa$ (line 48) as the number of digits to output. Next, we begin the outer loop to produce the individual columns of the product. We use the two aliases $tmpx$ and $tmpy$ (lines 62, 63) to point inside the two multiplicands quickly.

The inner loop (lines 71 to 73) of this implementation is where the trade–off come into play. Originally, this Comba implementation was "row–major," which means it adds to each of the columns in each pass. After the outer loop it would then fix the carries. This was very fast, except it had an annoying drawback. You had to read an mp_word and two mp_digits and write one mp_word per iteration. On processors such as the Athlon XP and P4 this did not matter much since the cache bandwidth is very high and it can keep the ALU fed with data. It did, however, matter on older and embedded CPUs where cache is often slower and often does not exist. This new algorithm only performs two reads per iteration under the assumption that the compiler has aliased $\_\hat{W}$ to a CPU register.

After the inner loop we store the current accumulator in $W$ and shift $\_\hat{W}$ (lines 76, 79) to forward it as a carry for the next pass. After the outer loop we use the final carry (line 76) as the last digit of the product.

### 5.2.3   Even Faster Multiplication

In the realm of $O(n^2)$ multipliers, we can actually do better than Comba multipliers. In the case of the portable code, only $lg(\beta)$ bits of each digit are being used. This is only because accessing carry bits from the CPU flags is not efficient in portable C.

In the TomsFastMath[2] project, a triple–precision register is used to accumulate products. The multiplication algorithm produces digits of the result at a time. The benefit of this algorithm is that we are packing more bits per digit resulting in fewer single precision multiplications. For example, a 1024–bit multiplication on a 32–bit platform involves 1024 single precision multiplications with TomsFastMath and $37^2 == 1369$ with LibTomMath (33% more).

---

[2]See `http://tfm.libtomcrypt.com`.

---

Algorithm **fast_mult**.
**Input**. mp_int $a$ and mp_int $b$
**Output**. $c \leftarrow |a| \cdot |b|$.

---

Let $c0$, $c1$, $c2$ be three single precision variables.
Let $tmp$ represent an mp_int.
1. Allocate tmp, an mp_int of $a.used + b.used$ digits. ($mp\_init\_size$)
2. $pa \leftarrow a.used + b.used$
3. for $ix$ from 0 to $pa - 1$ do
   3.1 $ty \leftarrow \text{MIN}(ix, b.used - 1)$
   3.2 $tx \leftarrow ix - ty$
   3.3 $iy \leftarrow \text{MIN}(a.used - tx, ty + 1)$
   3.4 $\{c2 : c1 : c0\} \leftarrow \{0 : c2 : c1\}$
   3.5 for $iz$ from 0 to $iy - 1$ do
      3.5.1 $\{c2 : c1 : c0\} \leftarrow \{c2 : c1 : c0\} + a_{tx+iz} b_{ty-iz}$
   3.6 $tmp_{ix} \leftarrow c0$
4. $tmp.used \leftarrow a.used + b.used$
5. Clamp $tmp$
6. Exchange $c$ and $tmp$
7. Clear $tmp$

---

Figure 5.6: Algorithm fast_mult

**Algorithm fast_mult.** This algorithm performs a multiplication using the full precision of the digits (Figure 5.6). It is not strictly part of LibTomMath, instead this is part of TomsFastMath. Quite literally the TomsFastMath library was a port of LibTomMath.

The first noteworthy change from our LibTomMath conventions is that we are indeed using the full precision of the digits. For example, on a 32–bit platform, a 1024–bit number would require 32 digits to be fully represented (instead of the 37 that LibTomMath would require).

The shuffle in step 3.4 is effectively a triple–precision shift right by the size of one digit. Similarly, in step 3.5.1, a double–precision product is being accumulated in the triple–precision array $\{c2 : c1 : c0\}$.

The TomsFastMath library gets its significant speed increase over LibTomMath not only due to the use of full precision digits, but also the fact that the multipliers are unrolled and use inline assembler. It unrolls the multipliers in steps of 1 through 16, 20, 24, 28, 32, 48 and 64 digits. The unrolling takes considerable space, but the savings in time from not having all of the loop control overhead is significant. The use of inline assembler also lets us perform the inner loop with code such as the following x86 assembler.

```
#define MULADD(i, j)                                          \
asm(                                                          \
      "movl   %6,%%eax      \n\t"                             \
      "mull   %7            \n\t"                             \
      "addl   %%eax,%0      \n\t"                             \
      "adcl   %%edx,%1      \n\t"                             \
      "adcl   $0,%2         \n\t"                             \
      :"=r"(c0), "=r"(c1), "=r"(c2):                          \
      "0"(c0), "1"(c1), "2"(c2), "m"(i), "m"(j) :            \
      "%eax","%edx","%cc");
```

This performs the $32 \times 32$ multiplication and accumulates it in the 96–bit array $\{c2 : c1 : c0\}$, as required in step 3.5.1. A particular feature of the TomsFastMath approach is to use these functional macro blocks instead of hand–tuning the implementation for a given platform. As a result, we can change the macro to the following and produce a math library for ARM processors.

```
#define MULADD(i, j)                                        \
asm(                                                        \
   "UMULL   r0,r1,%6,%7        \n\t"                        \
   "ADDS    %0,%0,r0           \n\t"                        \
   "ADCS    %1,%1,r1           \n\t"                        \
   "ADC     %2,%2,#0           \n\t"                        \
   :"=r"(c0), "=r"(c1), "=r"(c2) :                          \
     "0"(c0), "1"(c1), "2"(c2), "r"(i), "r"(j) :           \
     "r0", "r1", "%cc");
```

In total, TomsFastMath supports four distinct hardware architectures covering x86, PPC32 and ARM platforms from a relatively consistent code base. Adding new ports for most platforms is usually a matter of implementing the macros, and then choosing a suitable level of loop unrolling to match the processor cache.

When fully unrolled, the x86 assembly code achieves very high performance on the AMD K8 series of processors. An "instructions per cycle" count close to 2 can be observed through 1024–bit multiplications. This means that, on average, more than one processor pipeline is actively processing opcodes. This is particularly significant due to the long delay of the single precision multiplication instruction.

Unfortunately, while this routine could be adapted to LibTomMath (using a more complicated right shift in step 3.4), it would not help as we still have to perform the same number of single precision multiplications. Readers are encouraged to investigate the TomsFastMath library on its own to see how far these optimizations can push performance.

## 5.2.4 Polynomial Basis Multiplication

To break the $O(n^2)$ barrier in multiplication requires a completely different look at integer multiplication. In the following algorithms the use of polynomial basis representation for two integers $a$ and $b$ as $f(x) = \sum_{i=0}^{n} a_i x^i$ and $g(x) = \sum_{i=0}^{n} b_i x^i$, respectively, is required. In this system, both $f(x)$ and $g(x)$ have $n+1$ terms and are of the $n$'th degree.

The product $a \cdot b \equiv f(x)g(x)$ is the polynomial $W(x) = \sum_{i=0}^{2n} w_i x^i$. The coefficients $w_i$ will directly yield the desired product when $\beta$ is substituted for $x$. The direct solution to solve for the $2n + 1$ coefficients requires $O(n^2)$ time and would in practice be slower than the Comba technique.

However, numerical analysis theory indicates that only $2n + 1$ distinct points in $W(x)$ are required to determine the values of the $2n + 1$ unknown coefficients. This means by finding $\zeta_y = W(y)$ for $2n + 1$ small values of $y$, the coefficients of $W(x)$ can be found with Gaussian elimination. This technique is also occasionally referred to as the *interpolation technique* [20], since in effect an interpolation based on $2n + 1$ points will yield a polynomial equivalent to $W(x)$.

The coefficients of the polynomial $W(x)$ are unknown, which makes finding $W(y)$ for any value of $y$ impossible. However, since $W(x) = f(x)g(x)$, the equivalent $\zeta_y = f(y)g(y)$ can be used in its place. The benefit of this technique stems from the fact that $f(y)$ and $g(y)$ are much smaller than either $a$ or $b$, respectively. As a result, finding the $2n + 1$ relations required by multiplying $f(y)g(y)$ involves multiplying integers that are much smaller than either of the inputs.

When you are picking points to gather relations, there are always three obvious points to choose, $y = 0, 1$, and $\infty$. The $\zeta_0$ term is simply the product $W(0) = w_0 = a_0 \cdot b_0$. The $\zeta_1$ term is the product $W(1) = \left( \sum_{i=0}^{n} a_i \right) \left( \sum_{i=0}^{n} b_i \right)$. The third point $\zeta_\infty$ is less obvious but rather simple to explain. The $2n+1$'th coefficient of $W(x)$ is numerically equivalent to the most significant column in an integer multiplication. The point at $\infty$ is used symbolically to represent the most significant column– $W(\infty) = w_{2n} = a_n b_n$. Note that the points at $y = 0$ and $\infty$ yield the coefficients $w_0$ and $w_{2n}$ directly.

If more points are required they should be of small values and powers of two

| Split into $n$ Parts | Exponent | Notes |
|:---:|:---:|:---|
| 2 | 1.584962501 | This is Karatsuba Multiplication. |
| 3 | 1.464973520 | This is Toom-Cook 3-Way Multiplication. |
| 4 | 1.403677461 | |
| 5 | 1.365212389 | |
| 10 | 1.278753601 | |
| 100 | 1.149426538 | Beyond this point Fourier Transforms are used. |
| 1000 | 1.100270931 | |
| 10000 | 1.075252070 | |

Figure 5.7: Asymptotic Running Time of Polynomial Basis Multiplication

such as $2^q$ and the related *mirror points* $(2^q)^{2n} \cdot \zeta_{2-q}$ for small values of $q$. The term "mirror point" stems from the fact that $(2^q)^{2n} \cdot \zeta_{2-q}$ can be calculated in the exact opposite fashion as $\zeta_{2q}$. For example, when $n = 2$ and $q = 1$, the following two equations are equivalent to the point $\zeta_2$ and its mirror.

$$\zeta_2 = f(2)g(2) = (4a_2 + 2a_1 + a_0)(4b_2 + 2b_1 + b_0)$$
$$16 \cdot \zeta_{\frac{1}{2}} = 4f(\frac{1}{2}) \cdot 4g(\frac{1}{2}) = (a_2 + 2a_1 + 4a_0)(b_2 + 2b_1 + 4b_0) \tag{5.5}$$

Using such points will allow the values of $f(y)$ and $g(y)$ to be independently calculated using only left shifts. For example, when $n = 2$ the polynomial $f(2^q)$ is equal to $2^q((2^q a_2) + a_1) + a_0$. This technique of polynomial representation is known as Horner's method.

As a general rule of the algorithm when the inputs are split into $n$ parts each, there are $2n - 1$ multiplications. Each multiplication is of multiplicands that have $n$ times fewer digits than the inputs. The asymptotic running time of this algorithm is $O\left(k^{lg_n(2n-1)}\right)$ for $k$ digit inputs (*assuming they have the same number of digits*). Figure 5.7 summarizes the exponents for various values of $n$.

At first, it may seem like a good idea to choose $n = 1000$ since the exponent is approximately 1.1. However, the overhead of solving for the 2001 terms of $W(x)$ will certainly consume any savings the algorithm could offer for all but exceedingly large numbers.

**Cutoff Point**

The polynomial basis multiplication algorithms all require fewer single precision multiplications than a straight Comba approach. However, the algorithms incur an overhead (*at the $O(n)$ work level*) since they require a system of equations to be solved. This makes the polynomial basis approach more costly to use with small inputs.

Let $m$ represent the number of digits in the multiplicands (*assume both multiplicands have the same number of digits*). There exists a point $y$ such that when $m < y$, the polynomial basis algorithms are more costly than Comba; when $m = y$, they are roughly the same cost; and when $m > y$, the Comba methods are slower than the polynomial basis algorithms.

The exact location of $y$ depends on several key architectural elements of the computer platform in question.

1. The ratio of clock cycles for single precision multiplication versus other simpler operations such as addition, shifting, etc. For example on the AMD Athlon the ratio is roughly 17 : 1, while on the Intel P4 it is 29 : 1. The higher the ratio in favor of multiplication, the lower the cutoff point $y$ will be.

2. The complexity of the linear system of equations (*for the coefficients of $W(x)$*) is, generally speaking, as the number of splits grows the complexity grows substantially. Ideally, solving the system will only involve addition, subtraction, and shifting of integers. This directly reflects on the ratio previously mentioned.

3. To a lesser extent, memory bandwidth and function call overhead affect the location of $y$. Provided the values and code are in the processor cache, this is less of an influence over the cutoff point.

A clean cutoff point separation occurs when a point $y$ is found such that all the cutoff point conditions are met. For example, if the point is too low, there will be values of $m$ such that $m > y$ and the Comba method is still faster. Finding the cutoff points is fairly simple when a high–resolution timer is available.

## 5.2.5 Karatsuba Multiplication

Karatsuba [19] multiplication when originally proposed in 1962 was among the first set of algorithms to break the $O(n^2)$ barrier for general–purpose multiplication.

Given two polynomial basis representations $f(x) = ax + b$ and $g(x) = cx + d$, Karatsuba proved with light algebra [5] that the following polynomial is equivalent to multiplication of the two integers the polynomials represent.

$$f(x) \cdot g(x) = acx^2 + ((a + b)(c + d) - (ac + bd))x + bd \qquad (5.6)$$

Using the observation that $ac$ and $bd$ could be re-used, only three half–sized multiplications would be required to produce the product. Applying this algorithm recursively the work factor becomes $O(n^{lg(3)})$, which is substantially better than the work factor $O(n^2)$ of the Comba technique. It turns out what Karatsuba did not know or at least did not publish was that this is simply polynomial basis multiplication with the points $\zeta_0$, $\zeta_\infty$, and $\zeta_1$. Consider the resultant system of equations.

$$
\begin{array}{rcl}
\zeta_0 & = & w_0 \\
\zeta_1 & = & w_2 + w_1 + w_0 \\
\zeta_\infty & = & w_2
\end{array}
$$

By adding the first and last equation to the equation in the middle, the term $w_1$ can be isolated and all three coefficients solved for. The simplicity of this system of equations has made Karatsuba fairly popular. In fact, the cutoff point is often fairly low[3], making it an ideal algorithm to speed up certain public key cryptosystems such as RSA and Diffie-Hellman.

---

[3]With LibTomMath 0.18 it is 70 and 109 digits for the Intel P4 and AMD Athlon, respectively.

---

Algorithm **mp_karatsuba_mul**.
**Input**. mp_int $a$ and mp_int $b$
**Output**. $c \leftarrow |a| \cdot |b|$

---

1. Init the following mp_int variables: $x0$, $x1$, $y0$, $y1$, $t1$, $x0y0$, $x1y1$.
2. If step 2 failed, then return($MP\_MEM$).

Split the input. e.g. $a = x1 \cdot \beta^B + x0$
3. $B \leftarrow \min(a.used, b.used)/2$
4. $x0 \leftarrow a \pmod{\beta^B}$ ($mp\_mod\_2d$)
5. $y0 \leftarrow b \pmod{\beta^B}$
6. $x1 \leftarrow \lfloor a/\beta^B \rfloor$ ($mp\_rshd$)
7. $y1 \leftarrow \lfloor b/\beta^B \rfloor$

Calculate the three products.
8. $x0y0 \leftarrow x0 \cdot y0$ ($mp\_mul$)
9. $x1y1 \leftarrow x1 \cdot y1$
10. $t1 \leftarrow x1 + x0$ ($mp\_add$)
11. $x0 \leftarrow y1 + y0$
12. $t1 \leftarrow t1 \cdot x0$

Calculate the middle term.
13. $x0 \leftarrow x0y0 + x1y1$
14. $t1 \leftarrow t1 - x0$ ($s\_mp\_sub$)

Calculate the final product.
15. $t1 \leftarrow t1 \cdot \beta^B$ ($mp\_lshd$)
16. $x1y1 \leftarrow x1y1 \cdot \beta^{2B}$
17. $t1 \leftarrow x0y0 + t1$
18. $c \leftarrow t1 + x1y1$
19. Clear all of the temporary variables.
20. Return($MP\_OKAY$).

---

Figure 5.8: Algorithm mp_karatsuba_mul

**Algorithm mp_karatsuba_mul.** This algorithm computes the unsigned product of two inputs using the Karatsuba multiplication algorithm. It is loosely based on the description from Knuth [1, pp. 294-295] (Figure 5.8).

To split the two inputs into their respective halves, a suitable *radix point* must be chosen. The radix point chosen must be used for both of the inputs, meaning that it must be smaller than the smallest input. Step 3 chooses the radix point $B$ as half of the smallest input **used** count. After the radix point is chosen, the inputs are split into lower and upper halves. Steps 4 and 5 compute the lower halves. Steps 6 and 7 compute the upper halves.

After the halves have been computed the three intermediate half-size products must be computed. Step 8 and 9 compute the trivial products $x0 \cdot y0$ and $x1 \cdot y1$. The mp_int $x0$ is used as a temporary variable after $x1 + x0$ has been computed. By using $x0$ instead of an additional temporary variable, the algorithm can avoid an addition memory allocation operation.

The remaining steps 13 through 18 compute the Karatsuba polynomial through a variety of digit shifting and addition operations.

```
File: bn_mp_karatsuba_mul.c
018    /* c = |a| * |b| using Karatsuba Multiplication using
019     * three half size multiplications
020     *
021     * Let B represent the radix [e.g. 2**DIGIT_BIT] and
022     * let n represent half of the number of digits in
023     * the min(a,b)
024     *
025     * a = a1 * B**n + a0
026     * b = b1 * B**n + b0
027     *
028     * Then, a * b =>
029       a1b1 * B**2n + ((a1 + a0)(b1 + b0) - (a0b0 + a1b1)) * B + a0b0
030     *
031     * Note that a1b1 and a0b0 are used twice and only need to be
032     * computed once.  So in total three half size (half # of
033     * digit) multiplications are performed, a0b0, a1b1 and
034     * (a1+b1)(a0+b0)
035     *
036     * Note that a multiplication of half the digits requires
037     * 1/4th the number of single precision multiplications so in
038     * total after one call 25% of the single precision multiplications
039     * are saved.  Note also that the call to mp_mul can end up back
040     * in this function if the a0, a1, b0, or b1 are above the threshold.
041     * This is known as divide-and-conquer and leads to the famous
042     * O(N**lg(3)) or O(N**1.584) work which is asymptopically lower than
043     * the standard O(N**2) that the baseline/comba methods use.
044     * Generally though the overhead of this method doesn't pay off
045     * until a certain size (N ~ 80) is reached.
```

```
046     */
047     int mp_karatsuba_mul (mp_int * a, mp_int * b, mp_int * c)
048     {
049       mp_int  x0, x1, y0, y1, t1, x0y0, x1y1;
050       int     B, err;
051
052       /* default the return code to an error */
053       err = MP_MEM;
054
055       /* min # of digits */
056       B = MIN (a->used, b->used);
057
058       /* now divide in two */
059       B = B >> 1;
060
061       /* init copy all the temps */
062       if (mp_init_size (&x0, B) != MP_OKAY)
063         goto ERR;
064       if (mp_init_size (&x1, a->used - B) != MP_OKAY)
065         goto X0;
066       if (mp_init_size (&y0, B) != MP_OKAY)
067         goto X1;
068       if (mp_init_size (&y1, b->used - B) != MP_OKAY)
069         goto Y0;
070
071       /* init temps */
072       if (mp_init_size (&t1, B * 2) != MP_OKAY)
073         goto Y1;
074       if (mp_init_size (&x0y0, B * 2) != MP_OKAY)
075         goto T1;
076       if (mp_init_size (&x1y1, B * 2) != MP_OKAY)
077         goto X0Y0;
078
079       /* now shift the digits */
080       x0.used = y0.used = B;
081       x1.used = a->used - B;
082       y1.used = b->used - B;
083
084       {
085         register int x;
086         register mp_digit *tmpa, *tmpb, *tmpx, *tmpy;
```

```
087
088    /* we copy the digits directly instead of using higher level functions
089     * since we also need to shift the digits
090     */
091    tmpa = a->dp;
092    tmpb = b->dp;
093
094    tmpx = x0.dp;
095    tmpy = y0.dp;
096    for (x = 0; x < B; x++) {
097       *tmpx++ = *tmpa++;
098       *tmpy++ = *tmpb++;
099    }
100
101    tmpx = x1.dp;
102    for (x = B; x < a->used; x++) {
103       *tmpx++ = *tmpa++;
104    }
105
106    tmpy = y1.dp;
107    for (x = B; x < b->used; x++) {
108       *tmpy++ = *tmpb++;
109    }
110    }
111
112    /* only need to clamp the lower words since by definition the
113     * upper words x1/y1 must have a known number of digits
114     */
115    mp_clamp (&x0);
116    mp_clamp (&y0);
117
118    /* now calc the products x0y0 and x1y1 */
119    /* after this x0 is no longer required, free temp [x0==t2]! */
120    if (mp_mul (&x0, &y0, &x0y0) != MP_OKAY)
121       goto X1Y1;          /* x0y0 = x0*y0 */
122    if (mp_mul (&x1, &y1, &x1y1) != MP_OKAY)
123       goto X1Y1;          /* x1y1 = x1*y1 */
124
125    /* now calc x1+x0 and y1+y0 */
126    if (s_mp_add (&x1, &x0, &t1) != MP_OKAY)
127       goto X1Y1;          /* t1 = x1 - x0 */
```

```
128      if (s_mp_add (&y1, &y0, &x0) != MP_OKAY)
129        goto X1Y1;               /* t2 = y1 - y0 */
130      if (mp_mul (&t1, &x0, &t1) != MP_OKAY)
131        goto X1Y1;               /* t1 = (x1 + x0) * (y1 + y0) */
132
133      /* add x0y0 */
134      if (mp_add (&x0y0, &x1y1, &x0) != MP_OKAY)
135        goto X1Y1;               /* t2 = x0y0 + x1y1 */
136      if (s_mp_sub (&t1, &x0, &t1) != MP_OKAY)
137        goto X1Y1;               /* t1 = (x1+x0)*(y1+y0) - (x1y1 + x0y0) */
138
139      /* shift by B */
140      if (mp_lshd (&t1, B) != MP_OKAY)
141        goto X1Y1;               /* t1 = (x0y0 + x1y1 - (x1-x0)*(y1-y0))<<B */
142      if (mp_lshd (&x1y1, B * 2) != MP_OKAY)
143        goto X1Y1;               /* x1y1 = x1y1 << 2*B */
144
145      if (mp_add (&x0y0, &t1, &t1) != MP_OKAY)
146        goto X1Y1;               /* t1 = x0y0 + t1 */
147      if (mp_add (&t1, &x1y1, c) != MP_OKAY)
148        goto X1Y1;               /* t1 = x0y0 + t1 + x1y1 */
149
150      /* Algorithm succeeded set the return code to MP_OKAY */
151      err = MP_OKAY;
152
153   X1Y1:mp_clear (&x1y1);
154   X0Y0:mp_clear (&x0y0);
155   T1:mp_clear (&t1);
156   Y1:mp_clear (&y1);
157   Y0:mp_clear (&y0);
158   X1:mp_clear (&x1);
159   X0:mp_clear (&x0);
160   ERR:
161      return err;
162   }
163
```

The new coding element in this routine, not seen in previous routines, is the usage of goto statements. The conventional wisdom is that goto statements should be avoided. This is generally true; however, when every single function call can fail, it makes sense to handle error recovery with a single piece of code. Lines 62 to 76 handle initializing all of the temporary variables required. Note how each of the if statements goes to a different label in case of failure. This allows the routine to correctly free only the temporaries that have been successfully allocated so far.

The temporary variables are all initialized using the mp_init_size routine since they are expected to be large. This saves the additional reallocation that would have been necessary. Moreover, $x0$, $x1$, $y0$, and $y1$ have to be able to hold at least their respective number of digits for the next section of code.

The first algebraic portion of the algorithm is to split the two inputs into their halves. However, instead of using mp_mod_2d and mp_rshd to extract the halves, the respective code has been placed inline within the body of the function. To initialize the halves, the **used** and **sign** members are copied first. The first for loop on line 96 copies the lower halves. Since they are both the same magnitude, it is simpler to calculate both lower halves in a single loop. The for loop on lines 102 and 107 calculate the upper halves $x1$ and $y1$, respectively.

By inlining the calculation of the halves, the Karatsuba multiplier has a slightly lower overhead and can be used for smaller magnitude inputs.

When line 151 is reached, the algorithm has completed successfully. The "error status" variable *err* is set to **MP_OKAY** so the same code that handles errors can be used to clear the temporary variables and return.

## 5.2.6   Toom-Cook 3-Way Multiplication

The 3–Way multiplication scheme, usually known as Toom–Cook, is actually a variation of the Toom–Cook multiplication [1, pp. 296–299] algorithm. In their combined approach, multiplication is essentially linearized by increasing the number of ways as the size of the inputs increase. The 3–Way approach is the polynomial basis algorithm for $n = 2$, except that the points are chosen such that $\zeta$ is easy to compute and the resulting system of equations easy to reduce. Here, the points $\zeta_0$, $16 \cdot \zeta_{\frac{1}{2}}$, $\zeta_1$, $\zeta_2$, and $\zeta_\infty$ make up the five required points to solve for the coefficients of $W(x)$.

With the five relations Toom-Cook specifies, the following system of equations is formed.

$$
\begin{aligned}
\zeta_0 &= 0w_4 + 0w_3 + 0w_2 + 0w_1 + 1w_0 \\
16 \cdot \zeta_{\frac{1}{2}} &= 1w_4 + 2w_3 + 4w_2 + 8w_1 + 16w_0 \\
\zeta_1 &= 1w_4 + 1w_3 + 1w_2 + 1w_1 + 1w_0 \\
\zeta_2 &= 16w_4 + 8w_3 + 4w_2 + 2w_1 + 1w_0 \\
\zeta_\infty &= 1w_4 + 0w_3 + 0w_2 + 0w_1 + 0w_0
\end{aligned}
$$

A trivial solution to this matrix requires 12 subtractions, two multiplications by a small power of two, two divisions by a small power of two, two divisions by three, and one multiplication by three. All of these 19 sub-operations require less than quadratic time, meaning that the algorithm can be faster than a baseline multiplication. However, the greater complexity of this algorithm places the cut-off point (**TOOM_MUL_CUTOFF**) where Toom-Cook becomes more efficient much higher than the Karatsuba cutoff point.

---

Algorithm **mp_toom_mul**.
**Input**. mp_int $a$ and mp_int $b$
**Output**. $c \leftarrow a \cdot b$

---

Split $a$ and $b$ into three pieces. E.g. $a = a_2 \beta^{2k} + a_1 \beta^k + a_0$
1. $k \leftarrow \lfloor \min(a.used, b.used)/3 \rfloor$
2. $a_0 \leftarrow a \pmod{\beta^k}$
3. $a_1 \leftarrow \lfloor a/\beta^k \rfloor$, $a_1 \leftarrow a_1 \pmod{\beta^k}$
4. $a_2 \leftarrow \lfloor a/\beta^{2k} \rfloor$, $a_2 \leftarrow a_2 \pmod{\beta^k}$
5. $b_0 \leftarrow a \pmod{\beta^k}$
6. $b_1 \leftarrow \lfloor a/\beta^k \rfloor$, $b_1 \leftarrow b_1 \pmod{\beta^k}$
7. $b_2 \leftarrow \lfloor a/\beta^{2k} \rfloor$, $b_2 \leftarrow b_2 \pmod{\beta^k}$

Find the five equations for $w_0, w_1, ..., w_4$.
8. $w_0 \leftarrow a_0 \cdot b_0$
9. $w_4 \leftarrow a_2 \cdot b_2$
10. $tmp_1 \leftarrow 2 \cdot a_0$, $tmp_1 \leftarrow a_1 + tmp_1$, $tmp_1 \leftarrow 2 \cdot tmp_1$, $tmp_1 \leftarrow tmp_1 + a_2$
11. $tmp_2 \leftarrow 2 \cdot b_0$, $tmp_2 \leftarrow b_1 + tmp_2$, $tmp_2 \leftarrow 2 \cdot tmp_2$, $tmp_2 \leftarrow tmp_2 + b_2$
12. $w_1 \leftarrow tmp_1 \cdot tmp_2$
13. $tmp_1 \leftarrow 2 \cdot a_2$, $tmp_1 \leftarrow a_1 + tmp_1$, $tmp_1 \leftarrow 2 \cdot tmp_1$, $tmp_1 \leftarrow tmp_1 + a_0$
14. $tmp_2 \leftarrow 2 \cdot b_2$, $tmp_2 \leftarrow b_1 + tmp_2$, $tmp_2 \leftarrow 2 \cdot tmp_2$, $tmp_2 \leftarrow tmp_2 + b_0$
15. $w_3 \leftarrow tmp_1 \cdot tmp_2$
16. $tmp_1 \leftarrow a_0 + a_1$, $tmp_1 \leftarrow tmp_1 + a_2$, $tmp_2 \leftarrow b_0 + b_1$, $tmp_2 \leftarrow tmp_2 + b_2$
17. $w_2 \leftarrow tmp_1 \cdot tmp_2$

---

Continued on the next page.

---

---

Algorithm **mp_toom_mul** (continued).
**Input**. mp_int $a$ and mp_int $b$
**Output**. $c \leftarrow a \cdot b$

---

Now solve the system of equations.
18. $w_1 \leftarrow w_4 - w_1, w_3 \leftarrow w_3 - w_0$
19. $w_1 \leftarrow \lfloor w_1/2 \rfloor, w_3 \leftarrow \lfloor w_3/2 \rfloor$
20. $w_2 \leftarrow w_2 - w_0, w_2 \leftarrow w_2 - w_4$
21. $w_1 \leftarrow w_1 - w_2, w_3 \leftarrow w_3 - w_2$
22. $tmp_1 \leftarrow 8 \cdot w_0, w_1 \leftarrow w_1 - tmp_1, tmp_1 \leftarrow 8 \cdot w_4, w_3 \leftarrow w_3 - tmp_1$
23. $w_2 \leftarrow 3 \cdot w_2, w_2 \leftarrow w_2 - w_1, w_2 \leftarrow w_2 - w_3$
24. $w_1 \leftarrow w_1 - w_2, w_3 \leftarrow w_3 - w_2$
25. $w_1 \leftarrow \lfloor w_1/3 \rfloor, w_3 \leftarrow \lfloor w_3/3 \rfloor$

Now substitute $\beta^k$ for $x$ by shifting $w_0, w_1, ..., w_4$.
26. for $n$ from 1 to 4 do
    26.1 $w_n \leftarrow w_n \cdot \beta^{nk}$
27. $c \leftarrow w_0 + w_1, c \leftarrow c + w_2, c \leftarrow c + w_3, c \leftarrow c + w_4$
28. Return($MP\_OKAY$)

---

Figure 5.9: Algorithm mp_toom_mul

**Algorithm mp_toom_mul.** This algorithm computes the product of two mp_int variables $a$ and $b$ using the Toom-Cook approach. Compared to the Karatsuba multiplication, this algorithm has a lower asymptotic running time of approximately $O(n^{1.464})$ but at an obvious cost in overhead. In this description, several statements have been compounded to save space. The intention is that the statements are executed from left to right across any given step (Figure 5.9).

The two inputs $a$ and $b$ are first split into three $k$-digit integers $a_0, a_1, a_2$ and $b_0, b_1, b_2$, respectively. From these smaller integers the coefficients of the polynomial basis representations $f(x)$ and $g(x)$ are known and can be used to find the relations required.

The first two relations $w_0$ and $w_4$ are the points $\zeta_0$ and $\zeta_\infty$, respectively. The relation $w_1, w_2$, and $w_3$ correspond to the points $16 \cdot \zeta_{\frac{1}{2}}, \zeta_2$ and $\zeta_1$, respectively. These are found using logical shifts to independently find $f(y)$ and $g(y)$, which significantly speeds up the algorithm.

After the five relations $w_0, w_1, \ldots, w_4$ have been computed, the system they represent must be solved in order for the unknown coefficients $w_1, w_2$, and $w_3$ to be isolated. Steps 18 through 25 perform the system reduction required as previously described. Each step of the reduction represents the comparable matrix operation that would be performed had this been performed by pencil. For example, step 18 indicates that row 1 must be subtracted from row 4, and simultaneously row 0 subtracted from row 3.

Once the coefficients have been isolated, the polynomial $W(x) = \sum_{i=0}^{2n} w_i x^i$ is known. By substituting $\beta^k$ for $x$, the integer result $a \cdot b$ is produced.

```
File: bn_mp_toom_mul.c
018    /* multiplication using the Toom-Cook 3-way algorithm
019     *
020     * Much more complicated than Karatsuba but has a lower
021     * asymptotic running time of O(N**1.464).  This algorithm is
022     * only particularly useful on VERY large inputs
023     * (we're talking 1000s of digits here...).
024     */
025    int mp_toom_mul(mp_int *a, mp_int *b, mp_int *c)
026    {
027        mp_int w0, w1, w2, w3, w4, tmp1, tmp2, a0, a1, a2, b0, b1, b2;
028        int res, B;
029
030        /* init temps */
031        if ((res = mp_init_multi(&w0, &w1, &w2, &w3, &w4,
032                                 &a0, &a1, &a2, &b0, &b1,
033                                 &b2, &tmp1, &tmp2, NULL)) != MP_OKAY) {
034            return res;
035        }
036
037        /* B */
038        B = MIN(a->used, b->used) / 3;
039
040        /* a = a2 * B**2 + a1 * B + a0 */
041        if ((res = mp_mod_2d(a, DIGIT_BIT * B, &a0)) != MP_OKAY) {
042            goto ERR;
043        }
044
045        if ((res = mp_copy(a, &a1)) != MP_OKAY) {
046            goto ERR;
047        }
048        mp_rshd(&a1, B);
049        mp_mod_2d(&a1, DIGIT_BIT * B, &a1);
```

```
050
051        if ((res = mp_copy(a, &a2)) != MP_OKAY) {
052           goto ERR;
053        }
054        mp_rshd(&a2, B*2);
055
056        /* b = b2 * B**2 + b1 * B + b0 */
057        if ((res = mp_mod_2d(b, DIGIT_BIT * B, &b0)) != MP_OKAY) {
058           goto ERR;
059        }
060
061        if ((res = mp_copy(b, &b1)) != MP_OKAY) {
062           goto ERR;
063        }
064        mp_rshd(&b1, B);
065        mp_mod_2d(&b1, DIGIT_BIT * B, &b1);
066
067        if ((res = mp_copy(b, &b2)) != MP_OKAY) {
068           goto ERR;
069        }
070        mp_rshd(&b2, B*2);
071
072        /* w0 = a0*b0 */
073        if ((res = mp_mul(&a0, &b0, &w0)) != MP_OKAY) {
074           goto ERR;
075        }
076
077        /* w4 = a2 * b2 */
078        if ((res = mp_mul(&a2, &b2, &w4)) != MP_OKAY) {
079           goto ERR;
080        }
081
082        /* w1 = (a2 + 2(a1 + 2a0))(b2 + 2(b1 + 2b0)) */
083        if ((res = mp_mul_2(&a0, &tmp1)) != MP_OKAY) {
084           goto ERR;
085        }
086        if ((res = mp_add(&tmp1, &a1, &tmp1)) != MP_OKAY) {
087           goto ERR;
088        }
089        if ((res = mp_mul_2(&tmp1, &tmp1)) != MP_OKAY) {
090           goto ERR;
```

```
091         }
092         if ((res = mp_add(&tmp1, &a2, &tmp1)) != MP_OKAY) {
093            goto ERR;
094         }
095
096         if ((res = mp_mul_2(&b0, &tmp2)) != MP_OKAY) {
097            goto ERR;
098         }
099         if ((res = mp_add(&tmp2, &b1, &tmp2)) != MP_OKAY) {
100            goto ERR;
101         }
102         if ((res = mp_mul_2(&tmp2, &tmp2)) != MP_OKAY) {
103            goto ERR;
104         }
105         if ((res = mp_add(&tmp2, &b2, &tmp2)) != MP_OKAY) {
106            goto ERR;
107         }
108
109         if ((res = mp_mul(&tmp1, &tmp2, &w1)) != MP_OKAY) {
110            goto ERR;
111         }
112
113         /* w3 = (a0 + 2(a1 + 2a2))(b0 + 2(b1 + 2b2)) */
114         if ((res = mp_mul_2(&a2, &tmp1)) != MP_OKAY) {
115            goto ERR;
116         }
117         if ((res = mp_add(&tmp1, &a1, &tmp1)) != MP_OKAY) {
118            goto ERR;
119         }
120         if ((res = mp_mul_2(&tmp1, &tmp1)) != MP_OKAY) {
121            goto ERR;
122         }
123         if ((res = mp_add(&tmp1, &a0, &tmp1)) != MP_OKAY) {
124            goto ERR;
125         }
126
127         if ((res = mp_mul_2(&b2, &tmp2)) != MP_OKAY) {
128            goto ERR;
129         }
130         if ((res = mp_add(&tmp2, &b1, &tmp2)) != MP_OKAY) {
131            goto ERR;
```

```
132        }
133        if ((res = mp_mul_2(&tmp2, &tmp2)) != MP_OKAY) {
134           goto ERR;
135        }
136        if ((res = mp_add(&tmp2, &b0, &tmp2)) != MP_OKAY) {
137           goto ERR;
138        }
139
140        if ((res = mp_mul(&tmp1, &tmp2, &w3)) != MP_OKAY) {
141           goto ERR;
142        }
143
144
145        /* w2 = (a2 + a1 + a0)(b2 + b1 + b0) */
146        if ((res = mp_add(&a2, &a1, &tmp1)) != MP_OKAY) {
147           goto ERR;
148        }
149        if ((res = mp_add(&tmp1, &a0, &tmp1)) != MP_OKAY) {
150           goto ERR;
151        }
152        if ((res = mp_add(&b2, &b1, &tmp2)) != MP_OKAY) {
153           goto ERR;
154        }
155        if ((res = mp_add(&tmp2, &b0, &tmp2)) != MP_OKAY) {
156           goto ERR;
157        }
158        if ((res = mp_mul(&tmp1, &tmp2, &w2)) != MP_OKAY) {
159           goto ERR;
160        }
161
162        /* now solve the matrix
163
164           0  0  0  0  1
165           1  2  4  8  16
166           1  1  1  1  1
167           16 8  4  2  1
168           1  0  0  0  0
169
170           using 12 subtractions, 4 shifts,
171                   2 small divisions and 1 small multiplication
172         */
```

```
173
174         /* r1 - r4 */
175         if ((res = mp_sub(&w1, &w4, &w1)) != MP_OKAY) {
176            goto ERR;
177         }
178         /* r3 - r0 */
179         if ((res = mp_sub(&w3, &w0, &w3)) != MP_OKAY) {
180            goto ERR;
181         }
182         /* r1/2 */
183         if ((res = mp_div_2(&w1, &w1)) != MP_OKAY) {
184            goto ERR;
185         }
186         /* r3/2 */
187         if ((res = mp_div_2(&w3, &w3)) != MP_OKAY) {
188            goto ERR;
189         }
190         /* r2 - r0 - r4 */
191         if ((res = mp_sub(&w2, &w0, &w2)) != MP_OKAY) {
192            goto ERR;
193         }
194         if ((res = mp_sub(&w2, &w4, &w2)) != MP_OKAY) {
195            goto ERR;
196         }
197         /* r1 - r2 */
198         if ((res = mp_sub(&w1, &w2, &w1)) != MP_OKAY) {
199            goto ERR;
200         }
201         /* r3 - r2 */
202         if ((res = mp_sub(&w3, &w2, &w3)) != MP_OKAY) {
203            goto ERR;
204         }
205         /* r1 - 8r0 */
206         if ((res = mp_mul_2d(&w0, 3, &tmp1)) != MP_OKAY) {
207            goto ERR;
208         }
209         if ((res = mp_sub(&w1, &tmp1, &w1)) != MP_OKAY) {
210            goto ERR;
211         }
212         /* r3 - 8r4 */
213         if ((res = mp_mul_2d(&w4, 3, &tmp1)) != MP_OKAY) {
```

```
214            goto ERR;
215        }
216        if ((res = mp_sub(&w3, &tmp1, &w3)) != MP_OKAY) {
217            goto ERR;
218        }
219        /* 3r2 - r1 - r3 */
220        if ((res = mp_mul_d(&w2, 3, &w2)) != MP_OKAY) {
221            goto ERR;
222        }
223        if ((res = mp_sub(&w2, &w1, &w2)) != MP_OKAY) {
224            goto ERR;
225        }
226        if ((res = mp_sub(&w2, &w3, &w2)) != MP_OKAY) {
227            goto ERR;
228        }
229        /* r1 - r2 */
230        if ((res = mp_sub(&w1, &w2, &w1)) != MP_OKAY) {
231            goto ERR;
232        }
233        /* r3 - r2 */
234        if ((res = mp_sub(&w3, &w2, &w3)) != MP_OKAY) {
235            goto ERR;
236        }
237        /* r1/3 */
238        if ((res = mp_div_3(&w1, &w1, NULL)) != MP_OKAY) {
239            goto ERR;
240        }
241        /* r3/3 */
242        if ((res = mp_div_3(&w3, &w3, NULL)) != MP_OKAY) {
243            goto ERR;
244        }
245
246        /* at this point shift W[n] by B*n */
247        if ((res = mp_lshd(&w1, 1*B)) != MP_OKAY) {
248            goto ERR;
249        }
250        if ((res = mp_lshd(&w2, 2*B)) != MP_OKAY) {
251            goto ERR;
252        }
253        if ((res = mp_lshd(&w3, 3*B)) != MP_OKAY) {
254            goto ERR;
```

```
255        }
256        if ((res = mp_lshd(&w4, 4*B)) != MP_OKAY) {
257            goto ERR;
258        }
259
260        if ((res = mp_add(&w0, &w1, c)) != MP_OKAY) {
261            goto ERR;
262        }
263        if ((res = mp_add(&w2, &w3, &tmp1)) != MP_OKAY) {
264            goto ERR;
265        }
266        if ((res = mp_add(&w4, &tmp1, &tmp1)) != MP_OKAY) {
267            goto ERR;
268        }
269        if ((res = mp_add(&tmp1, c, c)) != MP_OKAY) {
270            goto ERR;
271        }
272
273    ERR:
274        mp_clear_multi(&w0, &w1, &w2, &w3, &w4,
275                       &a0, &a1, &a2, &b0, &b1,
276                       &b2, &tmp1, &tmp2, NULL);
277        return res;
278    }
279
280
```

The first obvious thing to note is that this algorithm is complicated. The complexity is worth it if you are multiplying very large numbers. For example, a 10,000 digit multiplication takes approximately 99,282,205 fewer single precision multiplications with Toom–Cook than a Comba or baseline approach (a savings of more than 99%). For most "crypto" sized numbers this algorithm is not practical, as Karatsuba has a much lower cutoff point.

First, we split $a$ and $b$ into three roughly equal portions. This has been accomplished (lines 41 to 70) with combinations of mp_rshd() and mp_mod_2d() function calls. At this point, $a = a2 \cdot \beta^2 + a1 \cdot \beta + a0$, and similarly for $b$.

Next, we compute the five points $w0, w1, w2, w3$, and $w4$. Recall that $w0$ and $w4$ can be computed directly from the portions so we get those out of the way first (lines 73 and 78). Next, we compute $w1, w2$, and $w3$ using Horner's method.

After this point we solve for the actual values of $w1, w2$, and $w3$ by reducing the $5 \times 5$ system, which is relatively straightforward.

## 5.2.7   Signed Multiplication

Now that algorithms to handle multiplications of every useful dimensions have been developed, a rather simple finishing touch is required. So far, all of the multiplication algorithms have been unsigned multiplications, which leaves only a signed multiplication algorithm to be established.

---

Algorithm **mp_mul**.
**Input**. mp_int $a$ and mp_int $b$
**Output**. $c \leftarrow a \cdot b$

---

1. If $a.sign = b.sign$ then
   1.1 $sign = MP\_ZPOS$
2. else
   2.1 $sign = MP\_ZNEG$
3. If $\min(a.used, b.used) \geq TOOM\_MUL\_CUTOFF$ then
   3.1 $c \leftarrow a \cdot b$ using algorithm mp_toom_mul
4. else if $\min(a.used, b.used) \geq KARATSUBA\_MUL\_CUTOFF$ then
   4.1 $c \leftarrow a \cdot b$ using algorithm mp_karatsuba_mul
5. else
   5.1 $digs \leftarrow a.used + b.used + 1$
   5.2 If $digs < MP\_ARRAY$ and $\min(a.used, b.used) \leq \delta$ then
      5.2.1 $c \leftarrow a \cdot b \pmod{\beta^{digs}}$ using algorithm fast_s_mp_mul_digs.
   5.3 else
      5.3.1 $c \leftarrow a \cdot b \pmod{\beta^{digs}}$ using algorithm s_mp_mul_digs.
6. $c.sign \leftarrow sign$
7. Return the result of the unsigned multiplication performed.

---

Figure 5.10: Algorithm mp_mul

**Algorithm mp_mul.** This algorithm performs the signed multiplication of two inputs (Figure 5.10). It will make use of any of the three unsigned multiplication algorithms available when the input is of appropriate size. The **sign** of the result is not set until the end of the algorithm, since algorithm s_mp_mul_digs (Figure 5.1) will clear it.

File: bn_mp_mul.c

```
018   /* high level multiplication (handles sign) */
019   int mp_mul (mp_int * a, mp_int * b, mp_int * c)
020   {
021     int     res, neg;
022     neg = (a->sign == b->sign) ? MP_ZPOS : MP_NEG;
023
024     /* use Toom-Cook? */
025   #ifdef BN_MP_TOOM_MUL_C
026     if (MIN (a->used, b->used) >= TOOM_MUL_CUTOFF) {
027       res = mp_toom_mul(a, b, c);
028     } else
029   #endif
030   #ifdef BN_MP_KARATSUBA_MUL_C
031     /* use Karatsuba? */
032     if (MIN (a->used, b->used) >= KARATSUBA_MUL_CUTOFF) {
033       res = mp_karatsuba_mul (a, b, c);
034     } else
035   #endif
036     {
037       /* can we use the fast multiplier?
038        *
039        * The fast multiplier can be used if the output will
040        * have less than MP_WARRAY digits and the number of
041        * digits won't affect carry propagation
042        */
043       int     digs = a->used + b->used + 1;
044
045   #ifdef BN_FAST_S_MP_MUL_DIGS_C
046       if ((digs < MP_WARRAY) &&
047           MIN(a->used, b->used) <=
048           (1 << ((CHAR_BIT * sizeof (mp_word)) - (2 * DIGIT_BIT)))) {
049         res = fast_s_mp_mul_digs (a, b, c, digs);
050       } else
051   #endif
052   #ifdef BN_S_MP_MUL_DIGS_C
053         res = s_mp_mul (a, b, c); /* uses s_mp_mul_digs */
054   #else
055         res = MP_VAL;
056   #endif
057
```

```
058       }
059       c->sign = (c->used > 0) ? neg : MP_ZPOS;
060       return res;
061   }
062
```

The implementation is rather simplistic and is not particularly noteworthy. Line 22 computes the sign of the result using the "?" operator from the C programming language. Line 48 computes $\delta$ using the fact that $1 << k$ is equal to $2^k$.

## 5.3  Squaring

Squaring is a special case of multiplication where both multiplicands are equal. At first, it may seem like there is no significant optimization available, but in fact there is. Consider the multiplication of 576 against 241. In total there will be nine single precision multiplications performed–$1 \cdot 6$, $1 \cdot 7$, $1 \cdot 5$, $4 \cdot 6$, $4 \cdot 7$, $4 \cdot 5$, $2 \cdot 6$, $2 \cdot 7$, and $2 \cdot 5$. Now consider the multiplication of 123 against 123. The nine products are $3 \cdot 3$, $3 \cdot 2$, $3 \cdot 1$, $2 \cdot 3$, $2 \cdot 2$, $2 \cdot 1$, $1 \cdot 3$, $1 \cdot 2$, and $1 \cdot 1$. On closer inspection some of the products are equivalent; for example, $3 \cdot 2 = 2 \cdot 3$ and $3 \cdot 1 = 1 \cdot 3$.

For any $n$-digit input, there are $\frac{(n^2+n)}{2}$ possible unique single precision multiplications required compared to the $n^2$ required for multiplication. Figure 5.11 gives an example of the operations required.

|  |  | 1 | 2 | 3 |  |
|---|---|---|---|---|---|
| $\times$ |  | 1 | 2 | 3 |  |
|  |  | $3 \cdot 1$ | $3 \cdot 2$ | $3 \cdot 3$ | Row 0 |
|  | $2 \cdot 1$ | $2 \cdot 2$ | $2 \cdot 3$ |  | Row 1 |
| $1 \cdot 1$ | $1 \cdot 2$ | $1 \cdot 3$ |  |  | Row 2 |

Figure 5.11: Squaring Optimization Diagram

Starting from zero and numbering the columns from right to left, you will see a very simple pattern become obvious. For the purposes of this discussion, let $x$ represent the number being squared. The first observation is that in row $k$, the $2k$'th column of the product has a $(x_k)^2$ term in it.

The second observation is that every column $j$ in row $k$ where $j \neq 2k$ is part of a double product. Every non-square term of a column will appear twice, hence the name "double product." Every odd column is made up entirely of double products. In fact, every column is made up of double products and at most one square (*see the Exercise section*).

The third and final observation is that for row $k$ the first unique non-square term–that is, one that hasn't already appeared in an earlier row–occurs at column $2k + 1$. For example, on row 1 of the previous squaring, column one is part of the double product with column one from row zero. Column two of row one is a square, and column three is the first unique column.

### 5.3.1  The Baseline Squaring Algorithm

The baseline squaring algorithm is meant to be a catch-all squaring algorithm. It will handle any of the input sizes that the faster routines will not handle.

---

Algorithm **s_mp_sqr**.
**Input**. mp_int $a$
**Output**. $b \leftarrow a^2$

---

1. Init a temporary mp_int of at least $2 \cdot a.used + 1$ digits. ($mp\_init\_size$)
2. If step 1 failed return($MP\_MEM$)
3. $t.used \leftarrow 2 \cdot a.used + 1$
4. For $ix$ from 0 to $a.used - 1$ do
   Calculate the square.
   4.1 $\hat{r} \leftarrow t_{2ix} + (a_{ix})^2$
   4.2 $t_{2ix} \leftarrow \hat{r} \pmod{\beta}$
   Calculate the double products after the square.
   4.3 $u \leftarrow \lfloor \hat{r}/\beta \rfloor$
   4.4 For $iy$ from $ix + 1$ to $a.used - 1$ do
      4.4.1 $\hat{r} \leftarrow 2 \cdot a_{ix} a_{iy} + t_{ix+iy} + u$
      4.4.2 $t_{ix+iy} \leftarrow \hat{r} \pmod{\beta}$
      4.4.3 $u \leftarrow \lfloor \hat{r}/\beta \rfloor$
   Set the last carry.
   4.5 While $u > 0$ do
      4.5.1 $iy \leftarrow iy + 1$
      4.5.2 $\hat{r} \leftarrow t_{ix+iy} + u$
      4.5.3 $t_{ix+iy} \leftarrow \hat{r} \pmod{\beta}$
      4.5.4 $u \leftarrow \lfloor \hat{r}/\beta \rfloor$
5. Clamp excess digits of $t$. ($mp\_clamp$)
6. Exchange $b$ and $t$.
7. Clear $t$ ($mp\_clear$)
8. Return($MP\_OKAY$)

---

Figure 5.12: Algorithm s_mp_sqr

**Algorithm s_mp_sqr.** This algorithm computes the square of an input using the three observations on squaring. It is based fairly faithfully on algorithm 14.16 of HAC [2, pp.596-597]. Similar to algorithm s_mp_mul_digs, a temporary mp_int is allocated to hold the result of the squaring. This allows the destination mp_int to be the same as the source mp_int (Figure 5.12).

The outer loop of this algorithm begins on step 4. It is best to think of the outer loop as walking down the rows of the partial results, while the inner loop computes the columns of the partial result. Steps 4.1 and 4.2 compute the square term for each row, and steps 4.3 and 4.4 propagate the carry and compute the double products.

The requirement that an mp_word be able to represent the range $0 \leq x < 2\beta^2$ arises from this very algorithm. The product $a_{ix}a_{iy}$ will lie in the range $0 \leq x \leq \beta^2 - 2\beta + 1$, which is obviously less than $\beta^2$, meaning that when it is multiplied by two, it can be properly represented by an mp_word.

Similar to algorithm s_mp_mul_digs, after every pass of the inner loop, the destination is correctly set to the sum of all of the partial results calculated so far. This involves expensive carry propagation, which will be eliminated in the next algorithm.

```
File: bn_s_mp_sqr.c
018    /* low level squaring, b = a*a, HAC pp.596-597, Algorithm 14.16 */
019    int s_mp_sqr (mp_int * a, mp_int * b)
020    {
021      mp_int   t;
022      int      res, ix, iy, pa;
023      mp_word r;
024      mp_digit u, tmpx, *tmpt;
025
026      pa = a->used;
027      if ((res = mp_init_size (&t, 2*pa + 1)) != MP_OKAY) {
028        return res;
029      }
030
031      /* default used is maximum possible size */
032      t.used = 2*pa + 1;
033
034      for (ix = 0; ix < pa; ix++) {
035        /* first calculate the digit at 2*ix */
036        /* calculate double precision result */
037        r = ((mp_word) t.dp[2*ix]) +
038            ((mp_word)a->dp[ix])*((mp_word)a->dp[ix]);
039
040        /* store lower part in result */
041        t.dp[ix+ix] = (mp_digit) (r & ((mp_word) MP_MASK));
042
043        /* get the carry */
044        u          = (mp_digit)(r >> ((mp_word) DIGIT_BIT));
045
046        /* left hand side of A[ix] * A[iy] */
047        tmpx       = a->dp[ix];
```

```
048
049          /* alias for where to store the results */
050          tmpt        = t.dp + (2*ix + 1);
051
052          for (iy = ix + 1; iy < pa; iy++) {
053            /* first calculate the product */
054            r        = ((mp_word)tmpx) * ((mp_word)a->dp[iy]);
055
056            /* now calculate the double precision result, note we use
057             * addition instead of *2 since it's easier to optimize
058             */
059            r        = ((mp_word) *tmpt) + r + r + ((mp_word) u);
060
061            /* store lower part */
062            *tmpt++ = (mp_digit) (r & ((mp_word) MP_MASK));
063
064            /* get carry */
065            u        = (mp_digit)(r >> ((mp_word) DIGIT_BIT));
066          }
067          /* propagate upwards */
068          while (u != ((mp_digit) 0)) {
069            r        = ((mp_word) *tmpt) + ((mp_word) u);
070            *tmpt++ = (mp_digit) (r & ((mp_word) MP_MASK));
071            u        = (mp_digit) (r >> ((mp_word) DIGIT_BIT));
072          }
073        }
074
075     mp_clamp (&t);
076     mp_exch (&t, b);
077     mp_clear (&t);
078     return MP_OKAY;
079   }
080
```

Inside the outer loop (line 34) the square term is calculated on line 37. The carry (line 44) has been extracted from the mp_word accumulator using a right shift. Aliases for $a_{ix}$ and $t_{ix+iy}$ are initialized (lines 47 and 50) to simplify the inner loop. The doubling is performed using two additions (line 59), since it is usually faster than shifting, if not at least as fast.

The important observation is that the inner loop does not begin at $iy = 0$ like for multiplication. As such, the inner loops get progressively shorter as the algorithm proceeds. This is what leads to the savings compared to using a multiplication to square a number.

## 5.3.2 Faster Squaring by the "Comba" Method

A major drawback to the baseline method is the requirement for single precision shifting inside the $O(n^2)$ nested loop. Squaring has an additional drawback in that it must double the product inside the inner loop as well. As for multiplication, the Comba technique can be used to eliminate these performance hazards.

The first obvious solution is to make an array of mp_words that will hold all the columns. This will indeed eliminate all of the carry propagation operations from the inner loop. However, the inner product must still be doubled $O(n^2)$ times. The solution stems from the simple fact that $2a + 2b + 2c = 2(a + b + c)$. That is, the sum of all of the double products is equal to double the sum of all the products. For example, $ab + ba + ac + ca = 2ab + 2ac = 2(ab + ac)$.

However, we cannot simply double all the columns, since the squares appear only once per row. The most practical solution is to have two mp_word arrays. One array will hold the squares, and the other will hold the double products. With both arrays, the doubling and carry propagation can be moved to a $O(n)$ work level outside the $O(n^2)$ level. In this case, we have an even simpler solution in mind.

---

Algorithm **fast_s_mp_sqr**.
**Input**. mp_int $a$
**Output**. $b \leftarrow a^2$

---

Place an array of **MP_WARRAY** mp_digits named $W$ on the stack.
1. If $b.alloc < 2a.used + 1$ then grow $b$ to $2a.used + 1$ digits. ($mp\_grow$).
2. If step 1 failed return($MP\_MEM$).

3. $pa \leftarrow 2 \cdot a.used$
4. $\hat{W}1 \leftarrow 0$
5. for $ix$ from 0 to $pa - 1$ do
   5.1 $\_\hat{W} \leftarrow 0$
   5.2 $ty \leftarrow \text{MIN}(a.used - 1, ix)$
   5.3 $tx \leftarrow ix - ty$
   5.4 $iy \leftarrow \text{MIN}(a.used - tx, ty + 1)$
   5.5 $iy \leftarrow \text{MIN}(iy, \lfloor (ty - tx + 1)/2 \rfloor)$
   5.6 for $iz$ from 0 to $iz - 1$ do
      5.6.1 $\_\hat{W} \leftarrow \_\hat{W} + a_{tx+iz}a_{ty-iz}$
   5.7 $\_\hat{W} \leftarrow 2 \cdot \_\hat{W} + \hat{W}1$
   5.8 if $ix$ is even then
      5.8.1 $\_\hat{W} \leftarrow \_\hat{W} + \left(a_{\lfloor ix/2 \rfloor}\right)^2$
   5.9 $W_{ix} \leftarrow \_\hat{W} (\text{mod } \beta)$
   5.10 $\hat{W}1 \leftarrow \lfloor \_\hat{W}/\beta \rfloor$

6. $oldused \leftarrow b.used$
7. $b.used \leftarrow 2 \cdot a.used$
8. for $ix$ from 0 to $pa - 1$ do
   8.1 $b_{ix} \leftarrow W_{ix}$
9. for $ix$ from $pa$ to $oldused - 1$ do
   9.1 $b_{ix} \leftarrow 0$
10. Clamp excess digits from $b$. ($mp\_clamp$)
11. Return($MP\_OKAY$).

---

Figure 5.13: Algorithm fast_s_mp_sqr

**Algorithm fast_s_mp_sqr.** This algorithm computes the square of an input using the Comba technique. It is designed to be a replacement for algorithm s_mp_sqr when the number of input digits is less than **MP_WARRAY** and less than $\frac{\delta}{2}$. This algorithm is very similar to the Comba multiplier, except with a few key differences we shall make note of (Figure 5.13).

First, we have an accumulator and carry variables $\_\hat{W}$ and $\hat{W}1$, respectively. This is because the inner loop products are to be doubled. If we had added the previous carry in we would be doubling too much. Next, we perform an addition MIN condition on $iy$ (step 5.5) to prevent overlapping digits. For example, $a_3 \cdot a_5$ is equal $a_5 \cdot a_3$, whereas in the multiplication case we would have $5 < a.used$, and $3 \geq 0$ is maintained since we double the sum of the products just outside the inner loop, which we have to avoid doing. This is also a good thing since we perform fewer multiplications and the routine ends up being faster.

The last difference is the addition of the "square" term outside the inner loop (step 5.8). We add in the square only to even outputs, and it is the square of the term at the $\lfloor ix/2 \rfloor$ position.

```
File: bn_fast_s_mp_sqr.c
018    /* the gist of squaring...
019     * you do like mult except the offset of the tmpx [one that
020     * starts closer to zero] can't equal the offset of tmpy.
021     * So basically you set up iy like before then you min it with
022     * (ty-tx) so that it never happens.  You double all those
023     * you add in the inner loop
024
025    After that loop you do the squares and add them in.
026     */
027
028    int fast_s_mp_sqr (mp_int * a, mp_int * b)
029    {
030      int        olduse, res, pa, ix, iz;
031      mp_digit   W[MP_WARRAY], *tmpx;
032      mp_word    W1;
033
034      /* grow the destination as required */
035      pa = a->used + a->used;
036      if (b->alloc < pa) {
037        if ((res = mp_grow (b, pa)) != MP_OKAY) {
038          return res;
039        }
040      }
041
042      /* number of output digits to produce */
043      W1 = 0;
```

```
044    for (ix = 0; ix < pa; ix++) {
045        int      tx, ty, iy;
046        mp_word  _W;
047        mp_digit *tmpy;
048
049        /* clear counter */
050        _W = 0;
051
052        /* get offsets into the two bignums */
053        ty = MIN(a->used-1, ix);
054        tx = ix - ty;
055
056        /* setup temp aliases */
057        tmpx = a->dp + tx;
058        tmpy = a->dp + ty;
059
060        /* this is the number of times the loop will iterate, essentially
061            while (tx++ < a->used && ty-- >= 0) { ... }
062         */
063        iy = MIN(a->used-tx, ty+1);
064
065        /* now for squaring tx can never equal ty
066         * we halve the distance since they approach at a rate of 2x
067         * and we have to round because odd cases need to be executed
068         */
069        iy = MIN(iy, (ty-tx+1)>>1);
070
071        /* execute loop */
072        for (iz = 0; iz < iy; iz++) {
073            _W += ((mp_word)*tmpx++)*((mp_word)*tmpy--);
074        }
075
076        /* double the inner product and add carry */
077        _W = _W + _W + W1;
078
079        /* even columns have the square term in them */
080        if ((ix&1) == 0) {
081            _W += ((mp_word)a->dp[ix>>1])*((mp_word)a->dp[ix>>1]);
082        }
083
084        /* store it */
```

```
085            W[ix] = (mp_digit)(_W & MP_MASK);
086
087            /* make next carry */
088            W1 = _W >> ((mp_word)DIGIT_BIT);
089        }
090
091    /* setup dest */
092    olduse  = b->used;
093    b->used = a->used+a->used;
094
095    {
096      mp_digit *tmpb;
097      tmpb = b->dp;
098      for (ix = 0; ix < pa; ix++) {
099        *tmpb++ = W[ix] & MP_MASK;
100      }
101
102      /* clear unused digits [that existed in the old copy of c] */
103      for (; ix < olduse; ix++) {
104        *tmpb++ = 0;
105      }
106    }
107    mp_clamp (b);
108    return MP_OKAY;
109  }
110
```

This implementation is essentially a copy of Comba multiplication with the appropriate changes added to make it faster for the special case of squaring. The innermost loop (lines 72 to 74) computes the products the same way the multiplication routine does. The sum of the products is doubled separately (line 77) outside the innermost loop. The square term is added if $ix$ is even (lines 80 to 82), indicating column with a square.

### 5.3.3   Even Faster Squaring

Just like the case of algorithm fast_mult (Section 5.2.3), squaring can be performed using the full precision of single precision variables. This algorithm borrows much from the algorithm in Figure 5.13. Except that, in this case, we will be accumulating into a triple–precision accumulator. Similarly, loop unrolling can boost the performance of this operation significantly.

The TomsFastMath library incorporates fast squaring that is a direct port of algorithm fast_s_mp_sqr. Readers are encouraged to research this project to learn more.

### 5.3.4  Polynomial Basis Squaring

The same algorithm that performs optimal polynomial basis multiplication can be used to perform polynomial basis squaring. The minor exception is that $\zeta_y = f(y)g(y)$ is actually equivalent to $\zeta_y = f(y)^2$, since $f(y) = g(y)$. Instead of performing $2n + 1$ multiplications to find the $\zeta$ relations, squaring operations are performed instead.

### 5.3.5  Karatsuba Squaring

Let $f(x) = ax + b$ represent the polynomial basis representation of a number to square. Let $h(x) = (f(x))^2$ represent the square of the polynomial. The Karatsuba equation can be modified to square a number with the following equation.

$$h(x) = a^2 x^2 + \left( (a+b)^2 - (a^2 + b^2) \right) x + b^2 \tag{5.7}$$

Upon closer inspection, this equation only requires the calculation of three half-sized squares: $a^2$, $b^2$, and $(a+b)^2$. As in Karatsuba multiplication, this algorithm can be applied recursively on the input and will achieve an asymptotic running time of $O\left(n^{lg(3)}\right)$.

If the asymptotic times of Karatsuba squaring and multiplication are the same, why not simply use the multiplication algorithm instead? The answer to this arises from the cutoff point for squaring. As in multiplication, there exists a cutoff point, at which the time required for a Comba–based squaring and a Karatsuba–based squaring meet. Due to the overhead inherent in the Karatsuba method, the cutoff point is fairly high. For example, on an AMD Athlon XP processor with $\beta = 2^{28}$, the cutoff point is around 127 digits.

Consider squaring a 200–digit number with this technique. It will be split into two 100–digit halves that are subsequently squared. The 100–digit halves will not be squared using Karatsuba, but instead using the faster Comba–based squaring algorithm. If Karatsuba multiplication were used instead, the 100–digit numbers would be squared with a slower Comba–based multiplication.

---
Algorithm **mp_karatsuba_sqr**.
**Input**. mp_int $a$
**Output**. $b \leftarrow a^2$

---

1. Initialize the following temporary mp_ints: $x0$, $x1$, $t1$, $t2$, $x0x0$, and $x1x1$.
2. If any of the initializations on step 1 failed return($MP\_MEM$).

Split the input. e.g. $a = x1\beta^B + x0$
3. $B \leftarrow \lfloor a.used/2 \rfloor$
4. $x0 \leftarrow a \pmod{\beta^B}$ ($mp\_mod\_2d$)
5. $x1 \leftarrow \lfloor a/\beta^B \rfloor$ ($mp\_lshd$)

Calculate the three squares.
6. $x0x0 \leftarrow x0^2$ ($mp\_sqr$)
7. $x1x1 \leftarrow x1^2$
8. $t1 \leftarrow x1 + x0$ ($s\_mp\_add$)
9. $t1 \leftarrow t1^2$

Compute the middle term.
10. $t2 \leftarrow x0x0 + x1x1$ ($s\_mp\_add$)
11. $t1 \leftarrow t1 - t2$

Compute final product.
12. $t1 \leftarrow t1\beta^B$ ($mp\_lshd$)
13. $x1x1 \leftarrow x1x1\beta^{2B}$
14. $t1 \leftarrow t1 + x0x0$
15. $b \leftarrow t1 + x1x1$
16. Return($MP\_OKAY$).

---

Figure 5.14: Algorithm mp_karatsuba_sqr

**Algorithm mp_karatsuba_sqr.** This algorithm computes the square of an input $a$ using the Karatsuba technique. It is very similar to the Karatsuba–based multiplication algorithm with the exception that the three half-size multiplications have been replaced with three half-size squarings (Figure 5.14).

The radix point for squaring is simply placed exactly in the middle of the digits when the input has an odd number of digits; otherwise, it is placed just below the middle. Steps 3, 4, and 5 compute the two halves required using $B$ as the radix point. The first two squares in steps 6 and 7 are straightforward, while the last square is of a more compact form.

By expanding $(x1 + x0)^2$, the $x1^2$ and $x0^2$ terms in the middle disappear; that is, $(x0 - x1)^2 - (x1^2 + x0^2) = 2 \cdot x0 \cdot x1$. Now if $5n$ single precision additions and a squaring of $n$-digits is faster than multiplying two $n$-digit numbers and doubling, then this method is faster. Assuming no further recursions occur, the difference can be estimated with the following inequality.

Let $p$ represent the cost of a single precision addition and $q$ the cost of a single precision multiplication both in terms of time[4].

$$5pn + \frac{q(n^2 + n)}{2} \leq pn + qn^2 \qquad (5.8)$$

For example, on an AMD Athlon XP processor, $p = \frac{1}{3}$ and $q = 6$. This implies that the following inequality should hold.

$$\begin{array}{ccc} \frac{5n}{3} + 3n^2 + 3n & < & \frac{n}{3} + 6n^2 \\ \frac{5}{3} + 3n + 3 & < & \frac{1}{3} + 6n \\ \frac{13}{9} & < & n \end{array}$$

This results in a cutoff point around $n = 2$. As a consequence, it is actually faster to compute the middle term the "long way" on processors where multiplication is substantially slower[5] than simpler operations such as addition.

```
File: bn_mp_karatsuba_sqr.c
018   /* Karatsuba squaring, computes b = a*a using three
019    * half size squarings
020    *
021    * See comments of karatsuba_mul for details.  It
022    * is essentially the same algorithm but merely
023    * tuned to perform recursive squarings.
024    */
025   int mp_karatsuba_sqr (mp_int * a, mp_int * b)
026   {
027       mp_int  x0, x1, t1, t2, x0x0, x1x1;
028       int     B, err;
029
030       err = MP_MEM;
```

---

[4] Or machine clock cycles.

[5] On the Athlon there is a 1:17 ratio between clock cycles for addition and multiplication. On the Intel P4 processor this ratio is 1:29, making this method even more beneficial. The only common exception is the ARMv4 processor, which has a ratio of 1:7.

```
031
032        /* min # of digits */
033        B = a->used;
034
035        /* now divide in two */
036        B = B >> 1;
037
038        /* init copy all the temps */
039        if (mp_init_size (&x0, B) != MP_OKAY)
040          goto ERR;
041        if (mp_init_size (&x1, a->used - B) != MP_OKAY)
042          goto X0;
043
044        /* init temps */
045        if (mp_init_size (&t1, a->used * 2) != MP_OKAY)
046          goto X1;
047        if (mp_init_size (&t2, a->used * 2) != MP_OKAY)
048          goto T1;
049        if (mp_init_size (&x0x0, B * 2) != MP_OKAY)
050          goto T2;
051        if (mp_init_size (&x1x1, (a->used - B) * 2) != MP_OKAY)
052          goto X0X0;
053
054        {
055          register int x;
056          register mp_digit *dst, *src;
057
058          src = a->dp;
059
060          /* now shift the digits */
061          dst = x0.dp;
062          for (x = 0; x < B; x++) {
063            *dst++ = *src++;
064          }
065
066          dst = x1.dp;
067          for (x = B; x < a->used; x++) {
068            *dst++ = *src++;
069          }
070        }
071
```

```
072      x0.used = B;
073      x1.used = a->used - B;
074
075      mp_clamp (&x0);
076
077      /* now calc the products x0*x0 and x1*x1 */
078      if (mp_sqr (&x0, &x0x0) != MP_OKAY)
079        goto X1X1;                 /* x0x0 = x0*x0 */
080      if (mp_sqr (&x1, &x1x1) != MP_OKAY)
081        goto X1X1;                 /* x1x1 = x1*x1 */
082
083      /* now calc (x1+x0)**2 */
084      if (s_mp_add (&x1, &x0, &t1) != MP_OKAY)
085        goto X1X1;                 /* t1 = x1 - x0 */
086      if (mp_sqr (&t1, &t1) != MP_OKAY)
087        goto X1X1;                    /* t1 = (x1 - x0) * (x1 - x0) */
088
089      /* add x0y0 */
090      if (s_mp_add (&x0x0, &x1x1, &t2) != MP_OKAY)
091        goto X1X1;                   /* t2 = x0x0 + x1x1 */
092      if (s_mp_sub (&t1, &t2, &t1) != MP_OKAY)
093        goto X1X1;                    /* t1 = (x1+x0)**2 - (x0x0 + x1x1) */
094
095      /* shift by B */
096      if (mp_lshd (&t1, B) != MP_OKAY)
097        goto X1X1;                   /* t1 = (x0x0 + x1x1 - (x1-x0)*(x1-x0))<<B */
098      if (mp_lshd (&x1x1, B * 2) != MP_OKAY)
099        goto X1X1;                   /* x1x1 = x1x1 << 2*B */
100
101      if (mp_add (&x0x0, &t1, &t1) != MP_OKAY)
102        goto X1X1;                   /* t1 = x0x0 + t1 */
103      if (mp_add (&t1, &x1x1, b) != MP_OKAY)
104        goto X1X1;                   /* t1 = x0x0 + t1 + x1x1 */
105
106    err = MP_OKAY;
107
108  X1X1:mp_clear (&x1x1);
109  X0X0:mp_clear (&x0x0);
110  T2:mp_clear (&t2);
111  T1:mp_clear (&t1);
112  X1:mp_clear (&x1);
```

```
113    X0:mp_clear (&x0);
114    ERR:
115      return err;
116    }
117
```

This implementation is largely based on the implementation of algorithm mp_karatsuba_mul. It uses the same inline style to copy and shift the input into the two halves. The loop from line 54 to line 70 has been modified since only one input exists. The **used** count of both $x0$ and $x1$ is fixed up, and $x0$ is clamped before the calculations begin. At this point, $x1$ and $x0$ are valid equivalents to the respective halves as if mp_rshd and mp_mod_2d had been used.

By inlining the copy and shift operations, the cutoff point for Karatsuba multiplication can be lowered. On the Athlon, the cutoff point is exactly at the point where Comba squaring can no longer be used (*128 digits*). On slower processors such as the Intel P4, it is actually below the Comba limit (*at 110 digits*).

This routine uses the same error trap coding style as mp_karatsuba_sqr. As the temporary variables are initialized, errors are redirected to the error trap higher up. If the algorithm completes without error, the error code is set to **MP_OKAY** and mp_clears are executed normally.

### 5.3.6  Toom-Cook Squaring

The Toom-Cook squaring algorithm mp_toom_sqr is heavily based on the algorithm mp_toom_mul, with the exception that squarings are used instead of multiplication to find the five relations. Readers are encouraged to read the description of the latter algorithm and try to derive their own Toom-Cook squaring algorithm.

### 5.3.7 High Level Squaring

---

Algorithm **mp_sqr**.
**Input**. mp_int $a$
**Output**. $b \leftarrow a^2$

---

1. If $a.used \geq TOOM\_SQR\_CUTOFF$ then
   1.1 $b \leftarrow a^2$ using algorithm mp_toom_sqr
2. else if $a.used \geq KARATSUBA\_SQR\_CUTOFF$ then
   2.1 $b \leftarrow a^2$ using algorithm mp_karatsuba_sqr
3. else
   3.1 $digs \leftarrow a.used + b.used + 1$
   3.2 If $digs < MP\_ARRAY$ and $a.used \leq \delta$ then
      3.2.1 $b \leftarrow a^2$ using algorithm fast_s_mp_sqr.
   3.3 else
      3.3.1 $b \leftarrow a^2$ using algorithm s_mp_sqr.
4. $b.sign \leftarrow MP\_ZPOS$
5. Return the result of the unsigned squaring performed.

---

Figure 5.15: Algorithm mp_sqr

**Algorithm mp_sqr.** This algorithm computes the square of the input using one of four different algorithms. If the input is very large and has at least **TOOM_SQR_CUTOFF** or **KARATSUBA_SQR_CUTOFF** digits, then either the Toom-Cook or the Karatsuba Squaring algorithm is used. If neither of the polynomial basis algorithms should be used, then either the Comba or baseline algorithm is used (Figure 5.15).

```
File: bn_mp_sqr.c
018   /* computes b = a*a */
019   int
020   mp_sqr (mp_int * a, mp_int * b)
021   {
022     int     res;
023
024   #ifdef BN_MP_TOOM_SQR_C
025     /* use Toom-Cook? */
026     if (a->used >= TOOM_SQR_CUTOFF) {
027       res = mp_toom_sqr(a, b);
```

```
028    /* Karatsuba? */
029    } else
030  #endif
031  #ifdef BN_MP_KARATSUBA_SQR_C
032  if (a->used >= KARATSUBA_SQR_CUTOFF) {
033      res = mp_karatsuba_sqr (a, b);
034    } else
035  #endif
036    {
037  #ifdef BN_FAST_S_MP_SQR_C
038      /* can we use the fast comba multiplier? */
039      if ((a->used * 2 + 1) < MP_WARRAY &&
040          a->used <
041          (1 << (sizeof(mp_word) * CHAR_BIT - 2*DIGIT_BIT - 1))) {
042        res = fast_s_mp_sqr (a, b);
043      } else
044  #endif
045  #ifdef BN_S_MP_SQR_C
046        res = s_mp_sqr (a, b);
047  #else
048        res = MP_VAL;
049  #endif
050    }
051    b->sign = MP_ZPOS;
052    return res;
053  }
054
```

# Exercises

[3]  Devise an efficient algorithm for selection of the radix point to handle inputs
     that have different numbers of digits in Karatsuba multiplication.

[2]  In section 5.3, we stated, that every column of a squaring is made up
     of double products and at most one square is stated. Prove this statement.

[3]  Prove the equation for Karatsuba squaring.

[1]  Prove that Karatsuba squaring requires $O\left(n^{lg(3)}\right)$ time.

[3]  Implement a threaded version of Comba multiplication (and squaring) where you
     compute subsets of the columns in each thread. Determine a cutoff point where
     it is effective, and add the logic to mp_mul() and mp_sqr().

[4]  Same as the previous, but also modify the Karatsuba and Toom-Cook. You must
     increase the throughput of mp_exptmod() for random odd moduli in the range
     $512 \ldots 4096$ bits significantly ($> 2x$) to complete this challenge.

# Chapter 6

# Modular Reduction

## 6.1 Basics of Modular Reduction

Modular reduction arises quite often within public key cryptography algorithms and various number theoretic algorithms, such as factoring. Modular reduction algorithms are the third class of algorithms of the "multipliers" set. A number $a$ is said to be *reduced* modulo another number $b$ by finding the remainder of the division $a/b$. Full integer division with remainder is covered in Section 8.1.

Modular reduction is equivalent to solving for $r$ in the following equation: $a = bq + r$ where $q = \lfloor a/b \rfloor$. The result $r$ is said to be "congruent to $a$ modulo $b$," which is also written as $r \equiv a \pmod{b}$. In other vernacular, $r$ is known as the "modular residue," which leads to "quadratic residue"[1] and other forms of residues.

Modular reductions are normally used to create finite groups, rings, or fields. The most common usage for performance driven modular reductions is in modular exponentiation algorithms; that is, to compute $d = a^b \pmod{c}$ as fast as possible. This operation is used in the RSA and Diffie-Hellman public key algorithms, for example. Modular multiplication and squaring also appears as a fundamental operation in elliptic curve cryptographic algorithms. As will be discussed in the subsequent chapter, there exist fast algorithms for computing modular exponentiations without having to perform (*in this example*) $b - 1$ multiplications. These algorithms will produce partial results in the range $0 \le x < c^2$, which can be taken

---

[1] That's fancy talk for $b \equiv a^2 \pmod{p}$.

147

advantage of to create several efficient algorithms. They have also been used to create redundancy check algorithms known as CRCs, error correction codes such as Reed-Solomon, and solve a variety of number theoretic problems.

# 6.2   The Barrett Reduction

The Barrett reduction algorithm [6] was inspired by fast division algorithms that multiply by the reciprocal to emulate division. Barrett's observation was that the residue $c$ of $a$ modulo $b$ is equal to

$$c = a - b \cdot \lfloor a/b \rfloor \qquad (6.1)$$

Since algorithms such as modular exponentiation would be using the same modulus extensively, typical DSP[2] intuition would indicate the next step would be to replace $a/b$ by a multiplication by the reciprocal. However, DSP intuition on its own will not work, as these numbers are considerably larger than the precision of common DSP floating point data types. It would take another common optimization to optimize the algorithm.

## 6.2.1   Fixed Point Arithmetic

The trick used to optimize equation 6.1 is based on a technique of emulating floating point data types with fixed precision integers. Fixed point arithmetic would become very popular, as it greatly optimized the "3D–shooter" genre of games in the mid 1990s when floating point units were fairly slow, if not unavailable. The idea behind fixed point arithmetic is to take a normal $k$-bit integer data type and break it into $p$-bit integer and a $q$-bit fraction part (*where $p + q = k$*).

In this system, a $k$-bit integer $n$ would actually represent $n/2^q$. For example, with $q = 4$ the integer $n = 37$ would actually represent the value 2.3125. To multiply two fixed point numbers, the integers are multiplied using traditional arithmetic and subsequently normalized by moving the implied decimal point back to where it should be. For example, with $q = 4$, to multiply the integers 9 and 5 they must be converted to fixed point first by multiplying by $2^q$. Let $a = 9(2^q)$ represent the fixed point representation of 9, and $b = 5(2^q)$ represent the fixed point representation of 5. The product $ab$ is equal to $45(2^{2q})$, which when normalized by dividing by $2^q$ produces $45(2^q)$.

---

[2]It is worth noting that Barrett's paper targeted the DSP56K processor.

This technique became popular since a normal integer multiplication and logical shift right are the only required operations to perform a multiplication of two fixed point numbers. Using fixed point arithmetic, division can be easily approximated by multiplying by the reciprocal. If $2^q$ is equivalent to one, then, $2^q/b$ is equivalent to the fixed point approximation of $1/b$ using real arithmetic. Using this fact, dividing an integer $a$ by another integer $b$ can be achieved with the following expression.

$$\lfloor a/b \rfloor \sim \lfloor (a \cdot \lfloor 2^q/b \rfloor)/2^q \rfloor \qquad (6.2)$$

The precision of the division is proportional to the value of $q$. If the divisor $b$ is used frequently, as is the case with modular exponentiation, pre-computing $2^q/b$ will allow a division to be performed with a multiplication and a right shift. Both operations are considerably faster than division on most processors.

Consider dividing 19 by 5. The correct result is $\lfloor 19/5 \rfloor = 3$. With $q = 3$, the reciprocal is $\lfloor 2^q/5 \rfloor = 1$, which leads to a product of 19, which when divided by $2^q$ produces 2. However, with $q = 4$ the reciprocal is $\lfloor 2^q/5 \rfloor = 3$ and the result of the emulated division is $\lfloor 3 \cdot 19/2^q \rfloor = 3$, which is correct. The value of $2^q$ must be close to or ideally larger than the dividend. In effect, if $a$ is the dividend, then $q$ should allow $0 \le \lfloor a/2^q \rfloor \le 1$ for this approach to work correctly. Plugging this form of division into the original equation, the following modular residue equation arises.

$$c = a - b \cdot \lfloor (a \cdot \lfloor 2^q/b \rfloor)/2^q \rfloor \qquad (6.3)$$

Using the notation from [6], the value of $\lfloor 2^q/b \rfloor$ will be represented by the $\mu$ symbol. Using the $\mu$ variable also helps reinforce the idea that it is meant to be computed once and re-used.

$$c = a - b \cdot \lfloor (a \cdot \mu)/2^q \rfloor \qquad (6.4)$$

Provided that $2^q \ge a$, this algorithm will produce a quotient that is either exactly correct or off by a value of one. In the context of Barrett reduction the value of $a$ is bound by $0 \le a \le (b-1)^2$, meaning that $2^q \ge b^2$ is sufficient to ensure the reciprocal will have enough precision.

Let $n$ represent the number of digits in $b$. This algorithm requires approximately $2n^2$ single precision multiplications to produce the quotient, and another $n^2$ single precision multiplications to find the residue. In total, $3n^2$ single precision multiplications are required to reduce the number.

For example, if $b = 1179677$ and $q = 41$ $(2^q > b^2)$, the reciprocal $\mu$ is equal to $\lfloor 2^q/b \rfloor = 1864089$. Consider reducing $a = 180388626447$ modulo $b$ using the preceding reduction equation. The quotient using the new formula is $\lfloor (a \cdot \mu)/2^q \rfloor = 152913$. By subtracting $152913b$ from $a$, the correct residue $a \equiv 677346 \pmod{b}$ is found.

## 6.2.2   Choosing a Radix Point

Using the fixed point representation, a modular reduction can be performed with $3n^2$ single precision multiplications[3]. If that were the best that could be achieved. a full division[4] might as well be used in its place. The key to optimizing the reduction is to reduce the precision of the initial multiplication that finds the quotient.

Let $a$ represent the number of which the residue is sought. Let $b$ represent the modulus used to find the residue. Let $m$ represent the number of digits in $b$. For the purposes of this discussion we will assume that the number of digits in $a$ is $2m$, which is generally true if two $m$-digit numbers have been multiplied. Dividing $a$ by $b$ is the same as dividing a $2m$ digit integer by an $m$ digit integer. Digits below the $m - 1$'th digit of $a$ will contribute at most a value of 1 to the quotient, because $\beta^k < b$ for any $0 \leq k \leq m - 1$. Another way to express this is by re-writing $a$ as two parts. If $a' \equiv a \pmod{b^m}$ and $a'' = a - a'$, then $\frac{a}{b} = \frac{a'+a''}{b}$, which is equivalent to $\frac{a'}{b} + \frac{a''}{b}$. Since $a'$ is bound to be less than $b$, the quotient is bound by $0 \leq \frac{a'}{b} < 1$.

Since the digits of $a'$ do not contribute much to the quotient the observation is that they might as well be zero. However, if the digits "might as well be zero," they might as well not be there in the first place. Let $q_0 = \lfloor a/\beta^{m-1} \rfloor$ represent the input with the irrelevant digits trimmed. Now the modular reduction is trimmed to the almost equivalent equation

$$c = a - b \cdot \lfloor (q_0 \cdot \mu)/\beta^{m+1} \rfloor \tag{6.5}$$

Note that the original divisor $2^q$ has been replaced with $\beta^{m+1}$ where in this case $q$ is a multiple of $lg(\beta)$. Also note that the exponent on the divisor when added to the amount $q_0$ was shifted by equals $2m$. If the optimization had not been performed the divisor would have the exponent $2m$, so in the end the exponents

---

[3]One division and two multiplications require $3n^2$ single precision multiplications.

[4]A division requires approximately $O(2cn^2)$ single precision multiplications for a small value of $c$. See 8.1 for further details.

do "add up." Using equation 6.5 the quotient $\lfloor (q_0 \cdot \mu)/\beta^{m+1} \rfloor$ can be off from the true quotient by at most two. The original fixed point quotient can be off by as much as one (*provided the radix point is chosen suitably*), and now that the lower irrelevant digits have been trimmed the quotient can be off by an additional value of one for a total of at most two. This implies that $0 \leq a - b \cdot \lfloor (q_0 \cdot \mu)/\beta^{m+1} \rfloor < 3b$. By first subtracting $b$ times the quotient and then conditionally subtracting $b$ once or twice the residue is found.

The quotient is now found using $(m+1)(m) = m^2 + m$ single precision multiplications and the residue with an additional $m^2$ single precision multiplications, ignoring the subtractions required. In total, $2m^2 + m$ single precision multiplications are required to find the residue. This is considerably faster than the original attempt.

For example, let $\beta = 10$ represent the radix of the digits. Let $b = 9999$ represent the modulus, which implies $m = 4$. Let $a = 99929878$ represent the value of which the residue is desired; in this case, $q = 8$ since $10^7 < 9999^2$, meaning that $\mu = \lfloor \beta^q/b \rfloor = 10001$. With the new observation the multiplicand for the quotient is equal to $q_0 = \lfloor a/\beta^{m-1} \rfloor = 99929$. The quotient is then $\lfloor (q_0 \cdot \mu)/\beta^{m+1} \rfloor = 9993$. Subtract $9993b$ from $a$ and the correct residue $a \equiv 9871 \pmod{b}$ is found.

### 6.2.3   Trimming the Quotient

So far, the reduction algorithm has been optimized from $3m^2$ single precision multiplications down to $2m^2 + m$ single precision multiplications. As it stands now, the algorithm is already fairly fast compared to a full integer division algorithm. However, there is still room for optimization.

After the first multiplication inside the quotient $(q_0 \cdot \mu)$ the value is shifted right by $m+1$ places, effectively nullifying the lower half of the product. It would be nice to be able to remove those digits from the product to effectively cut down the number of single precision multiplications. If the number of digits in the modulus $m$ is far less than $\beta$, a full product is not required for the algorithm to work properly. In fact, the lower $m-2$ digits will not affect the upper half of the product at all and do not need to be computed.

The value of $\mu$ is an $m$-digit number and $q_0$ is an $m+1$ digit number. Using a full multiplier $(m+1)(m) = m^2 + m$ single precision multiplications would be required. Using a multiplier that will only produce digits at and above the $m-1$'th digit reduces the number of single precision multiplications to $\frac{m^2 + m}{2}$ single precision multiplications.

### 6.2.4   Trimming the Residue

After the quotient has been calculated it is used to reduce the input. As previously noted, the algorithm is not exact and can be off by a small multiple of the modulus; that is, $0 \leq a - b \cdot \lfloor (q_0 \cdot \mu)/\beta^{m+1} \rfloor < 3b$. If $b$ is $m$ digits, the result of reduction equation is a value of at most $m + 1$ digits (*provided* $3 < \beta$) implying that the upper $m - 1$ digits are implicitly zero.

The next optimization arises from this very fact. Instead of computing $b \cdot \lfloor (q_0 \cdot \mu)/\beta^{m+1} \rfloor$ using a full $O(m^2)$ multiplication algorithm, only the lower $m + 1$ digits of the product have to be computed. Similarly, the value of $a$ can be reduced modulo $\beta^{m+1}$ before the multiple of $b$ is subtracted, which simplifies the subtraction as well. A multiplication that produces only the lower $m + 1$ digits requires $\frac{m^2 + 3m - 2}{2}$ single precision multiplications.

With both optimizations in place the algorithm is the algorithm Barrett proposed. It requires $m^2 + 2m - 1$ single precision multiplications, which are considerably faster than the straightforward $3m^2$ method.

## 6.2.5 The Barrett Algorithm

---

Algorithm **mp_reduce**.
**Input**. mp_int $a$, mp_int $b$ and $\mu = \lfloor \beta^{2m}/b \rfloor$, $m = \lceil lg_\beta(b) \rceil$, $(0 \le a < b^2, b > 1)$
**Output**. $a \pmod{b}$

---

Let $m$ represent the number of digits in $b$.
1. Make a copy of $a$ and store it in $q$. (*mp_init_copy*)
2. $q \leftarrow \lfloor q/\beta^{m-1} \rfloor$ (*mp_rshd*)

Produce the quotient.
3. $q \leftarrow q \cdot \mu$ (*note: only produce digits at or above $m-1$*)
4. $q \leftarrow \lfloor q/\beta^{m+1} \rfloor$

Subtract the multiple of modulus from the input.
5. $a \leftarrow a \pmod{\beta^{m+1}}$ (*mp_mod_2d*)
6. $q \leftarrow q \cdot b \pmod{\beta^{m+1}}$ (*s_mp_mul_digs*)
7. $a \leftarrow a - q$ (*mp_sub*)

Add $\beta^{m+1}$ if a carry occurred.
8. If $a < 0$ then (*mp_cmp_d*)
   8.1 $q \leftarrow 1$ (*mp_set*)
   8.2 $q \leftarrow q \cdot \beta^{m+1}$ (*mp_lshd*)
   8.3 $a \leftarrow a + q$

Now subtract the modulus if the residue is too large (e.g., quotient too small).
9. While $a \ge b$ do (*mp_cmp*)
   9.1 $c \leftarrow a - b$
10. Clear $q$.
11. Return(*MP_OKAY*)

---

Figure 6.1: Algorithm mp_reduce

**Algorithm mp_reduce.** This algorithm will reduce the input $a$ modulo $b$ in place using the Barrett algorithm. It is loosely based on algorithm 14.42 of HAC [2, pp. 602], which is based on the paper from Paul Barrett [6]. The algorithm has several restrictions and assumptions that must be adhered to for the algorithm to work (Figure 6.1).

First, the modulus $b$ is assumed positive and greater than one. If the modulus were less than or equal to one, subtracting a multiple of it would either accomplish nothing or actually enlarge the input. The input $a$ must be in the range $0 \le a < b^2$ for the quotient to have enough precision. If $a$ is the product of two numbers that were already reduced modulo $b$, this will not be a problem. Technically, the algorithm will still work if $a \ge b^2$ but it will take much longer to finish. The value of $\mu$ is passed as an argument to this algorithm and is assumed calculated and stored before the algorithm is used.

Recall that the multiplication for the quotient in step 3 must only produce digits at or above the $m-1$'th position. An algorithm called *s_mp_mul_high_digs* that has not been presented is used to accomplish this task. The algorithm is based on *s_mp_mul_digs*, except that instead of stopping at a given level of precision it starts at a given level of precision. This optimal algorithm can only be used if the number of digits in $b$ is much smaller than $\beta$.

While it is known that $a \ge b \cdot \lfloor (q_0 \cdot \mu)/\beta^{m+1} \rfloor$, only the lower $m+1$ digits are being used to compute the residue, so an implied "borrow" from the higher digits might leave a negative result. After the multiple of the modulus has been subtracted from $a$, the residue must be fixed up in case it is negative. The invariant $\beta^{m+1}$ must be added to the residue to make it positive again.

The while loop in step 9 will subtract $b$ until the residue is less than $b$. If the algorithm is performed correctly, this step is performed at most twice, and on average once. However, if $a \ge b^2$, it will iterate substantially more times than it should.

File: **bn_mp_reduce.c**

```
018    /* reduces x mod m, assumes 0 < x < m**2, mu is
019     * precomputed via mp_reduce_setup.
020     * From HAC pp.604 Algorithm 14.42
021     */
022    int mp_reduce (mp_int * x, mp_int * m, mp_int * mu)
023    {
024      mp_int   q;
025      int      res, um = m->used;
026
027      /* q = x */
028      if ((res = mp_init_copy (&q, x)) != MP_OKAY) {
029        return res;
030      }
031
032      /* q1 = x / b**(k-1)   */
033      mp_rshd (&q, um - 1);
```

```
034
035      /* according to HAC this optimization is ok */
036      if (((unsigned long) um) > (((mp_digit)1) << (DIGIT_BIT - 1))) {
037        if ((res = mp_mul (&q, mu, &q)) != MP_OKAY) {
038          goto CLEANUP;
039        }
040      } else {
041  #ifdef BN_S_MP_MUL_HIGH_DIGS_C
042        if ((res = s_mp_mul_high_digs (&q, mu, &q, um)) != MP_OKAY) {
043          goto CLEANUP;
044        }
045  #elif defined(BN_FAST_S_MP_MUL_HIGH_DIGS_C)
046        if ((res = fast_s_mp_mul_high_digs (&q, mu, &q, um)) != MP_OKAY) {
047          goto CLEANUP;
048        }
049  #else
050        {
051          res = MP_VAL;
052          goto CLEANUP;
053        }
054  #endif
055      }
056
057      /* q3 = q2 / b**(k+1) */
058      mp_rshd (&q, um + 1);
059
060      /* x = x mod b**(k+1), quick (no division) */
061      if ((res = mp_mod_2d (x, DIGIT_BIT * (um + 1), x)) != MP_OKAY) {
062        goto CLEANUP;
063      }
064
065      /* q = q * m mod b**(k+1), quick (no division) */
066      if ((res = s_mp_mul_digs (&q, m, &q, um + 1)) != MP_OKAY) {
067        goto CLEANUP;
068      }
069
070      /* x = x - q */
071      if ((res = mp_sub (x, &q, x)) != MP_OKAY) {
072        goto CLEANUP;
073      }
074
```

```
075      /* If x < 0, add b**(k+1) to it */
076      if (mp_cmp_d (x, 0) == MP_LT) {
077        mp_set (&q, 1);
078        if ((res = mp_lshd (&q, um + 1)) != MP_OKAY)
079          goto CLEANUP;
080        if ((res = mp_add (x, &q, x)) != MP_OKAY)
081          goto CLEANUP;
082      }
083
084      /* Back off if it's too big */
085      while (mp_cmp (x, m) != MP_LT) {
086        if ((res = s_mp_sub (x, m, x)) != MP_OKAY) {
087          goto CLEANUP;
088        }
089      }
090
091   CLEANUP:
092        mp_clear (&q);
093
094        return res;
095   }
096
```

The first multiplication that determines the quotient can be performed by only producing the digits from $m - 1$ and up. This essentially halves the number of single precision multiplications required. However, the optimization is only safe if $\beta$ is much larger than the number of digits in the modulus. In the source code, this is evaluated on lines 36 to 44 where algorithm s_mp_mul_high_digs is used when it is safe to do so.

## 6.2.6   The Barrett Setup Algorithm

To use algorithm mp_reduce, the value of $\mu$ must be calculated in advance. Ideally, this value should be computed once and stored for future use so the Barrett algorithm can be used without delay.

---

Algorithm **mp_reduce_setup**.
**Input**. mp_int $a$ ($a > 1$)
**Output**. $\mu \leftarrow \lfloor \beta^{2m}/a \rfloor$

---

1. $\mu \leftarrow 2^{2 \cdot lg(\beta) \cdot m}$ (*mp_2expt*)
2. $\mu \leftarrow \lfloor \mu/b \rfloor$ (*mp_div*)
3. Return(*MP_OKAY*)

---

Figure 6.2: Algorithm mp_reduce_setup

**Algorithm mp_reduce_setup.** This algorithm computes the reciprocal $\mu$ required for Barrett reduction. First, $\beta^{2m}$ is calculated as $2^{2 \cdot lg(\beta) \cdot m}$, which is equivalent and much faster. The final value is computed by taking the integer quotient of $\lfloor \mu/b \rfloor$ (Figure 6.2).

```
File: bn_mp_reduce_setup.c
018    /* pre-calculate the value required for Barrett reduction
019     * For a given modulus "b" it calculates the value required in "a"
020     */
021    int mp_reduce_setup (mp_int * a, mp_int * b)
022    {
023      int      res;
024
025      if ((res = mp_2expt (a, b->used * 2 * DIGIT_BIT)) != MP_OKAY) {
026        return res;
027      }
028      return mp_div (a, b, a, NULL);
029    }
030
```

This simple routine calculates the reciprocal $\mu$ required by Barrett reduction. Note the extended usage of algorithm mp_div where the variable that would receive the remainder is passed as NULL. As will be discussed in 8.1, the division routine allows both the quotient and the remainder to be passed as NULL, meaning to ignore the value.

# 6.3   The Montgomery Reduction

Montgomery reduction[5] [7] is by far the most interesting form of reduction in common use. It computes a modular residue that is not actually equal to the residue of the input, yet instead equal to a residue times a constant. However, as perplexing as this may sound, the algorithm is relatively simple and very efficient.

Throughout this entire section the variable $n$ will represent the modulus used to form the residue. As will be discussed shortly, the value of $n$ must be odd. The variable $x$ will represent the quantity of which the residue is sought. Similar to the Barrett algorithm, the input is restricted to $0 \le x < n^2$. To begin the description, some simple number theory facts must be established.

**Fact 1.** Adding $n$ to $x$ does not change the residue, since in effect it adds one to the quotient $\lfloor x/n \rfloor$. Another way to explain this is that $n$ is (*or multiples of n are*) congruent to zero modulo $n$. Adding zero will not change the value of the residue.

**Fact 2.** If $x$ is even, then performing a division by two in $\mathbb{Z}$ is congruent to $x \cdot 2^{-1} \pmod{n}$. Actually, this is an application of the fact that if $x$ is evenly divisible by any $k \in \mathbb{Z}$, then division in $\mathbb{Z}$ will be congruent to multiplication by $k^{-1}$ modulo $n$.

From these two simple facts the following simple algorithm can be derived.

---
Algorithm **Montgomery Reduction**.
**Input**. Integer $x$, $n$ and $k$
**Output**. $2^{-k}x \pmod{n}$

---

1. for $t$ from 1 to $k$ do
   1.1 If $x$ is odd then
      1.1.1 $x \leftarrow x + n$
   1.2 $x \leftarrow x/2$
2. Return $x$.

Figure 6.3: Algorithm Montgomery Reduction

The algorithm in Figure 6.3 reduces the input one bit at a time using the two congruencies stated previously. Inside the loop $n$, which is odd, is added to $x$ if $x$ is odd. This forces $x$ to be even, which allows the division by two in $\mathbb{Z}$ to be congruent to a modular division by two. Since $x$ is assumed initially much larger

---

[5]Thanks to Niels Ferguson for his insightful explanation of the algorithm.

than $n$, the addition of $n$ will contribute an insignificant magnitude to $x$. Let $r$ represent the result of the Montgomery algorithm. If $k > lg(n)$ and $0 \le x < n^2$, then the result is limited to $0 \le r < \lfloor x/2^k \rfloor + n$. At most, a single subtraction is required to get the residue desired.

| Step number $(t)$ | Result $(x)$ |
|:---:|:---|
| 1 | $x + n = 5812,\ x/2 = 2906$ |
| 2 | $x/2 = 1453$ |
| 3 | $x + n = 1710,\ x/2 = 855$ |
| 4 | $x + n = 1112,\ x/2 = 556$ |
| 5 | $x/2 = 278$ |
| 6 | $x/2 = 139$ |
| 7 | $x + n = 396,\ x/2 = 198$ |
| 8 | $x/2 = 99$ |
| 9 | $x + n = 356,\ x/2 = 178$ |

Figure 6.4: Example of Montgomery Reduction (I)

Consider the example in Figure 6.4, which reduces $x = 5555$ modulo $n = 257$ when $k = 9$ (note $\beta^k = 512$, which is larger than $n$). The result of the algorithm $r = 178$ is congruent to the value of $2^{-9} \cdot 5555 \pmod{257}$. When $r$ is multiplied by $2^9$ modulo 257, the correct residue $r \equiv 158$ is produced.

Let $k = \lfloor lg(n) \rfloor + 1$ represent the number of bits in $n$. The current algorithm requires $2k^2$ single precision shifts and $k^2$ single precision additions. At this rate, the algorithm is most certainly slower than Barrett reduction and not terribly useful. Fortunately, there exists an alternative representation of the algorithm.

---

Algorithm **Montgomery Reduction** (modified I).
**Input.** Integer $x$, $n$ and $k$ ($2^k > n$)
**Output.** $2^{-k}x \pmod{n}$

---

1. for $t$ from 1 to $k$ do
   1.1 If the $t$'th bit of $x$ is one then
      1.1.1 $x \leftarrow x + 2^t n$
2. Return $x/2^k$.

---

Figure 6.5: Algorithm Montgomery Reduction (modified I)

This algorithm is equivalent since $2^t n$ is a multiple of $n$ and the lower $k$ bits of $x$ are zero by step 2. The number of single precision shifts has now been reduced from $2k^2$ to $k^2 + k$, which is only a small improvement (Figure 6.5).

| Step number $(t)$ | Result $(x)$ | Result $(x)$ in Binary |
|---|---|---|
| – | 5555 | 1010110110011 |
| 1 | $x + 2^0 n = 5812$ | 1011010110100 |
| 2 | 5812 | 1011010110100 |
| 3 | $x + 2^2 n = 6840$ | 1101010111000 |
| 4 | $x + 2^3 n = 8896$ | 10001011000000 |
| 5 | 8896 | 10001011000000 |
| 6 | 8896 | 10001011000000 |
| 7 | $x + 2^6 n = 25344$ | 110001100000000 |
| 8 | 25344 | 110001100000000 |
| 9 | $x + 2^7 n = 91136$ | 10110010000000000 |
| – | $x/2^k = 178$ | |

Figure 6.6: Example of Montgomery Reduction (II)

Figure 6.6 demonstrates the modified algorithm reducing $x = 5555$ modulo $n = 257$ with $k = 9$. With this algorithm, a single shift right at the end is the only right shift required to reduce the input instead of $k$ right shifts inside the loop. Note that for the iterations $t = 2, 5, 6,$ and $8$ where the result $x$ is not changed. In those iterations the $t$'th bit of $x$ is zero and the appropriate multiple of $n$ does not need to be added to force the $t$'th bit of the result to zero.

## 6.3.1 Digit Based Montgomery Reduction

Instead of computing the reduction on a bit-by-bit basis it is much faster to compute it on digit-by-digit basis. Consider the previous algorithm re-written to compute the Montgomery reduction in this new fashion (Figure 6.7).

---
Algorithm **Montgomery Reduction** (modified II).
**Input.** Integer $x$, $n$ and $k$ $(\beta^k > n)$
**Output.** $\beta^{-k}x$ (mod $n$)

---

1. for $t$ from 0 to $k - 1$ do
   1.1 $x \leftarrow x + \mu n \beta^t$
2. Return $x/\beta^k$.

---

Figure 6.7: Algorithm Montgomery Reduction (modified II)

The value $\mu n \beta^t$ is a multiple of the modulus $n$, meaning that it will not change the residue. If the first digit of the value $\mu n \beta^t$ equals the negative (modulo $\beta$) of the $t$'th digit of $x$, then the addition will result in a zero digit. This problem breaks down to solving the following congruency.

$$
\begin{aligned}
x_t + \mu n_0 &\equiv 0 \ (\text{mod } \beta) \\
\mu n_0 &\equiv -x_t \ (\text{mod } \beta) \\
\mu &\equiv -x_t/n_0 \ (\text{mod } \beta)
\end{aligned}
$$

In each iteration of the loop in step 1 a new value of $\mu$ must be calculated. The value of $-1/n_0$ (mod $\beta$) is used extensively in this algorithm and should be precomputed. Let $\rho$ represent the negative of the modular inverse of $n_0$ modulo $\beta$.

For example, let $\beta = 10$ represent the radix. Let $n = 17$ represent the modulus, which implies $k = 2$ and $\rho \equiv 7$. Let $x = 33$ represent the value to reduce.

The result in Figure 6.8 of 900 is then divided by $\beta^k$ to produce the result 9. The first observation is that $9 \not\equiv x$ (mod $n$), which implies the result is not the modular residue of $x$ modulo $n$. However, recall that the residue is actually multiplied by $\beta^{-k}$ in the algorithm. To get the true residue the value must be

| Step ($t$) | Value of $x$ | Value of $\mu$ |
|:---:|:---:|:---:|
| – | 33 | – |
| 0 | $33 + \mu n = 50$ | 1 |
| 1 | $50 + \mu n \beta = 900$ | 5 |

Figure 6.8: Example of Montgomery Reduction

multiplied by $\beta^k$. In this case, $\beta^k \equiv 15 \pmod{n}$ and the correct residue is $9 \cdot 15 \equiv 16 \pmod{n}$.

## 6.3.2 Baseline Montgomery Reduction

The baseline Montgomery reduction algorithm will produce the residue for any size input. It is designed to be a catch-all algorithm for Montgomery reductions.

---

Algorithm **mp_montgomery_reduce**.
**Input**. mp_int $x$, mp_int $n$ and a digit $\rho \equiv -1/n_0 \pmod{n}$.
$\quad (0 \leq x < n^2, n > 1, (n, \beta) = 1, \beta^k > n)$
**Output**. $\beta^{-k}x \pmod{n}$

---

1. $digs \leftarrow 2n.used + 1$
2. If $digs < MP\_ARRAY$ and $m.used < \delta$ then
    2.1 Use algorithm fast_mp_montgomery_reduce instead.

Setup $x$ for the reduction.
3. If $x.alloc < digs$ then grow $x$ to $digs$ digits.
4. $x.used \leftarrow digs$

Eliminate the lower $k$ digits.
5. For $ix$ from 0 to $k - 1$ do
    5.1 $\mu \leftarrow x_{ix} \cdot \rho \pmod{\beta}$
    5.2 $u \leftarrow 0$
    5.3 For $iy$ from 0 to $k - 1$ do
        5.3.1 $\hat{r} \leftarrow \mu n_{iy} + x_{ix+iy} + u$
        5.3.2 $x_{ix+iy} \leftarrow \hat{r} \pmod{\beta}$
        5.3.3 $u \leftarrow \lfloor \hat{r}/\beta \rfloor$
    5.4 While $u > 0$ do
        5.4.1 $iy \leftarrow iy + 1$
        5.4.2 $x_{ix+iy} \leftarrow x_{ix+iy} + u$
        5.4.3 $u \leftarrow \lfloor x_{ix+iy}/\beta \rfloor$
        5.4.4 $x_{ix+iy} \leftarrow x_{ix+iy} \pmod{\beta}$

Divide by $\beta^k$ and fix up as required.
6. $x \leftarrow \lfloor x/\beta^k \rfloor$
7. If $x \geq n$ then
    7.1 $x \leftarrow x - n$
8. Return($MP\_OKAY$).

---

Figure 6.9: Algorithm mp_montgomery_reduce

**Algorithm mp_montgomery_reduce.** This algorithm reduces the input $x$ modulo $n$ in place using the Montgomery reduction algorithm. The algorithm is loosely based on algorithm 14.32 of [2, pp.601], except it merges the multiplication of $\mu n \beta^t$ with the addition in the inner loop. The restrictions on this algorithm are fairly easy to adapt to. First, $0 \leq x < n^2$ bounds the input to numbers in the same range as for the Barrett algorithm. Additionally, if $n > 1$ and $n$ is odd there will exist a modular inverse $\rho$. $\rho$ must be calculated in advance of this algorithm. Finally, the variable $k$ is fixed and a pseudonym for $n.used$ (Figure 6.9).

Step 2 decides whether a faster Montgomery algorithm can be used. It is based on the Comba technique, meaning that there are limits on the size of the input. This algorithm is discussed in 7.9.

Step 5 is the main reduction loop of the algorithm. The value of $\mu$ is calculated once per iteration in the outer loop. The inner loop calculates $x + \mu n \beta^{ix}$ by multiplying $\mu n$ and adding the result to $x$ shifted by $ix$ digits. Both the addition and multiplication are performed in the same loop to save time and memory. Step 5.4 will handle any additional carries that escape the inner loop.

On quick inspection, this algorithm requires $n$ single precision multiplications for the outer loop and $n^2$ single precision multiplications in the inner loop for a total $n^2 + n$ single precision multiplications, which compares favorably to Barrett at $n^2 + 2n - 1$ single precision multiplications.

```
File: bn_mp_montgomery_reduce.c
018    /* computes xR**-1 (mod N) via Montgomery Reduction */
019    int
020    mp_montgomery_reduce (mp_int * x, mp_int * n, mp_digit rho)
021    {
022      int      ix, res, digs;
023      mp_digit mu;
024
025      /* can the fast reduction [comba] method be used?
026       *
027       * Note that unlike in mul you're safely allowed *less*
028       * than the available columns [255 per default] since carries
029       * are fixed up in the inner loop.
030       */
031      digs = n->used * 2 + 1;
032      if ((digs < MP_WARRAY) &&
033          n->used <
034          (1 << ((CHAR_BIT * sizeof (mp_word)) - (2 * DIGIT_BIT)))) {
035        return fast_mp_montgomery_reduce (x, n, rho);
036      }
037
038      /* grow the input as required */
039      if (x->alloc < digs) {
040        if ((res = mp_grow (x, digs)) != MP_OKAY) {
```

```
041            return res;
042          }
043        }
044        x->used = digs;
045
046        for (ix = 0; ix < n->used; ix++) {
047          /* mu = ai * rho mod b
048           *
049           * The value of rho must be precalculated via
050           * montgomery_setup() such that
051           * it equals -1/n0 mod b this allows the
052           * following inner loop to reduce the
053           * input one digit at a time
054           */
055          mu = (mp_digit) (((mp_word)x->dp[ix]) * ((mp_word)rho) & MP_MASK);
056
057          /* a = a + mu * m * b**i */
058          {
059            register int iy;
060            register mp_digit *tmpn, *tmpx, u;
061            register mp_word r;
062
063            /* alias for digits of the modulus */
064            tmpn = n->dp;
065
066            /* alias for the digits of x [the input] */
067            tmpx = x->dp + ix;
068
069            /* set the carry to zero */
070            u = 0;
071
072            /* Multiply and add in place */
073            for (iy = 0; iy < n->used; iy++) {
074              /* compute product and sum */
075              r       = ((mp_word)mu) * ((mp_word)*tmpn++) +
076                         ((mp_word) u) + ((mp_word) * tmpx);
077
078              /* get carry */
079              u       = (mp_digit)(r >> ((mp_word) DIGIT_BIT));
080
081              /* fix digit */
```

```
082            *tmpx++ = (mp_digit)(r & ((mp_word) MP_MASK));
083          }
084          /* At this point the ix'th digit of x should be zero */
085
086
087          /* propagate carries upwards as required*/
088          while (u) {
089            *tmpx    += u;
090            u        = *tmpx >> DIGIT_BIT;
091            *tmpx++ &= MP_MASK;
092          }
093        }
094      }
095
096      /* at this point the n.used'th least
097       * significant digits of x are all zero
098       * which means we can shift x to the
099       * right by n.used digits and the
100       * residue is unchanged.
101       */
102
103      /* x = x/b**n.used */
104      mp_clamp(x);
105      mp_rshd (x, n->used);
106
107      /* if x >= n then x = x - n */
108      if (mp_cmp_mag (x, n) != MP_LT) {
109        return s_mp_sub (x, n, x);
110      }
111
112      return MP_OKAY;
113    }
114
```

This is the baseline implementation of the Montgomery reduction algorithm. Lines 31 to 36 determine if the Comba–based routine can be used instead. Line 47 computes the value of $\mu$ for that particular iteration of the outer loop.

The multiplication $\mu n \beta^{ix}$ is performed in one step in the inner loop. The alias *tmpx* refers to the $ix$'th digit of $x$, and the alias *tmpn* refers to the modulus $n$.

### 6.3.3 Faster "Comba" Montgomery Reduction

The Montgomery reduction requires fewer single precision multiplications than a Barrett reduction; however, it is much slower due to the serial nature of the inner loop. The Barrett reduction algorithm requires two slightly modified multipliers, which can be implemented with the Comba technique. The Montgomery reduction algorithm cannot directly use the Comba technique to any significant advantage since the inner loop calculates a $k \times 1$ product $k$ times.

The biggest obstacle is that at the $ix$'th iteration of the outer loop, the value of $x_{ix}$ is required to calculate $\mu$. This means the carries from 0 to $ix - 1$ must have been propagated upwards to form a valid $ix$'th digit. The solution as it turns out is very simple. Perform a Comba–like multiplier, and inside the outer loop just after the inner loop, fix up the $ix + 1$'th digit by forwarding the carry.

With this change in place, the Montgomery reduction algorithm can be performed with a Comba–style multiplication loop, which substantially increases the speed of the algorithm.

---

Algorithm **fast_mp_montgomery_reduce**.
**Input**. mp_int $x$, mp_int $n$ and a digit $\rho \equiv -1/n_0 \pmod{n}$.
$$(0 \le x < n^2, n > 1, (n, \beta) = 1, \beta^k > n)$$
**Output**. $\beta^{-k}x \pmod{n}$

---

Place an array of **MP_WARRAY** mp_word variables called $\hat{W}$ on the stack.
1. if $x.alloc < n.used + 1$ then grow $x$ to $n.used + 1$ digits.
Copy the digits of $x$ into the array $\hat{W}$
2. For $ix$ from 0 to $x.used - 1$ do
    2.1 $\hat{W}_{ix} \leftarrow x_{ix}$
3. For $ix$ from $x.used$ to $2n.used - 1$ do
    3.1 $\hat{W}_{ix} \leftarrow 0$
Eliminate the lower $k$ digits.
4. for $ix$ from 0 to $n.used - 1$ do
    4.1 $\mu \leftarrow \hat{W}_{ix} \cdot \rho \pmod{\beta}$
    4.2 For $iy$ from 0 to $n.used - 1$ do
        4.2.1 $\hat{W}_{iy+ix} \leftarrow \hat{W}_{iy+ix} + \mu \cdot n_{iy}$
    4.3 $\hat{W}_{ix+1} \leftarrow \hat{W}_{ix+1} + \lfloor \hat{W}_{ix}/\beta \rfloor$
Propagate the rest of the carries upwards.
5. for $ix$ from $n.used$ to $2n.used + 1$ do
    5.1 $\hat{W}_{ix+1} \leftarrow \hat{W}_{ix+1} + \lfloor \hat{W}_{ix}/\beta \rfloor$
Shift right and reduce modulo $\beta$ simultaneously.
6. for $ix$ from 0 to $n.used + 1$ do
    6.1 $x_{ix} \leftarrow \hat{W}_{ix+n.used} \pmod{\beta}$
Zero excess digits and fixup $x$.
7. if $x.used > n.used + 1$ then do
    7.1 for $ix$ from $n.used + 1$ to $x.used - 1$ do
        7.1.1 $x_{ix} \leftarrow 0$
8. $x.used \leftarrow n.used + 1$
9. Clamp excessive digits of $x$.
10. If $x \ge n$ then
    10.1 $x \leftarrow x - n$
11. Return($MP\_OKAY$).

---

Figure 6.10: Algorithm fast_mp_montgomery_reduce

**Algorithm fast_mp_montgomery_reduce.** This algorithm will compute the Montgomery reduction of $x$ modulo $n$ using the Comba technique. It is on most computer platforms significantly faster than algorithm mp_montgomery_reduce and algorithm mp_reduce (*Barrett reduction*). The algorithm has the same restrictions on the input as the baseline reduction algorithm. An additional two restrictions are imposed on this algorithm. The number of digits $k$ in the modulus $n$ must not violate $MP\_WARRAY > 2k + 1$ and $n < \delta$. When $\beta = 2^{28}$, this algorithm can be used to reduce modulo a modulus of at most $3,556$ bits in length (Figure 6.10).

As in the other Comba reduction algorithms there is a $\hat{W}$ array that stores the columns of the product. It is initially filled with the contents of $x$ with the excess digits zeroed. The reduction loop is very similar the to the baseline loop at heart. The multiplication in step 4.1 can be single precision only, since $ab \pmod{\beta} \equiv (a \bmod \beta)(b \bmod \beta)$. Some multipliers such as those on the ARM processors take a variable length time to complete depending on the number of bytes of result it must produce. By performing a single precision multiplication instead, half the amount of time is spent.

Also note that digit $\hat{W}_{ix}$ must have the carry from the $ix-1$'th digit propagated upwards for this to work. That is what step 4.3 will do. In effect, over the *n.used* iterations of the outer loop the *n.used*'th lower columns all have their carries propagated forwards. Note how the upper bits of those same words are not reduced modulo $\beta$. This is because those values will be discarded shortly and there is no point.

Step 5 will propagate the remainder of the carries upwards. In step 6, the columns are reduced modulo $\beta$ and shifted simultaneously as they are stored in the destination $x$.

```
File: bn_fast_mp_montgomery_reduce.c
018    /* computes xR**-1 == x (mod N) via Montgomery Reduction
019     *
020     * This is an optimized implementation of montgomery_reduce
021     * which uses the comba method to quickly calculate the columns of the
022     * reduction.
023     *
024     * Based on Algorithm 14.32 on pp.601 of HAC.
025     */
026    int fast_mp_montgomery_reduce (mp_int * x, mp_int * n, mp_digit rho)
027    {
028       int      ix, res, olduse;
029       mp_word W[MP_WARRAY];
030
031       /* get old used count */
```

```
032    olduse = x->used;
033
034    /* grow a as required */
035    if (x->alloc < n->used + 1) {
036      if ((res = mp_grow (x, n->used + 1)) != MP_OKAY) {
037        return res;
038      }
039    }
040
041    /* first we have to get the digits of the input into
042     * an array of double precision words W[...]
043     */
044    {
045      register mp_word *_W;
046      register mp_digit *tmpx;
047
048      /* alias for the W[] array */
049      _W   = W;
050
051      /* alias for the digits of  x*/
052      tmpx = x->dp;
053
054      /* copy the digits of a into W[0..a->used-1] */
055      for (ix = 0; ix < x->used; ix++) {
056        *_W++ = *tmpx++;
057      }
058
059      /* zero the high words of W[a->used..m->used*2] */
060      for (; ix < n->used * 2 + 1; ix++) {
061        *_W++ = 0;
062      }
063    }
064
065    /* now we proceed to zero successive digits
066     * from the least significant upwards
067     */
068    for (ix = 0; ix < n->used; ix++) {
069      /* mu = ai * m' mod b
070       *
071       * We avoid a double precision multiplication (which isn't required)
072       * by casting the value down to a mp_digit.  Note this requires
```

```
073            * that W[ix-1] have  the carry cleared (see after the inner loop)
074            */
075           register mp_digit mu;
076           mu = (mp_digit) (((W[ix] & MP_MASK) * rho) & MP_MASK);
077
078           /* a = a + mu * m * b**i
079            *
080            * This is computed in place and on the fly.  The multiplication
081            * by b**i is handled by offsetting which columns the results
082            * are added to.
083            *
084            * Note the comba method normally doesn't handle carries in the
085            * inner loop In this case we fix the carry from the previous
086            * column since the Montgomery reduction requires digits of the
087            * result (so far) [see above] to work.  This is
088            * handled by fixing up one carry after the inner loop.  The
089            * carry fixups are done in order so after these loops the
090            * first m->used words of W[] have the carries fixed
091            */
092           {
093             register int iy;
094             register mp_digit *tmpn;
095             register mp_word *_W;
096
097             /* alias for the digits of the modulus */
098             tmpn = n->dp;
099
100             /* Alias for the columns set by an offset of ix */
101             _W = W + ix;
102
103             /* inner loop */
104             for (iy = 0; iy < n->used; iy++) {
105                 *_W++ += ((mp_word)mu) * ((mp_word)*tmpn++);
106             }
107           }
108
109           /* now fix carry for next digit, W[ix+1] */
110           W[ix + 1] += W[ix] >> ((mp_word) DIGIT_BIT);
111         }
112
113         /* now we have to propagate the carries and
```

```
114      * shift the words downward [all those least
115      * significant digits we zeroed].
116      */
117      {
118       register mp_digit *tmpx;
119       register mp_word *_W, *_W1;
120
121       /* nox fix rest of carries */
122
123       /* alias for current word */
124       _W1 = W + ix;
125
126       /* alias for next word, where the carry goes */
127       _W = W + ++ix;
128
129       for (; ix <= n->used * 2 + 1; ix++) {
130         *_W++ += *_W1++ >> ((mp_word) DIGIT_BIT);
131       }
132
133       /* copy out, A = A/b**n
134        *
135        * The result is A/b**n but instead of converting from an
136        * array of mp_word to mp_digit then calling mp_rshd
137        * we just copy them in the right order
138        */
139
140       /* alias for destination word */
141       tmpx = x->dp;
142
143       /* alias for shifted double precision result */
144       _W = W + n->used;
145
146       for (ix = 0; ix < n->used + 1; ix++) {
147         *tmpx++ = (mp_digit)(*_W++ & ((mp_word) MP_MASK));
148       }
149
150       /* zero oldused digits, if the input a was larger than
151        * m->used+1 we'll have to clear the digits
152        */
153       for (; ix < olduse; ix++) {
154         *tmpx++ = 0;
```

```
155        }
156      }
157
158      /* set the max used and clamp */
159      x->used = n->used + 1;
160      mp_clamp (x);
161
162      /* if A >= m then A = A - m */
163      if (mp_cmp_mag (x, n) != MP_LT) {
164        return s_mp_sub (x, n, x);
165      }
166      return MP_OKAY;
167    }
168
```

The $\hat{W}$ array is first filled with digits of $x$ on line 55, then the rest of the digits are zeroed on line 60. Both loops share the same alias variables to make the code easier to read.

The value of $\mu$ is calculated in an interesting fashion. First, the value $\hat{W}_{ix}$ is reduced modulo $\beta$ and cast to a mp_digit. This forces the compiler to use a single precision multiplication and prevents any concerns about loss of precision. Line 110 fixes the carry for the next iteration of the loop by propagating the carry from $\hat{W}_{ix}$ to $\hat{W}_{ix+1}$.

The for loop on line 129 propagates the rest of the carries upwards through the columns. The for loop on line 146 reduces the columns modulo $\beta$ and shifts them $k$ places at the same time. The alias $\_\hat{W}$ actually refers to the array $\hat{W}$ starting at the $n.used$'th digit, that is $\_\hat{W}_t = \hat{W}_{n.used+t}$.

### 6.3.4   Montgomery Setup

To calculate the variable $\rho$, a relatively simple algorithm will be required.

---

Algorithm **mp_montgomery_setup**.
**Input**. mp_int $n$ ($n > 1$ and $(n, 2) = 1$)
**Output**. $\rho \equiv -1/n_0 \pmod{\beta}$

---

1. $b \leftarrow n_0$
2. If $b$ is even return($MP\_VAL$)
3. $x \leftarrow (((b + 2) \text{ AND } 4) << 1) + b$
4. for $k$ from 0 to $\lceil lg(lg(\beta)) \rceil - 2$ do
   4.1 $x \leftarrow x \cdot (2 - bx)$
5. $\rho \leftarrow \beta - x \pmod{\beta}$
6. Return($MP\_OKAY$).

---

Figure 6.11: Algorithm mp_montgomery_setup

**Algorithm mp_montgomery_setup.** This algorithm will calculate the value of $\rho$ required within the Montgomery reduction algorithms. It uses a very interesting trick to calculate $1/n_0$ when $\beta$ is a power of two (Figure 6.11).

```
File: bn_mp_montgomery_setup.c
018    /* sets up the montgomery reduction stuff */
019    int
020    mp_montgomery_setup (mp_int * n, mp_digit * rho)
021    {
022      mp_digit x, b;
023
024    /* fast inversion mod 2**k
025     *
026     * Based on the fact that
027     *
028     * XA = 1 (mod 2**n)   =>   (X(2-XA)) A = 1 (mod 2**2n)
029     *                     =>   2*X*A - X*X*A*A = 1
030     *                     =>   2*(1) - (1)     = 1
031     */
032      b = n->dp[0];
033
034      if ((b & 1) == 0) {
035        return MP_VAL;
036      }
037
038      x = (((b + 2) & 4) << 1) + b; /* here x*a==1 mod 2**4 */
```

```
039        x *= 2 - b * x;                /* here x*a==1 mod 2**8 */
040    #if !defined(MP_8BIT)
041        x *= 2 - b * x;                /* here x*a==1 mod 2**16 */
042    #endif
043    #if defined(MP_64BIT) || !(defined(MP_8BIT) || defined(MP_16BIT))
044        x *= 2 - b * x;                /* here x*a==1 mod 2**32 */
045    #endif
046    #ifdef MP_64BIT
047        x *= 2 - b * x;                /* here x*a==1 mod 2**64 */
048    #endif
049
050        /* rho = -1/m mod b */
051        *rho = (((mp_word)1 << ((mp_word) DIGIT_BIT)) - x) & MP_MASK;
052
053        return MP_OKAY;
054    }
055
```

This source code computes the value of $\rho$ required to perform Montgomery reduction. It has been modified to avoid performing excess multiplications when $\beta$ is not the default 28 bits.

## 6.4 The Diminished Radix Algorithm

The Diminished Radix method of modular reduction [8] is a fairly clever technique that can be more efficient than either the Barrett or Montgomery methods for certain forms of moduli. The technique is based on the following simple congruence.

$$(x \bmod n) + k\lfloor x/n \rfloor \equiv x \; (\bmod \; (n - k)) \tag{6.6}$$

This observation was used in the MMB [9] block cipher to create a diffusion primitive. It used the fact that if $n = 2^{31}$ and $k = 1$, an x86 multiplier could produce the 62-bit product and use the "shrd" instruction to perform a double-precision right shift. The proof of equation 6.6 is very simple. First, write $x$ in the product form.

$$x = qn + r \tag{6.7}$$

Now reduce both sides modulo $(n - k)$.

$$x \equiv qk + r \pmod{(n-k)} \tag{6.8}$$

The variable $n$ reduces modulo $n - k$ to $k$. By putting $q = \lfloor x/n \rfloor$ and $r = x \bmod n$ into the equation the original congruence is reproduced, thus concluding the proof. The following algorithm is based on this observation.

---
Algorithm **Diminished Radix Reduction**.
**Input**. Integer $x$, $n$, $k$
**Output**. $x \bmod (n-k)$

---

1. $q \leftarrow \lfloor x/n \rfloor$
2. $q \leftarrow k \cdot q$
3. $x \leftarrow x \pmod{n}$
4. $x \leftarrow x + q$
5. If $x \geq (n-k)$ then
   5.1 $x \leftarrow x - (n-k)$
   5.2 Goto step 1.
6. Return $x$

---

Figure 6.12: Algorithm Diminished Radix Reduction

This algorithm will reduce $x$ modulo $n - k$ and return the residue. If $0 \leq x < (n-k)^2$, then the algorithm will loop almost always once or twice and occasionally three times. For simplicity's sake, the value of $x$ is bounded by the following simple polynomial.

$$0 \leq x < n^2 + k^2 - 2nk \tag{6.9}$$

The true bound is $0 \leq x < (n - k - 1)^2$, but this has quite a few more terms. The value of $q$ after step 1 is bounded by the following equation.

$$q < n - 2k - k^2/n \tag{6.10}$$

Since $k^2$ is going to be considerably smaller than $n$, that term will always be zero. The value of $x$ after step 3 is bounded trivially as $0 \leq x < n$. By step 4, the sum $x + q$ is bounded by

$$0 \leq q + x < (k+1)n - 2k^2 - 1 \tag{6.11}$$

| $x = 123456789, n = 256, k = 3$ |
| --- |
| $q \leftarrow \lfloor x/n \rfloor = 482253$ |
| $q \leftarrow q * k = 1446759$ |
| $x \leftarrow x \bmod n = 21$ |
| $x \leftarrow x + q = 1446780$ |
| $x \leftarrow x - (n - k) = 1446527$ |
| $q \leftarrow \lfloor x/n \rfloor = 5650$ |
| $q \leftarrow q * k = 16950$ |
| $x \leftarrow x \bmod n = 127$ |
| $x \leftarrow x + q = 17077$ |
| $x \leftarrow x - (n - k) = 16824$ |
| $q \leftarrow \lfloor x/n \rfloor = 65$ |
| $q \leftarrow q * k = 195$ |
| $x \leftarrow x \bmod n = 184$ |
| $x \leftarrow x + q = 379$ |
| $x \leftarrow x - (n - k) = 126$ |

Figure 6.13: Example Diminished Radix Reduction

With a second pass, $q$ will be loosely bounded by $0 \leq q < k^2$ after step 2, while $x$ will still be loosely bounded by $0 \leq x < n$ after step 3. After the second pass it is highly unlikely that the sum in step 4 will exceed $n - k$. In practice, fewer than three passes of the algorithm are required to reduce virtually every input in the range $0 \leq x < (n - k - 1)^2$.

Figure 6.13 demonstrates the reduction of $x = 123456789$ modulo $n - k = 253$ when $n = 256$ and $k = 3$. Note that even while $x$ is considerably larger than $(n - k - 1)^2 = 63504$, the algorithm still converges on the modular residue exceedingly fast. In this case, only three passes were required to find the residue $x \equiv 126$.

## 6.4.1  Choice of Moduli

On the surface, this algorithm looks very expensive. It requires a couple of subtractions followed by multiplication and other modular reductions. The usefulness of this algorithm becomes exceedingly clear when an appropriate modulus is chosen.

Division in general is a very expensive operation to perform. The one exception is when the division is by a power of the radix of representation used. Division by

10, for example, is simple for pencil and paper mathematics since it amounts to shifting the decimal place to the right. Similarly, division by 2 (*or powers of 2*) is very simple for binary computers to perform. It would therefore seem logical to choose $n$ of the form $2^p$, which would imply that $\lfloor x/n \rfloor$ is a simple shift of $x$ right $p$ bits.

However, there is one operation related to division of power of twos that is even faster. If $n = \beta^p$, then the division may be performed by moving whole digits to the right $p$ places. In practice, division by $\beta^p$ is much faster than division by $2^p$ for any $p$. Also, with the choice of $n = \beta^p$ reducing $x$ modulo $n$ merely requires zeroing the digits above the $p - 1$'th digit of $x$.

Throughout the next section the term *restricted modulus* will refer to a modulus of the form $\beta^p - k$, whereas the term *unrestricted modulus* will refer to a modulus of the form $2^p - k$. The word *restricted* in this case refers to the fact that it is based on the $2^p$ logic, except $p$ must be a multiple of $lg(\beta)$.

### 6.4.2   Choice of $k$

Now that division and reduction (*steps 1 and 3 of Figure 6.12*) have been optimized to simple digit operations, the multiplication by $k$ in step 2 is the most expensive operation. Fortunately, the choice of $k$ is not terribly limited. For all intents and purposes it might as well be a single digit. The smaller the value of $k$, the faster the algorithm will be.

### 6.4.3   Restricted Diminished Radix Reduction

The Restricted Diminished Radix algorithm can quickly reduce an input modulo a modulus of the form $n = \beta^p - k$. This algorithm can reduce an input $x$ within the range $0 \leq x < n^2$ using only a couple of passes of the algorithm demonstrated in Figure 6.12. The implementation of this algorithm has been optimized to avoid additional overhead associated with a division by $\beta^p$, the multiplication by $k$ or the addition of $x$ and $q$. The resulting algorithm is very efficient and can lead to substantial improvements over Barrett and Montgomery reduction when modular exponentiations are performed.

---

Algorithm **mp_dr_reduce**.
**Input**. mp_int $x$, $n$ and a mp_digit $k = \beta - n_0$
$\qquad (0 \leq x < n^2,\, n > 1,\, 0 < k < \beta)$
**Output**. $x \bmod n$

---

1. $m \leftarrow n.used$
2. If $x.alloc < 2m$ then grow $x$ to $2m$ digits.
3. $\mu \leftarrow 0$
4. for $i$ from 0 to $m - 1$ do
   4.1 $\hat{r} \leftarrow k \cdot x_{m+i} + x_i + \mu$
   4.2 $x_i \leftarrow \hat{r} \pmod{\beta}$
   4.3 $\mu \leftarrow \lfloor \hat{r}/\beta \rfloor$
5. $x_m \leftarrow \mu$
6. for $i$ from $m + 1$ to $x.used - 1$ do
   6.1 $x_i \leftarrow 0$
7. Clamp excess digits of $x$.
8. If $x \geq n$ then
   8.1 $x \leftarrow x - n$
   8.2 Goto step 3.
9. Return($MP\_OKAY$).

---

Figure 6.14: Algorithm mp_dr_reduce

**Algorithm mp_dr_reduce.** This algorithm will perform the Diminished Radix reduction of $x$ modulo $n$. It has similar restrictions to that of the Barrett reduction with the addition that $n$ must be of the form $n = \beta^m - k$ where $0 < k < \beta$ (Figure 6.14).

This algorithm essentially implements the pseudo-code in Figure 6.12, except with a slight optimization. The division by $\beta^m$, multiplication by $k$, and addition of $x \bmod \beta^m$ are all performed simultaneously inside the loop in step 4. The division by $\beta^m$ is emulated by accessing the term at the $m + i$'th position, which is subsequently multiplied by $k$ and added to the term at the $i$'th position. After the loop the $m$'th digit is set to the carry and the upper digits are zeroed. Steps 5 and 6 emulate the reduction modulo $\beta^m$ that should have happened to $x$ before the addition of the multiple of the upper half.

In step 8, if $x$ is still larger than $n$, another pass of the algorithm is required. First, $n$ is subtracted from $x$ and then the algorithm resumes at step 3.

File: bn_mp_dr_reduce.c

```
018    /* reduce "x" in place modulo "n" using the Diminished Radix algorithm.
019     *
020     * Based on algorithm from the paper
021     *
022     * "Generating Efficient Primes for Discrete Log Cryptosystems"
023     *                   Chae Hoon Lim, Pil Joong Lee,
024     *            POSTECH Information Research Laboratories
025     *
026     * The modulus must be of a special format [see manual]
027     *
028     * Has been modified to use algorithm 7.10 from the LTM book instead
029     *
030     * Input x must be in the range 0 <= x <= (n-1)**2
031     */
032    int
033    mp_dr_reduce (mp_int * x, mp_int * n, mp_digit k)
034    {
035      int       err, i, m;
036      mp_word   r;
037      mp_digit mu, *tmpx1, *tmpx2;
038
039      /* m = digits in modulus */
040      m = n->used;
041
042      /* ensure that "x" has at least 2m digits */
043      if (x->alloc < m + m) {
044        if ((err = mp_grow (x, m + m)) != MP_OKAY) {
045          return err;
046        }
047      }
048
049    /* top of loop, this is where the code resumes if
050     * another reduction pass is required.
051     */
052    top:
053      /* aliases for digits */
054      /* alias for lower half of x */
055      tmpx1 = x->dp;
056
057      /* alias for upper half of x, or x/B**m */
```

```
058        tmpx2 = x->dp + m;
059
060        /* set carry to zero */
061        mu = 0;
062
063        /* compute (x mod B**m) + k * [x/B**m] inline and inplace */
064        for (i = 0; i < m; i++) {
065            r           = ((mp_word)*tmpx2++) * ((mp_word)k) + *tmpx1 + mu;
066            *tmpx1++    = (mp_digit)(r & MP_MASK);
067            mu          = (mp_digit)(r >> ((mp_word)DIGIT_BIT));
068        }
069
070        /* set final carry */
071        *tmpx1++ = mu;
072
073        /* zero words above m */
074        for (i = m + 1; i < x->used; i++) {
075            *tmpx1++ = 0;
076        }
077
078        /* clamp, sub and return */
079        mp_clamp (x);
080
081        /* if x >= n then subtract and reduce again
082         * Each successive "recursion" makes the input smaller and smaller.
083         */
084        if (mp_cmp_mag (x, n) != MP_LT) {
085            s_mp_sub(x, n, x);
086            goto top;
087        }
088        return MP_OKAY;
089    }
090
```

The first step is to grow $x$ as required to $2m$ digits, since the reduction is performed in place on $x$. The label on line 52 is where the algorithm will resume if further reduction passes are required. In theory, it could be placed at the top of the function. However, the size of the modulus and question of whether $x$ is large enough are invariant after the first pass, meaning that it would be a waste of time.

The aliases *tmpx1* and *tmpx2* refer to the digits of $x$, where the latter is offset by $m$ digits. By reading digits from $x$ offset by $m$ digits, a division by $\beta^m$ can be simulated virtually for free. The loop on line 64 performs the bulk of the work (*corresponds to step 4 of algorithm 7.11*) in this algorithm.

By line 67 the pointer $tmpx1$ points to the $m$'th digit of $x$, which is where the final carry will be placed. Similarly, by line 74 the same pointer will point to the $m + 1$'th digit where the zeroes will be placed.

Since the algorithm is only valid if both $x$ and $n$ are greater than zero, an unsigned comparison suffices to determine if another pass is required. With the same logic at line 81 the value of $x$ is known to be greater than or equal to $n$, meaning that an unsigned subtraction can be used as well. Since the destination of the subtraction is the larger of the inputs, the call to algorithm s_mp_sub cannot fail and the return code does not need to be checked.

### Setup

To set up the Restricted Diminished Radix algorithm the value $k = \beta - n_0$ is required. This algorithm is not complicated but is provided for completeness (Figure 6.15).

---
Algorithm **mp_dr_setup**.
**Input**. mp_int $n$
**Output**. $k = \beta - n_0$

---

1. $k \leftarrow \beta - n_0$

---

Figure 6.15: Algorithm mp_dr_setup

```
File: bn_mp_dr_setup.c
018   /* determines the setup value */
019   void mp_dr_setup(mp_int *a, mp_digit *d)
020   {
021      /* the casts are required if DIGIT_BIT is one less than
022       * the number of bits in a mp_digit [e.g. DIGIT_BIT==31]
023       */
024      *d = (mp_digit)((((mp_word)1) << ((mp_word)DIGIT_BIT)) -
025          ((mp_word)a->dp[0]));
026   }
027
028
```

## Modulus Detection

Another useful algorithm gives the ability to detect a Restricted Diminished Radix modulus. An integer is said to be of Restricted Diminished Radix form if all the digits are equal to $\beta - 1$ except the trailing digit, which may be any value.

---
Algorithm **mp_dr_is_modulus**.
**Input**. mp_int $n$
**Output**. 1 if $n$ is in D.R form, 0 otherwise

---
1. If $n.used < 2$ then return(0).
2. for $ix$ from 1 to $n.used - 1$ do
   2.1 If $n_{ix} \neq \beta - 1$ return(0).
3. Return(1).

---

Figure 6.16: Algorithm mp_dr_is_modulus

**Algorithm mp_dr_is_modulus.** This algorithm determines if a value is in Diminished Radix form. Step 1 rejects obvious cases where fewer than two digits are in the mp_int. Step 2 tests all but the first digit to see if they are equal to $\beta - 1$. If the algorithm manages to get to step 3, then $n$ must be of Diminished Radix form (Figure 6.16).

```
File: bn_mp_dr_is_modulus.c
018    /* determines if a number is a valid DR modulus */
019    int mp_dr_is_modulus(mp_int *a)
020    {
021       int ix;
022
023       /* must be at least two digits */
024       if (a->used < 2) {
025          return 0;
026       }
027
028       /* must be of the form b**k - a [a <= b] so all
029        * but the first digit must be equal to -1 (mod b).
030        */
031       for (ix = 1; ix < a->used; ix++) {
032          if (a->dp[ix] != MP_MASK) {
033             return 0;
034          }
```

```
035        }
036        return 1;
037    }
038
039
```

## 6.4.4    Unrestricted Diminished Radix Reduction

The unrestricted Diminished Radix algorithm allows modular reductions to be performed when the modulus is of the form $2^p - k$. This algorithm is a straightforward adaptation of algorithm 6.12.

In general, the restricted Diminished Radix reduction algorithm is much faster since it has considerably lower overhead. However, this new algorithm is much faster than either Montgomery or Barrett reduction when the moduli are of the appropriate form.

---

Algorithm **mp_reduce_2k**.
**Input**. mp_int $a$ and $n$. mp_digit $k$
        ($a \geq 0$, $n > 1$, $0 < k < \beta$, $n + k$ is a power of two)
**Output**. $a \pmod{n}$

---

1. $p \leftarrow \lceil lg(n) \rceil$ (mp_count_bits)
2. While $a \geq n$ do
   2.1 $q \leftarrow \lfloor a/2^p \rfloor$ (mp_div_2d)
   2.2 $a \leftarrow a \pmod{2^p}$ (mp_mod_2d)
   2.3 $q \leftarrow q \cdot k$ (mp_mul_d)
   2.4 $a \leftarrow a - q$ (s_mp_sub)
   2.5 If $a \geq n$ then do
      2.5.1 $a \leftarrow a - n$
3. Return($MP\_OKAY$).

---

Figure 6.17: Algorithm mp_reduce_2k

**Algorithm mp_reduce_2k.** This algorithm quickly reduces an input $a$ modulo an unrestricted Diminished Radix modulus $n$. Division by $2^p$ is emulated with a right shift, which makes the algorithm fairly inexpensive to use (Figure 6.17).

```
File: bn_mp_reduce_2k.c
018    /* reduces a modulo n where n is of the form 2**p - d */
019    int mp_reduce_2k(mp_int *a, mp_int *n, mp_digit d)
```

```
020   {
021       mp_int q;
022       int   p, res;
023
024       if ((res = mp_init(&q)) != MP_OKAY) {
025          return res;
026       }
027
028       p = mp_count_bits(n);
029   top:
030      /* q = a/2**p, a = a mod 2**p */
031      if ((res = mp_div_2d(a, p, &q, a)) != MP_OKAY) {
032          goto ERR;
033      }
034
035      if (d != 1) {
036         /* q = q * d */
037         if ((res = mp_mul_d(&q, d, &q)) != MP_OKAY) {
038             goto ERR;
039         }
040      }
041
042      /* a = a + q */
043      if ((res = s_mp_add(a, &q, a)) != MP_OKAY) {
044          goto ERR;
045      }
046
047      if (mp_cmp_mag(a, n) != MP_LT) {
048         s_mp_sub(a, n, a);
049         goto top;
050      }
051
052   ERR:
053      mp_clear(&q);
054      return res;
055   }
056
057
```

The algorithm mp_count_bits calculates the number of bits in an mp_int, which is used to find the initial value of $p$. The call to mp_div_2d on line 31 calculates both the quotient $q$ and the remainder $a$ required. By doing both in a single function call, the code size is kept fairly small. The multiplication by $k$ is only performed if $k > 1$. This allows reductions modulo $2^p - 1$ to be performed without any multiplications.

The unsigned s_mp_add, mp_cmp_mag, and s_mp_sub are used in place of their full sign counterparts since the inputs are only valid if they are positive. By using the unsigned versions, the overhead is kept to a minimum.

### Unrestricted Setup

To set up this reduction algorithm, the value of $k = 2^p - n$ is required.

---

Algorithm **mp_reduce_2k_setup**.
**Input**. mp_int $n$
**Output**. $k = 2^p - n$

---
1. $p \leftarrow \lceil lg(n) \rceil$ $(mp\_count\_bits)$
2. $x \leftarrow 2^p$ $(mp\_2expt)$
3. $x \leftarrow x - n$ $(mp\_sub)$
4. $k \leftarrow x_0$
5. Return($MP\_OKAY$).

---

Figure 6.18: Algorithm mp_reduce_2k_setup

**Algorithm mp_reduce_2k_setup.** This algorithm computes the value of $k$ required for the algorithm mp_reduce_2k. By making a temporary variable $x$ equal to $2^p$, a subtraction is sufficient to solve for $k$. Alternatively if $n$ has more than one digit the value of $k$ is simply $\beta - n_0$ (Figure 6.18).

```
File: bn_mp_reduce_2k_setup.c
018   /* determines the setup value */
019   int mp_reduce_2k_setup(mp_int *a, mp_digit *d)
020   {
021      int res, p;
022      mp_int tmp;
023
024      if ((res = mp_init(&tmp)) != MP_OKAY) {
025         return res;
026      }
027
```

```
028        p = mp_count_bits(a);
029        if ((res = mp_2expt(&tmp, p)) != MP_OKAY) {
030           mp_clear(&tmp);
031           return res;
032        }
033
034        if ((res = s_mp_sub(&tmp, a, &tmp)) != MP_OKAY) {
035           mp_clear(&tmp);
036           return res;
037        }
038
039        *d = tmp.dp[0];
040        mp_clear(&tmp);
041        return MP_OKAY;
042     }
043
```

### Unrestricted Detection

An integer $n$ is a valid unrestricted Diminished Radix modulus if either of the following are true.

- The number has only one digit.

- The number has more than one digit, and every bit from the $\beta$'th to the most significant is one.

If either condition is true, there is a power of two $2^p$ such that $0 < 2^p - n < \beta$. If the input is only one digit, it will always be of the correct form. Otherwise, all of the bits above the first digit must be one. This arises from the fact that there will be value of $k$ that when added to the modulus causes a carry in the first digit that propagates all the way to the most significant bit. The resulting sum will be a power of two.

---

Algorithm **mp_reduce_is_2k**.
**Input**. mp_int $n$
**Output**. 1 if of proper form, 0 otherwise

---

1. If $n.used = 0$ then return(0).
2. If $n.used = 1$ then return(1).
3. $p \leftarrow \lceil lg(n) \rceil$ (mp_count_bits)
4. for $x$ from $lg(\beta)$ to $p$ do
   4.1 If the $(x \bmod lg(\beta))$'th bit of the $\lfloor x/lg(\beta) \rfloor$ of $n$ is zero then return(0).
5. Return(1).

---

Figure 6.19: Algorithm mp_reduce_is_2k

**Algorithm mp_reduce_is_2k.** This algorithm quickly determines if a modulus is of the form required for algorithm mp_reduce_2k to function properly (Figure 6.19).

```
File: bn_mp_reduce_is_2k.c
018    /* determines if mp_reduce_2k can be used */
019    int mp_reduce_is_2k(mp_int *a)
020    {
021       int ix, iy, iw;
022       mp_digit iz;
023
024       if (a->used == 0) {
025          return MP_NO;
026       } else if (a->used == 1) {
027          return MP_YES;
028       } else if (a->used > 1) {
029          iy = mp_count_bits(a);
030          iz = 1;
031          iw = 1;
032
033          /* Test every bit from the second digit up, must be 1 */
034          for (ix = DIGIT_BIT; ix < iy; ix++) {
035             if ((a->dp[iw] & iz) == 0) {
036                return MP_NO;
037             }
038             iz <<= 1;
039             if (iz > (mp_digit)MP_MASK) {
040                ++iw;
```

```
041                 iz = 1;
042             }
043         }
044     }
045     return MP_YES;
046 }
047
048
```

## 6.5 Algorithm Comparison

So far, three very different algorithms for modular reduction have been discussed. Each algorithm has its own strengths and weaknesses that make having such a selection very useful. The following table summarizes the three algorithms along with comparisons of work factors. Since all three algorithms have the restriction that $0 \le x < n^2$ and $n > 1$, those limitations are not included in the table.

| Method | Work Required | Limitations | $m = 8$ | $m = 32$ | $m = 64$ |
|--------|---------------|-------------|---------|----------|----------|
| Barrett | $m^2 + 2m - 1$ | None | 79 | 1087 | 4223 |
| Montgomery | $m^2 + m$ | $n$ must be odd | 72 | 1056 | 4160 |
| D.R. | $2m$ | $n = \beta^m - k$ | 16 | 64 | 128 |

In theory, Montgomery and Barrett reductions would require roughly the same amount of time to complete. However, in practice since Montgomery reduction can be written as a single function with the Comba technique, it is much faster. Barrett reduction suffers from the overhead of calling the half precision multipliers, addition and division by $\beta$ algorithms.

For almost every cryptographic algorithm, Montgomery reduction is the algorithm of choice. The one set of algorithms where Diminished Radix reduction truly shines is based on the discrete logarithm problem such as Diffie-Hellman and ElGamal. In these algorithms, primes of the form $\beta^m - k$ can be found and shared among users. These primes will allow the Diminished Radix algorithm to be used in modular exponentiation to greatly speed up the operation.

# Exercises

[3]  Prove that the "trick" in algorithm mp_montgomery_setup actually
     calculates the correct value of $\rho$.

[2]  Devise an algorithm to reduce modulo $n + k$ for small $k$ quickly.

[4]  Prove that the pseudo-code algorithm "Diminished Radix Reduction"
     (*Figure 6.12*) terminates. Also prove the probability that it will
     terminate within $1 \leq k \leq 10$ iterations.

# Chapter 7

# Exponentiation

Exponentiation is the operation of raising one variable to the power of another; for example, $a^b$. A variant of exponentiation, computed in a finite field or ring, is called modular exponentiation. This latter style of operation is typically used in public key cryptosystems such as RSA and Diffie-Hellman. The ability to quickly compute modular exponentiations is of great benefit to any such cryptosystem, and many methods have been sought to speed it up.

## 7.1  Exponentiation Basics

A trivial algorithm would simply multiply $a$ against itself $b-1$ times to compute the exponentiation desired. However, as $b$ grows in size the number of multiplications becomes prohibitive. Imagine what would happen if $b \sim 2^{1024}$, as is the case when computing an RSA signature with a 1024-bit key. Such a calculation could never be completed, as it would take far too long.

Fortunately, there is a very simple algorithm based on the laws of exponents. Recall that $lg_a(a^b) = b$ and that $lg_a(a^b a^c) = b+c$ which are two trivial relationships between the base and the exponent. Let $b_i$ represent the $i$'th bit of $b$ starting from the least significant bit. If $b$ is a $k$-bit integer, equation 7.1 is true.

$$a^b = \prod_{i=0}^{k-1} a^{2^i \cdot b_i} \qquad (7.1)$$

By taking the base $a$ logarithm of both sides of the equation, equation 7.2 is the result.

$$b = \sum_{i=0}^{k-1} 2^i \cdot b_i \qquad (7.2)$$

The term $a^{2^i}$ can be found from the $i-1$'th term by squaring the term, since $\left(a^{2^i}\right)^2$ is equal to $a^{2^{i+1}}$. This observation forms the basis of essentially all fast exponentiation algorithms. It requires $k$ squarings and on average $\frac{k}{2}$ multiplications to compute the result. This is indeed quite an improvement over simply multiplying by $a$ a total of $b-1$ times.

While this current method is considerably faster, there are further improvements to be made. For example, the $a^{2^i}$ term does not need to be computed in an auxiliary variable. Consider the equivalent algorithm in Figure 7.1.

---
Algorithm **Left to Right Exponentiation**.
**Input**. Integer $a$, $b$ and $k$
**Output**. $c = a^b$

---

1. $c \leftarrow 1$
2. for $i$ from $k-1$ to 0 do
      2.1 $c \leftarrow c^2$
      2.2 $c \leftarrow c \cdot a^{b_i}$
3. Return $c$.

---

Figure 7.1: Left to Right Exponentiation

This algorithm starts from the most significant bit and works toward the least significant bit. When the $i$'th bit of $b$ is set, $a$ is multiplied against the current product. In each iteration the product is squared, which doubles the exponent of the individual terms of the product.

For example, let $b = 101100_2 \equiv 44_{10}$. Figure 7.2 demonstrates the actions of the algorithm.

| Value of $i$ | Value of $c$ |
|:---:|:---:|
| - | 1 |
| 5 | $a$ |
| 4 | $a^2$ |
| 3 | $a^4 \cdot a$ |
| 2 | $a^8 \cdot a^2 \cdot a$ |
| 1 | $a^{16} \cdot a^4 \cdot a^2$ |
| 0 | $a^{32} \cdot a^8 \cdot a^4$ |

Figure 7.2: Example of Left to Right Exponentiation

When the product $a^{32} \cdot a^8 \cdot a^4$ is simplified, it is equal to $a^{44}$, which is the desired exponentiation. This particular algorithm is called "Left to Right" because it reads the exponent in that order. All the exponentiation algorithms that will be presented are of this nature.

### 7.1.1 Single Digit Exponentiation

The first algorithm in the series of exponentiation algorithms will be an unbounded algorithm where the exponent is a single digit. It is intended to be used when a small power of an input is required (*e.g.*, $a^5$). It is faster than simply multiplying $b - 1$ times for all values of $b$ that are greater than three.

---

Algorithm **mp_expt_d**.
**Input**. mp_int $a$ and mp_digit $b$
**Output**. $c = a^b$

---

1. $g \leftarrow a$ ($mp\_init\_copy$)
2. $c \leftarrow 1$ ($mp\_set$)
3. for $x$ from 1 to $lg(\beta)$ do
    3.1 $c \leftarrow c^2$ ($mp\_sqr$)
    3.2 If $b$ AND $2^{lg(\beta)-1} \neq 0$ then
        3.2.1 $c \leftarrow c \cdot g$ ($mp\_mul$)
    3.3 $b \leftarrow b << 1$
4. Clear $g$.
5. Return($MP\_OKAY$).

---

Figure 7.3: Algorithm mp_expt_d

**Algorithm mp_expt_d.** This algorithm computes the value of $a$ raised to the power of a single digit $b$. It uses the left to right exponentiation algorithm to quickly compute the exponentiation. It is loosely based on algorithm 14.79 of HAC [2, pp. 615], with the difference that the exponent is a fixed width (Figure 7.3).

A copy of $a$ is made first to allow destination variable $c$ be the same as the source variable $a$. The result is set to the initial value of 1 in the subsequent step.

Inside the loop the exponent is read from the most significant bit first down to the least significant bit. First, $c$ is invariably squared in step 3.1. In the following step, if the most significant bit of $b$ is one, the copy of $a$ is multiplied against $c$. The value of $b$ is shifted left one bit to make the next bit down from the most significant bit the new most significant bit. In effect, each iteration of the loop moves the bits of the exponent $b$ upwards to the most significant location.

```
File: bn_mp_expt_d.c
018    /* calculate c = a**b  using a square-multiply algorithm */
019    int mp_expt_d (mp_int * a, mp_digit b, mp_int * c)
020    {
021      int      res, x;
022      mp_int  g;
023
024      if ((res = mp_init_copy (&g, a)) != MP_OKAY) {
025        return res;
```

```
026        }
027
028        /* set initial result */
029        mp_set (c, 1);
030
031        for (x = 0; x < (int) DIGIT_BIT; x++) {
032          /* square */
033          if ((res = mp_sqr (c, c)) != MP_OKAY) {
034            mp_clear (&g);
035            return res;
036          }
037
038          /* if the bit is set multiply */
039          if ((b & (mp_digit) (((mp_digit)1) << (DIGIT_BIT - 1))) != 0) {
040            if ((res = mp_mul (c, &g, c)) != MP_OKAY) {
041              mp_clear (&g);
042              return res;
043            }
044          }
045
046          /* shift to next bit */
047          b <<= 1;
048        }
049
050        mp_clear (&g);
051        return MP_OKAY;
052      }
053
```

Line 29 sets the initial value of the result to 1. Next, the loop on line 31 steps through each bit of the exponent starting from the most significant down toward the least significant. The invariant squaring operation placed on line 33 is performed first. After the squaring the result $c$ is multiplied by the base $g$ if and only if the most significant bit of the exponent is set. The shift on line 47 moves all of the bits of the exponent upwards toward the most significant location.

## 7.2   $k$-ary Exponentiation

When you are calculating an exponentiation, the most time–consuming bottleneck is the multiplications, which are in general a small factor slower than squaring.

Recall from the previous algorithm that $b_i$ refers to the $i$'th bit of the exponent $b$. Suppose instead it referred to the $i$'th $k$-bit digit of the exponent of $b$. For $k = 1$ the definitions are synonymous, and for $k > 1$ algorithm 7.4 computes the same exponentiation. A group of $k$ bits from the exponent is called a *window*, a small window on only a portion of the entire exponent. Consider the modification in Figure 7.4 to the basic left to right exponentiation algorithm.

---

**Algorithm $k$-ary Exponentiation.**
**Input.** Integer $a$, $b$, $k$ and $t$
**Output.** $c = a^b$

---

1. $c \leftarrow 1$
2. for $i$ from $t - 1$ to $0$ do
   2.1 $c \leftarrow c^{2^k}$
   2.2 Extract the $i$'th $k$-bit word from $b$ and store it in $g$.
   2.3 $c \leftarrow c \cdot a^g$
3. Return $c$.

---

Figure 7.4: $k$-ary Exponentiation

The squaring in step 2.1 can be calculated by squaring the value $c$ successively $k$ times. If the values of $a^g$ for $0 < g < 2^k$ have been precomputed, this algorithm requires only $t$ multiplications and $tk$ squarings. The table can be generated with $2^{k-1} - 1$ squarings and $2^{k-1} + 1$ multiplications. This algorithm assumes that the number of bits in the exponent is evenly divisible by $k$. However, when it is not, the remaining $0 < x \leq k - 1$ bits can be handled with algorithm 7.1.

Suppose $k = 4$ and $t = 100$. This modified algorithm will require 109 multiplications and 408 squarings to compute the exponentiation. The original algorithm would on average have required 200 multiplications and 400 squarings to compute the same value. The total number of squarings has increased slightly but the number of multiplications has nearly halved.

## 7.2.1 Optimal Values of $k$

An optimal value of $k$ will minimize $2^k + \lceil n/k \rceil + n - 1$ for a fixed number of bits in the exponent $n$. The simplest approach is to brute force search among the values $k = 2, 3, \ldots, 8$ for the lowest result. Figure 7.5 lists optimal values of $k$ for various exponent sizes and compares the number of multiplication and squarings required against algorithm 7.1.

| Exponent (bits) | Optimal $k$ | Work at $k$ | Work with 7.1 |
|:---:|:---:|:---:|:---:|
| 16 | 2 | 27 | 24 |
| 32 | 3 | 49 | 48 |
| 64 | 3 | 92 | 96 |
| 128 | 4 | 175 | 192 |
| 256 | 4 | 335 | 384 |
| 512 | 5 | 645 | 768 |
| 1024 | 6 | 1257 | 1536 |
| 2048 | 6 | 2452 | 3072 |
| 4096 | 7 | 4808 | 6144 |

Figure 7.5: Optimal Values of $k$ for $k$-ary Exponentiation

## 7.2.2   Sliding Window Exponentiation

A simple modification to the previous algorithm is only generate the upper half of the table in the range $2^{k-1} \leq g < 2^k$. Essentially, this is a table for all values of $g$ where the most significant bit of $g$ is a one. However, for this to be allowed in the algorithm, values of $g$ in the range $0 \leq g < 2^{k-1}$ must be avoided.

Figure 7.6 lists optimal values of $k$ for various exponent sizes and compares the work required against algorithm 7.4.

| Exponent (bits) | Optimal $k$ | Work at $k$ | Work with 7.4 |
|:---:|:---:|:---:|:---:|
| 16 | 3 | 24 | 27 |
| 32 | 3 | 45 | 49 |
| 64 | 4 | 87 | 92 |
| 128 | 4 | 167 | 175 |
| 256 | 5 | 322 | 335 |
| 512 | 6 | 628 | 645 |
| 1024 | 6 | 1225 | 1257 |
| 2048 | 7 | 2403 | 2452 |
| 4096 | 8 | 4735 | 4808 |

Figure 7.6: Optimal Values of $k$ for Sliding Window Exponentiation

---

Algorithm **Sliding Window $k$-ary Exponentiation.**
**Input**. Integer $a$, $b$, $k$ and $t$
**Output**. $c = a^b$

---

1. $c \leftarrow 1$
2. for $i$ from $t - 1$ to 0 do
  2.1 If the $i$'th bit of $b$ is a zero then
    2.1.1 $c \leftarrow c^2$
  2.2 else do
    2.2.1 $c \leftarrow c^{2^k}$
    2.2.2 Extract the $k$ bits from $(b_i b_{i-1} \ldots b_{i-(k-1)})$ and store it in $g$.
    2.2.3 $c \leftarrow c \cdot a^g$
    2.2.4 $i \leftarrow i - (k - 1)$ (*We assume there is a decrement of $i$ before the loop re–iterates*)
3. Return $c$.

---

Figure 7.7: Sliding Window $k$-ary Exponentiation

Similar to the previous algorithm, this algorithm must have a special handler when fewer than $k$ bits are left in the exponent. While this algorithm requires the same number of squarings, it can potentially have fewer multiplications. The pre-computed table $a^g$ is also half the size as the previous table.

Consider the exponent $b = 111101011001000_2 \equiv 31432_{10}$, with $k = 3$ using both algorithms. The first algorithm will divide the exponent up as the following five 3-bit words $b \equiv (111, 101, 011, 001, 000)_2$. The second algorithm will break the exponent as $b \equiv (111, 101, 0, 110, 0, 100, 0)_2$. The single digit 0 in the second representation is where a single squaring took place instead of a squaring and multiplication. In total, the first method requires 10 multiplications and 18 squarings. The second method requires 8 multiplications and 18 squarings.

In general, the sliding window method is never slower than the generic $k$-ary method and often is slightly faster (Figure 7.7).

## 7.3 Modular Exponentiation

Modular exponentiation is essentially computing the power of a base within a finite field or ring. For example, computing $d \equiv a^b \pmod{c}$ is a modular exponentiation. Instead of first computing $a^b$ and then reducing it modulo $c$, the intermediate result is reduced modulo $c$ after every squaring or multiplication operation.

This guarantees that any intermediate result is bounded by $0 \leq d \leq c^2 - 2c + 1$ and can be reduced modulo $c$ quickly using one of the algorithms presented in Chapter 7.

Before the actual modular exponentiation algorithm can be written a wrapper algorithm must be written. This algorithm will allow the exponent $b$ to be negative, which is computed as $c \equiv (1/a)^{|b|} \pmod{d}$. The value of $(1/a) \bmod c$ is computed using the modular inverse (see Section 9.4). If no inverse exists, the algorithm terminates with an error.

---

Algorithm **mp_exptmod**.
**Input**. mp_int $a$, $b$ and $c$
**Output**. $y \equiv g^x \pmod{p}$

---

1. If $c.sign = MP\_NEG$ return($MP\_VAL$).
2. If $b.sign = MP\_NEG$ then
   2.1 $g' \leftarrow g^{-1} \pmod{c}$
   2.2 $x' \leftarrow |x|$
   2.3 Compute $d \equiv g'^{x'} \pmod{c}$ via recursion.
3. if $p$ is odd **OR** $p$ is a D.R. modulus then
   3.1 Compute $y \equiv g^x \pmod{p}$ via algorithm mp_exptmod_fast.
4. else
   4.1 Compute $y \equiv g^x \pmod{p}$ via algorithm s_mp_exptmod.

---

Figure 7.8: Algorithm mp_exptmod

**Algorithm mp_exptmod.** The first algorithm that actually performs modular exponentiation is a sliding window $k$-ary algorithm that uses Barrett reduction to reduce the product modulo $p$. The second algorithm mp_exptmod_fast performs the same operation, except it uses either Montgomery or Diminished Radix reduction. The two latter reduction algorithms are clumped in the same exponentiation algorithm since their arguments are essentially the same (*two mp_ints and one mp_digit*) (Figure 7.8).

```
File: bn_mp_exptmod.c
019   /* this is a shell function that calls either the normal or Montgomery
020    * exptmod functions.  Originally the call to the montgomery code was
021    * embedded in the normal function but that wasted alot of stack space
022    * for nothing (since 99% of the time the Montgomery code would be called)
023    */
```

```
024   int mp_exptmod (mp_int * G, mp_int * X, mp_int * P, mp_int * Y)
025   {
026     int dr;
027
028     /* modulus P must be positive */
029     if (P->sign == MP_NEG) {
030        return MP_VAL;
031     }
032
033     /* if exponent X is negative we have to recurse */
034     if (X->sign == MP_NEG) {
035   #ifdef BN_MP_INVMOD_C
036        mp_int tmpG, tmpX;
037        int err;
038
039        /* first compute 1/G mod P */
040        if ((err = mp_init(&tmpG)) != MP_OKAY) {
041           return err;
042        }
043        if ((err = mp_invmod(G, P, &tmpG)) != MP_OKAY) {
044           mp_clear(&tmpG);
045           return err;
046        }
047
048        /* now get |X| */
049        if ((err = mp_init(&tmpX)) != MP_OKAY) {
050           mp_clear(&tmpG);
051           return err;
052        }
053        if ((err = mp_abs(X, &tmpX)) != MP_OKAY) {
054           mp_clear_multi(&tmpG, &tmpX, NULL);
055           return err;
056        }
057
058        /* and now compute (1/G)**|X| instead of G**X [X < 0] */
059        err = mp_exptmod(&tmpG, &tmpX, P, Y);
060        mp_clear_multi(&tmpG, &tmpX, NULL);
061        return err;
062   #else
063        /* no invmod */
064        return MP_VAL;
```

```
065    #endif
066      }
067
068    /* modified diminished radix reduction */
069    #if defined(BN_MP_REDUCE_IS_2K_L_C) && defined(BN_MP_REDUCE_2K_L_C) && defin
       ed(BN_S_MP_EXPTMOD_C)
070      if (mp_reduce_is_2k_l(P) == MP_YES) {
071         return s_mp_exptmod(G, X, P, Y, 1);
072      }
073    #endif
074
075    #ifdef BN_MP_DR_IS_MODULUS_C
076      /* is it a DR modulus? */
077      dr = mp_dr_is_modulus(P);
078    #else
079      /* default to no */
080      dr = 0;
081    #endif
082
083    #ifdef BN_MP_REDUCE_IS_2K_C
084      /* if not, is it an unrestricted DR modulus? */
085      if (dr == 0) {
086         dr = mp_reduce_is_2k(P) << 1;
087      }
088    #endif
089
090      /* if the modulus is odd or dr != 0 use the montgomery method */
091    #ifdef BN_MP_EXPTMOD_FAST_C
092      if (mp_isodd (P) == 1 || dr != 0) {
093        return mp_exptmod_fast (G, X, P, Y, dr);
094      } else {
095    #endif
096    #ifdef BN_S_MP_EXPTMOD_C
097        /* otherwise use the generic Barrett reduction technique */
098        return s_mp_exptmod (G, X, P, Y, 0);
099    #else
100        /* no exptmod for evens */
101        return MP_VAL;
102    #endif
103    #ifdef BN_MP_EXPTMOD_FAST_C
104      }
```

```
105    #endif
106    }
107
108
```

To keep the algorithms in a known state, the first step on line 29 is to reject any negative modulus as input. If the exponent is negative, the algorithm tries to perform a modular exponentiation with the modular inverse of the base $G$. The temporary variable $tmpG$ is assigned the modular inverse of $G$, and $tmpX$ is assigned the absolute value of $X$. The algorithm will call itself with these new values with a positive exponent.

If the exponent is positive, the algorithm resumes the exponentiation. Line 77 determines if the modulus is of the restricted Diminished Radix form. If it is not, line 86 attempts to determine if it is of an unrestricted Diminished Radix form. The integer $dr$ will take on one of three values.

1. $dr = 0$ means that the modulus is not either restricted or unrestricted Diminished Radix form.

2. $dr = 1$ means that the modulus is of restricted Diminished Radix form.

3. $dr = 2$ means that the modulus is of unrestricted Diminished Radix form.

Line 49 determines if the fast modular exponentiation algorithm can be used. It is allowed if $dr \neq 0$ or if the modulus is odd. Otherwise, the slower s_mp_exptmod algorithm is used, which uses Barrett reduction.

## 7.3.1   Barrett Modular Exponentiation

---

Algorithm **s_mp_exptmod**.
**Input.** mp_int $a$, $b$ and $c$
**Output.** $y \equiv g^x \pmod{p}$

---

1. $k \leftarrow lg(x)$

2. $winsize \leftarrow \begin{cases} 2 & \text{if } k \leq 7 \\ 3 & \text{if } 7 < k \leq 36 \\ 4 & \text{if } 36 < k \leq 140 \\ 5 & \text{if } 140 < k \leq 450 \\ 6 & \text{if } 450 < k \leq 1303 \\ 7 & \text{if } 1303 < k \leq 3529 \\ 8 & \text{if } 3529 < k \end{cases}$

3. Initialize $2^{winsize}$ mp_ints in an array named $M$ and one mp_int named $\mu$
4. Calculate the $\mu$ required for Barrett Reduction (*mp_reduce_setup*).
5. $M_1 \leftarrow g \pmod{p}$

Set up the table of small powers of $g$. First find $g^{2^{winsize}}$ and then all the multiples of it.
6. $k \leftarrow 2^{winsize-1}$
7. $M_k \leftarrow M_1$
8. for $ix$ from 0 to $winsize - 2$ do
   8.1 $M_k \leftarrow (M_k)^2$ (*mp_sqr*)
   8.2 $M_k \leftarrow M_k \pmod{p}$ (*mp_reduce*)
9. for $ix$ from $2^{winsize-1} + 1$ to $2^{winsize} - 1$ do
   9.1 $M_{ix} \leftarrow M_{ix-1} \cdot M_1$ (*mp_mul*)
   9.2 $M_{ix} \leftarrow M_{ix} \pmod{p}$ (*mp_reduce*)
10. $res \leftarrow 1$

Start Sliding Window.
11. $mode \leftarrow 0, bitcnt \leftarrow 1, buf \leftarrow 0, digidx \leftarrow x.used - 1, bitcpy \leftarrow 0, bitbuf \leftarrow 0$
Continued on next page.

---

---

Algorithm **s_mp_exptmod** (*continued*).
**Input**. mp_int $a$, $b$ and $c$
**Output**. $y \equiv g^x \pmod{p}$

---

12. Loop
  12.1 $bitcnt \leftarrow bitcnt - 1$
  12.2 If $bitcnt = 0$ then do
    12.2.1 If $digidx = -1$ goto step 13.
    12.2.2 $buf \leftarrow x_{digidx}$
    12.2.3 $digidx \leftarrow digidx - 1$
    12.2.4 $bitcnt \leftarrow lg(\beta)$
  12.3 $y \leftarrow (buf >> (lg(\beta) - 1))$ AND 1
  12.4 $buf \leftarrow buf << 1$
  12.5 if $mode = 0$ and $y = 0$ then goto step 12.
  12.6 if $mode = 1$ and $y = 0$ then do
    12.6.1 $res \leftarrow res^2$
    12.6.2 $res \leftarrow res \pmod{p}$
    12.6.3 Goto step 12.
  12.7 $bitcpy \leftarrow bitcpy + 1$
  12.8 $bitbuf \leftarrow bitbuf + (y << (winsize - bitcpy))$
  12.9 $mode \leftarrow 2$
  12.10 If $bitcpy = winsize$ then do
  Window is full so perform the squarings and single multiplication.
    12.10.1 for $ix$ from 0 to $winsize - 1$ do
      12.10.1.1 $res \leftarrow res^2$
      12.10.1.2 $res \leftarrow res \pmod{p}$
    12.10.2 $res \leftarrow res \cdot M_{bitbuf}$
    12.10.3 $res \leftarrow res \pmod{p}$
  Reset the window.
    12.10.4 $bitcpy \leftarrow 0, bitbuf \leftarrow 0, mode \leftarrow 1$

---

Continued on the next page.

---

Algorithm **s_mp_exptmod** (*continued*).
**Input**. mp_int $a$, $b$ and $c$
**Output**. $y \equiv g^x \pmod{p}$

---

No more windows left. Check for residual bits of exponent.
13. If $mode = 2$ and $bitcpy > 0$ then do
   13.1 for $ix$ form 0 to $bitcpy - 1$ do
      13.1.1 $res \leftarrow res^2$
      13.1.2 $res \leftarrow res \pmod{p}$
      13.1.3 $bitbuf \leftarrow bitbuf << 1$
      13.1.4 If $bitbuf$ AND $2^{winsize} \neq 0$ then do
         13.1.4.1 $res \leftarrow res \cdot M_1$
         13.1.4.2 $res \leftarrow res \pmod{p}$
14. $y \leftarrow res$
15. Clear $res$, $mu$ and the $M$ array.
16. Return($MP\_OKAY$).

---

Figure 7.9: Algorithm s_mp_exptmod

**Algorithm s_mp_exptmod.** This algorithm computes the $x$'th power of $g$ modulo $p$ and stores the result in $y$. It takes advantage of the Barrett reduction algorithm to keep the product small throughout the algorithm (Figure 7.9).

The first two steps determine the optimal window size based on the number of bits in the exponent. The larger the exponent, the larger the window size becomes. After a window size $winsize$ has been chosen, an array of $2^{winsize}$ mp_int variables is allocated. This table will hold the values of $g^x \pmod{p}$ for $2^{winsize-1} \leq x < 2^{winsize}$.

After the table is allocated, the first power of $g$ is found. Since $g \geq p$ is allowed it must be first reduced modulo $p$ to make the rest of the algorithm more efficient. The first element of the table at $2^{winsize-1}$ is found by squaring $M_1$ successively $winsize - 2$ times. The rest of the table elements are found by multiplying the previous element by $M_1$ modulo $p$.

Now that the table is available, the sliding window may begin (Figure 7.10). The following list describes the functions of all the variables in the window.

1. The variable $mode$ dictates how the bits of the exponent are interpreted.

   (a) When $mode = 0$, the bits are ignored since no non-zero bit of the exponent has been seen yet. For example, if the exponent were simply

1, then there would be $lg(\beta) - 1$ zero bits before the first non-zero bit. In this case bits are ignored until a non-zero bit is found.

(b) When $mode = 1$, a non-zero bit has been seen before and a new *winsize*-bit window has not been formed yet. In this mode, leading 0 bits are read and a single squaring is performed. If a non-zero bit is read, a new window is created.

(c) When $mode = 2$, the algorithm is in the middle of forming a window and new bits are appended to the window from the most significant bit downwards.

2. The variable *bitcnt* indicates how many bits are left in the current digit of the exponent left to be read. When it reaches zero, a new digit is fetched from the exponent.

3. The variable *buf* holds the currently read digit of the exponent.

4. The variable *digidx* is an index into the exponent's digits. It starts at the leading digit $x.used - 1$ and moves toward the trailing digit.

5. The variable *bitcpy* indicates how many bits are in the currently formed window. When it reaches *winsize* the window is flushed and the appropriate operations performed.

6. The variable *bitbuf* holds the current bits of the window being formed.

Step 12 is the window processing loop. It will iterate while there are digits available form the exponent to read. The first step inside this loop is to extract a new digit if no more bits are available in the current digit. If there are no bits left, a new digit is read, and if there are no digits left, the loop terminates.

After a digit is made available, step 12.3 will extract the most significant bit of the current digit and move all other bits in the digit upwards. In effect, the digit is read from most significant bit to least significant bit, and since the digits are read from leading to trailing edges, the entire exponent is read from most significant bit to least significant bit.

At step 12.5, if the *mode* and currently extracted bit $y$ are both zero the bit is ignored and the next bit is read. This prevents the algorithm from having to perform trivial squaring and reduction operations before the first non-zero bit is read. Steps 12.6 and 12.7 through 12.10 handle the two cases of $mode = 1$ and $mode = 2$, respectively.

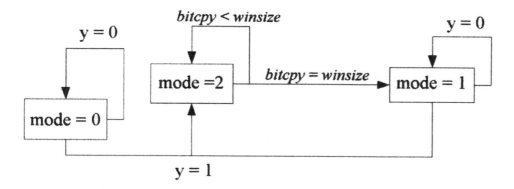

Figure 7.10: Sliding Window State Diagram

By step 13 there are no more digits left in the exponent. However, there may be partial bits in the window left. If $mode = 2$ then a Left-to-Right algorithm is used to process the remaining few bits.

```
File: bn_s_mp_exptmod.c
017   #ifdef MP_LOW_MEM
018      #define TAB_SIZE 32
019   #else
020      #define TAB_SIZE 256
021   #endif
022
023   int s_mp_exptmod (mp_int * G, mp_int * X, mp_int * P, mp_int * Y, int redmod
      e)
024   {
025     mp_int  M[TAB_SIZE], res, mu;
026     mp_digit buf;
027     int     err, bitbuf, bitcpy, bitcnt, mode, digidx, x, y, winsize;
028     int (*redux)(mp_int*,mp_int*,mp_int*);
029
030     /* find window size */
031     x = mp_count_bits (X);
032     if (x <= 7) {
033       winsize = 2;
```

```
034    } else if (x <= 36) {
035      winsize = 3;
036    } else if (x <= 140) {
037      winsize = 4;
038    } else if (x <= 450) {
039      winsize = 5;
040    } else if (x <= 1303) {
041      winsize = 6;
042    } else if (x <= 3529) {
043      winsize = 7;
044    } else {
045      winsize = 8;
046    }
047
048  #ifdef MP_LOW_MEM
049      if (winsize > 5) {
050          winsize = 5;
051      }
052  #endif
053
054    /* init M array */
055    /* init first cell */
056    if ((err = mp_init(&M[1])) != MP_OKAY) {
057      return err;
058    }
059
060    /* now init the second half of the array */
061    for (x = 1<<(winsize-1); x < (1 << winsize); x++) {
062      if ((err = mp_init(&M[x])) != MP_OKAY) {
063        for (y = 1<<(winsize-1); y < x; y++) {
064          mp_clear (&M[y]);
065        }
066        mp_clear(&M[1]);
067        return err;
068      }
069    }
070
071    /* create mu, used for Barrett reduction */
072    if ((err = mp_init (&mu)) != MP_OKAY) {
073      goto LBL_M;
074    }
```

```
075
076     if (redmode == 0) {
077        if ((err = mp_reduce_setup (&mu, P)) != MP_OKAY) {
078           goto LBL_MU;
079        }
080        redux = mp_reduce;
081     } else {
082        if ((err = mp_reduce_2k_setup_l (P, &mu)) != MP_OKAY) {
083           goto LBL_MU;
084        }
085        redux = mp_reduce_2k_l;
086     }
087
088     /* create M table
089      *
090      * The M table contains powers of the base,
091      * e.g. M[x] = G**x mod P
092      *
093      * The first half of the table is not
094      * computed except for M[0]=1 and M[1]=g
095      */
096     if ((err = mp_mod (G, P, &M[1])) != MP_OKAY) {
097       goto LBL_MU;
098     }
099
100     /* compute the value at M[1<<(winsize-1)] by squaring
101      * M[1] (winsize-1) times
102      */
103     if ((err = mp_copy (&M[1], &M[1 << (winsize - 1)])) != MP_OKAY) {
104       goto LBL_MU;
105     }
106
107     for (x = 0; x < (winsize - 1); x++) {
108       /* square it */
109       if ((err = mp_sqr (&M[1 << (winsize - 1)],
110                          &M[1 << (winsize - 1)])) != MP_OKAY) {
111         goto LBL_MU;
112       }
113
114       /* reduce modulo P */
115       if ((err = redux (&M[1 << (winsize - 1)], P, &mu)) != MP_OKAY) {
```

```
116        goto LBL_MU;
117      }
118    }
119
120    /* create upper table, that is M[x] = M[x-1] * M[1] (mod P)
121     * for x = (2**(winsize - 1) + 1) to (2**winsize - 1)
122     */
123    for (x = (1 << (winsize - 1)) + 1; x < (1 << winsize); x++) {
124      if ((err = mp_mul (&M[x - 1], &M[1], &M[x])) != MP_OKAY) {
125        goto LBL_MU;
126      }
127      if ((err = redux (&M[x], P, &mu)) != MP_OKAY) {
128        goto LBL_MU;
129      }
130    }
131
132    /* setup result */
133    if ((err = mp_init (&res)) != MP_OKAY) {
134      goto LBL_MU;
135    }
136    mp_set (&res, 1);
137
138    /* set initial mode and bit cnt */
139    mode   = 0;
140    bitcnt = 1;
141    buf    = 0;
142    digidx = X->used - 1;
143    bitcpy = 0;
144    bitbuf = 0;
145
146    for (;;) {
147      /* grab next digit as required */
148      if (--bitcnt == 0) {
149        /* if digidx == -1 we are out of digits */
150        if (digidx == -1) {
151          break;
152        }
153        /* read next digit and reset the bitcnt */
154        buf    = X->dp[digidx--];
155        bitcnt = (int) DIGIT_BIT;
156      }
```

```
157
158         /* grab the next msb from the exponent */
159         y     = (buf >> (mp_digit)(DIGIT_BIT - 1)) & 1;
160         buf <<= (mp_digit)1;
161
162         /* if the bit is zero and mode == 0 then we ignore it
163          * These represent the leading zero bits before the first 1 bit
164          * in the exponent.  Technically this opt is not required but it
165          * does lower the # of trivial squaring/reductions used
166          */
167         if (mode == 0 && y == 0) {
168           continue;
169         }
170
171         /* if the bit is zero and mode == 1 then we square */
172         if (mode == 1 && y == 0) {
173           if ((err = mp_sqr (&res, &res)) != MP_OKAY) {
174             goto LBL_RES;
175           }
176           if ((err = redux (&res, P, &mu)) != MP_OKAY) {
177             goto LBL_RES;
178           }
179           continue;
180         }
181
182         /* else we add it to the window */
183         bitbuf |= (y << (winsize - ++bitcpy));
184         mode    = 2;
185
186         if (bitcpy == winsize) {
187           /* ok window is filled so square as required and multiply  */
188           /* square first */
189           for (x = 0; x < winsize; x++) {
190             if ((err = mp_sqr (&res, &res)) != MP_OKAY) {
191               goto LBL_RES;
192             }
193             if ((err = redux (&res, P, &mu)) != MP_OKAY) {
194               goto LBL_RES;
195             }
196           }
197
```

```
198        /* then multiply */
199        if ((err = mp_mul (&res, &M[bitbuf], &res)) != MP_OKAY) {
200          goto LBL_RES;
201        }
202        if ((err = redux (&res, P, &mu)) != MP_OKAY) {
203          goto LBL_RES;
204        }
205
206        /* empty window and reset */
207        bitcpy = 0;
208        bitbuf = 0;
209        mode   = 1;
210      }
211    }
212
213    /* if bits remain then square/multiply */
214    if (mode == 2 && bitcpy > 0) {
215      /* square then multiply if the bit is set */
216      for (x = 0; x < bitcpy; x++) {
217        if ((err = mp_sqr (&res, &res)) != MP_OKAY) {
218          goto LBL_RES;
219        }
220        if ((err = redux (&res, P, &mu)) != MP_OKAY) {
221          goto LBL_RES;
222        }
223
224        bitbuf <<= 1;
225        if ((bitbuf & (1 << winsize)) != 0) {
226          /* then multiply */
227          if ((err = mp_mul (&res, &M[1], &res)) != MP_OKAY) {
228            goto LBL_RES;
229          }
230          if ((err = redux (&res, P, &mu)) != MP_OKAY) {
231            goto LBL_RES;
232          }
233        }
234      }
235    }
236
237    mp_exch (&res, Y);
238    err = MP_OKAY;
```

```
239    LBL_RES:mp_clear (&res);
240    LBL_MU:mp_clear (&mu);
241    LBL_M:
242      mp_clear(&M[1]);
243      for (x = 1<<(winsize-1); x < (1 << winsize); x++) {
244        mp_clear (&M[x]);
245      }
246      return err;
247    }
248
```

Lines 32 through 46 determine the optimal window size based on the length of the exponent in bits. The window divisions are sorted from smallest to greatest so that in each **if** statement, only one condition must be tested. For example, by the **if** statement on line 38 the value of $x$ is already known to be greater than 140.

The conditional piece of code beginning on line 48 allows the window size to be restricted to five bits. This logic is used to ensure the table of precomputed powers of $G$ remains relatively small.

The for loop on line 61 initializes the $M$ array, while lines 72 and 77 through 86 initialize the reduction function that will be used for this modulus. Next, we populate (lines 88 through 129) the $M$ table with the appropriate powers of $g$. At this point, we are ready to start the sliding window (lines 138 through 144), and begin processing bits of the exponent.

The first block of code inside the for loop extracts the next digit as required. We enter this loop initially in the state of requiring the next digit, which is why *bitcnt* is initially set to 1. Once we have a digit we can extract the most significant bit (line 159). If the bit is zero, and we have not seen a non–zero bit yet we jump to the top of the loop. Otherwise, we either square and loop (lines 171 through 179) or add the bit to the window.

Note on line 176 how we call the reduction function through our callback pointer *redux*. Provided the function has a consistent calling interface, it could be literally any sort of reduction function.

The block of code starting on line 213 is used to handle cases where the window was not complete. In this case, we use a left–to–right exponentiation on single bits. Since the windows are small, this will involve doing at most 4 to 7 square–multiply steps which is acceptable given the runtime of the remainder of the algorithm.

## 7.4   Quick Power of Two

Calculating $b = 2^a$ can be performed much quicker than with any of the previous algorithms. Recall that a logical shift left $m << k$ is equivalent to $m \cdot 2^k$. By this logic, when $m = 1$ a quick power of two can be achieved.

---

Algorithm **mp_2expt**.
**Input**. integer $b$
**Output**. $a \leftarrow 2^b$

---

1. $a \leftarrow 0$
2. If $a.alloc < \lfloor b/lg(\beta) \rfloor + 1$ then grow $a$ appropriately.
3. $a.used \leftarrow \lfloor b/lg(\beta) \rfloor + 1$
4. $a_{\lfloor b/lg(\beta) \rfloor} \leftarrow 1 << (b \bmod lg(\beta))$
5. Return($MP\_OKAY$).

---

Figure 7.11: Algorithm mp_2expt

**Algorithm mp_2expt.** This algorithm computes a quick power of two by setting the desired bit of the result. It is used by various reduction functions such as Barrett and Montgomery (Figure 7.11).

```
File: bn_mp_2expt.c
018    /* computes a = 2**b
019     *
020     * Simple algorithm which zeroes the int, grows it then just sets one bit
021     * as required.
022     */
023    int
024    mp_2expt (mp_int * a, int b)
025    {
026      int     res;
027
028      /* zero a as per default */
029      mp_zero (a);
030
031      /* grow a to accommodate the single bit */
032      if ((res = mp_grow (a, b / DIGIT_BIT + 1)) != MP_OKAY) {
033        return res;
034      }
```

```
035
036      /* set the used count of where the bit will go */
037      a->used = b / DIGIT_BIT + 1;
038
039      /* put the single bit in its place */
040      a->dp[b / DIGIT_BIT] = ((mp_digit)1) << (b % DIGIT_BIT);
041
042      return MP_OKAY;
043    }
044
```

# Exercises

[2]   Devise an algorithm to perform square and multiply exponentiation
       by reading the exponent from right to left.

[5]   Explore the use of exponent recoding (such as signed representations).
       Describe situations where it could be beneficial.

[5]   Devise an exponentiation algorithm which is does not leak timing information.
       Try to avoid using randomization.

[5]   Explore the use of vector addition chains. Develop a greedy encoding algorithm
       which can beat algorithm s_mp_exptmod for static (fixed), and then random exponent

# Chapter 8

# Higher Level Algorithms

This chapter discusses the various higher level algorithms that are required to complete a well–rounded multiple precision integer package. These routines are less performance oriented than the algorithms in Chapters 5, 6, and 7, but are no less important.

The first section describes a method of integer division with remainder that is universally well known. It provides the signed division logic for the package. The subsequent section discusses a set of algorithms that allow a single digit to be the 2nd operand for a variety of operations. These algorithms serve mostly to simplify other algorithms where small constants are required. The last two sections discuss how to manipulate various representations of integers; for example, converting from an mp_int to a string of character.

## 8.1 Integer Division with Remainder

Integer division aside from modular exponentiation is the most intensive algorithm to compute. Like addition, subtraction, and multiplication, the basis of this algorithm is the long-hand division algorithm taught to schoolchildren. Throughout this discussion several common variables will be used. Let $x$ represent the divisor and $y$ represent the dividend. Let $q$ represent the integer quotient $\lfloor y/x \rfloor$ and let $r$ represent the remainder $r = y - x\lfloor y/x \rfloor$. The following simple algorithm will be used to start the discussion (Figure 8.1).

---

Algorithm **Radix-$\beta$ Integer Division.**
**Input.** integer $x$ and $y$
**Output.** $q = \lfloor y/x \rfloor, r = y - xq$

---

1. $q \leftarrow 0$
2. $n \leftarrow ||y|| - ||x||$
3. for $t$ from $n$ down to 0 do
   3.1 Maximize $k$ such that $kx\beta^t$ is less than or equal to $y$ and $(k+1)x\beta^t$ is greater.
   3.2 $q \leftarrow q + k\beta^t$
   3.3 $y \leftarrow y - kx\beta^t$
4. $r \leftarrow y$
5. Return$(q, r)$

---

Figure 8.1: Algorithm Radix-$\beta$ Integer Division

As children we are taught this very simple algorithm for the case of $\beta = 10$. Almost instinctively, several optimizations are taught for which their reason of existing are never explained. For this example, let $y = 5471$ represent the dividend and $x = 23$ represent the divisor.

To find the first digit of the quotient the value of $k$ must be maximized such that $kx\beta^t$ is less than or equal to $y$, and simultaneously $(k+1)x\beta^t$ is greater than $y$. Implicitly, $k$ is the maximum value the $t$'th digit of the quotient may have. The habitual method used to find the maximum is to "eyeball" the two numbers, typically only the leading digits, and quickly estimate a quotient. By only using leading digits, a much simpler division may be used to form an educated guess at what the value must be. In this case, $k = \lfloor 54/23 \rfloor = 2$ quickly arises as a possible solution. Indeed, $2x\beta^2 = 4600$ is less than $y = 5471$, and simultaneously $(k+1)x\beta^2 = 6900$ is larger than $y$. As a result, $k\beta^2$ is added to the quotient which now equals $q = 200$, and 4600 is subtracted from $y$ to give a remainder of $y = 841$.

This process is repeated to produce the quotient digit $k = 3$, which makes the quotient $q = 200 + 3\beta = 230$ and the remainder $y = 841 - 3x\beta = 181$. Finally, the last iteration of the loop produces $k = 7$, which leads to the quotient $q = 230 + 7 = 237$ and the remainder $y = 181 - 7x = 20$. The final quotient and remainder found are $q = 237$ and $r = y = 20$, which are indeed correct since $237 \cdot 23 + 20 = 5471$ is true.

### 8.1.1 Quotient Estimation

As alluded to earlier, the quotient digit $k$ can be estimated from only the leading digits of both the divisor and dividend. When $p$ leading digits are used from both the divisor and dividend to form an estimation, the accuracy of the estimation rises as $p$ grows. Technically speaking, the estimation is based on assuming the lower $||y|| - p$ and $||x|| - p$ lower digits of the dividend and divisor are zero.

The value of the estimation may off by a few values in either direction and in general is fairly correct. A simplification [1, pp. 271] of the estimation technique is to use $t + 1$ digits of the dividend and $t$ digits of the divisor, particularly when $t = 1$. The estimate using this technique is never too small. For the following proof, let $t = ||y|| - 1$ and $s = ||x|| - 1$ represent the most significant digits of the dividend and divisor, respectively.

**Theorem.** *The quotient $\hat{k} = \lfloor (y_t \beta + y_{t-1})/x_s \rfloor$ is greater than or equal to* $k = \lfloor y/(x \cdot \beta^{||y|| - ||x|| - 1}) \rfloor$.

**Proof.** Adapted from [1, pp. 271]. The first obvious case is when $\hat{k} = \beta - 1$, in which case the proof is concluded since the real quotient cannot be larger. For all other cases $\hat{k} = \lfloor (y_t \beta + y_{t-1})/x_s \rfloor$ and $\hat{k} x_s \geq y_t \beta + y_{t-1} - x_s + 1$. The latter portion of the inequality $-x_s + 1$ arises from the fact that a truncated integer division will give the same quotient for at most $x_s - 1$ values. Next, a series of inequalities will prove the hypothesis.

$$y - \hat{k}x \leq y - \hat{k} x_s \beta^s \tag{8.1}$$

This is trivially true since $x \geq x_s \beta^s$. Next, we replace $\hat{k} x_s \beta^s$ by the previous inequality for $\hat{k} x_s$.

$$y - \hat{k}x \leq y_t \beta^t + \ldots + y_0 - (y_t \beta^t + y_{t-1} \beta^{t-1} - x_s \beta^t + \beta^s) \tag{8.2}$$

By simplifying the previous inequality the following inequality is formed.

$$y - \hat{k}x \leq y_{t-2} \beta^{t-2} + \ldots + y_0 + x_s \beta^s - \beta^s \tag{8.3}$$

Subsequently,

$$y_{t-2} \beta^{t-2} + \ldots + y_0 + x_s \beta^s - \beta^s < x_s \beta^s \leq x \tag{8.4}$$

which proves that $y - \hat{k}x \leq x$ and by consequence $\hat{k} \geq k$, which concludes the proof.

**QED**

### 8.1.2 Normalized Integers

For the purposes of division, a normalized input is when the divisor's leading digit $x_n$ is greater than or equal to $\beta/2$. By multiplying both $x$ and $y$ by $j = \lfloor (\beta/2)/x_n \rfloor$, the quotient remains unchanged and the remainder is simply $j$ times the original remainder. The purpose of normalization is to ensure the leading digit of the divisor is sufficiently large such that the estimated quotient will lie in the domain of a single digit. Consider the maximum dividend $(\beta - 1) \cdot \beta + (\beta - 1)$ and the minimum divisor $\beta/2$.

$$\frac{\beta^2 - 1}{\beta/2} \leq 2\beta - \frac{2}{\beta} \tag{8.5}$$

At most, the quotient approaches $2\beta$; however, in practice this will not occur since that would imply the previous quotient digit was too small.

## 8.1.3 Radix-$\beta$ Division with Remainder

---

Algorithm **mp_div**.
**Input**. mp_int $a, b$
**Output**. $c = \lfloor a/b \rfloor$, $d = a - bc$

---

1. If $b = 0$ return($MP\_VAL$).
2. If $|a| < |b|$ then do
   2.1 $d \leftarrow a$
   2.2 $c \leftarrow 0$
   2.3 Return($MP\_OKAY$).

Setup the quotient to receive the digits.
3. Grow $q$ to $a.used + 2$ digits.
4. $q \leftarrow 0$
5. $x \leftarrow |a|, y \leftarrow |b|$
6. $sign \leftarrow \begin{cases} MP\_ZPOS & \text{if } a.sign = b.sign \\ MP\_NEG & \text{otherwise} \end{cases}$

Normalize the inputs such that the leading digit of $y$ is greater than or equal to $\beta/2$.
7. $norm \leftarrow (lg(\beta) - 1) - (\lceil lg(y) \rceil \ (\text{mod } lg(\beta)))$
8. $x \leftarrow x \cdot 2^{norm}, y \leftarrow y \cdot 2^{norm}$

Find the leading digit of the quotient.
9. $n \leftarrow x.used - 1, t \leftarrow y.used - 1$
10. $y \leftarrow y \cdot \beta^{n-t}$
11. While ($x \geq y$) do
    11.1 $q_{n-t} \leftarrow q_{n-t} + 1$
    11.2 $x \leftarrow x - y$
12. $y \leftarrow \lfloor y/\beta^{n-t} \rfloor$

---

Continued on the next page.

---

---

Algorithm **mp_div** (continued).
**Input**. mp_int $a, b$
**Output**. $c = \lfloor a/b \rfloor$, $d = a - bc$

---

Now find the remainder fo the digits.

13. for $i$ from $n$ down to $(t+1)$ do
    13.1 If $i > x.used$ then jump to the next iteration of this loop.
    13.2 If $x_i = y_t$ then
        13.2.1 $q_{i-t-1} \leftarrow \beta - 1$
    13.3 else
        13.3.1 $\hat{r} \leftarrow x_i \cdot \beta + x_{i-1}$
        13.3.2 $\hat{r} \leftarrow \lfloor \hat{r}/y_t \rfloor$
        13.3.3 $q_{i-t-1} \leftarrow \hat{r}$
    13.4 $q_{i-t-1} \leftarrow q_{i-t-1} + 1$

Fixup quotient estimation.
    13.5 Loop
        13.5.1 $q_{i-t-1} \leftarrow q_{i-t-1} - 1$
        13.5.2 $t1 \leftarrow 0$
        13.5.3 $t1_0 \leftarrow y_{t-1}$, $t1_1 \leftarrow y_t$, $t1.used \leftarrow 2$
        13.5.4 $t1 \leftarrow t1 \cdot q_{i-t-1}$
        13.5.5 $t2_0 \leftarrow x_{i-2}$, $t2_1 \leftarrow x_{i-1}$, $t2_2 \leftarrow x_i$, $t2.used \leftarrow 3$
        13.5.6 If $|t1| > |t2|$ then goto step 13.5.
    13.6 $t1 \leftarrow y \cdot q_{i-t-1}$
    13.7 $t1 \leftarrow t1 \cdot \beta^{i-t-1}$
    13.8 $x \leftarrow x - t1$
    13.9 If $x.sign = MP\_NEG$ then
        13.10 $t1 \leftarrow y$
        13.11 $t1 \leftarrow t1 \cdot \beta^{i-t-1}$
        13.12 $x \leftarrow x + t1$
        13.13 $q_{i-t-1} \leftarrow q_{i-t-1} - 1$

---

Continued on the next page.

---

---
Algorithm **mp_div** (continued).
**Input**. mp_int $a, b$
**Output**. $c = \lfloor a/b \rfloor$, $d = a - bc$

---

Finalize the result.
14. Clamp excess digits of $q$
15. $c \leftarrow q, c.sign \leftarrow sign$
16. $x.sign \leftarrow a.sign$
17. $d \leftarrow \lfloor x/2^{norm} \rfloor$
18. Return($MP\_OKAY$).

---

Figure 8.2: Algorithm mp_div

**Algorithm mp_div.** This algorithm will calculate the quotient and remainder from an integer division given a dividend and divisor. The algorithm is a signed division and will produce a fully qualified quotient and remainder (Figure 8.2).

First, the divisor $b$ must be non-zero, which is enforced in step 1. If the divisor is larger than the dividend, the quotient is implicitly zero and the remainder is the dividend.

After the first two trivial cases of inputs are handled, the variable $q$ is set up to receive the digits of the quotient. Two unsigned copies of the divisor $y$ and dividend $x$ are made as well. The core of the division algorithm is an unsigned division and will only work if the values are positive. Now the two values $x$ and $y$ must be normalized such that the leading digit of $y$ is greater than or equal to $\beta/2$. This is performed by shifting both to the left by enough bits to get the desired normalization.

At this point, the division algorithm can begin producing digits of the quotient. Recall that maximum value of the estimation used is $2\beta - \frac{2}{\beta}$, which means that a digit of the quotient must be first produced by another means. In this case, $y$ is shifted to the left (*step 10*) so that it has the same number of digits as $x$. The loop in step 11 will subtract multiples of the shifted copy of $y$ until $x$ is smaller. Since the leading digit of $y$ is greater than or equal to $\beta/2$, this loop will iterate at most two times to produce the desired leading digit of the quotient.

Now the remainder of the digits can be produced. The equation $\hat{q} = \lfloor \frac{x_i\beta + x_{i-1}}{y_t} \rfloor$ is used to fairly accurately approximate the true quotient digit. The estimation can in theory produce an estimation as high as $2\beta - \frac{2}{\beta}$, but by induction the upper quotient digit is correct (*as established in step 11*) and the estimate must be less than $\beta$.

Recall from section 8.1.1 that the estimation is never too low but may be too high. The next step of the estimation process is to refine the estimation. The loop in step 13.5 uses $x_i\beta^2 + x_{i-1}\beta + x_{i-2}$ and $q_{i-t-1}(y_t\beta + y_{t-1})$ as a higher order approximation to adjust the quotient digit.

After both phases of estimation the quotient digit may still be off by a value of one[1]. Steps 13.6 and 13.7 subtract the multiple of the divisor from the dividend (*similar to step 3.3 of algorithm 8.1*) and then add a multiple of the divisor if the quotient was too large.

Now that the quotient has been determined, finalizing the result is a matter of clamping the quotient, fixing the sizes, and de-normalizing the remainder. An important aspect of this algorithm seemingly overlooked in other descriptions such as that of Algorithm 14.20 HAC [2, pp. 598] is that when the estimations are being made (*inside the loop in step 13.5*), that the digits $y_{t-1}$, $x_{i-2}$ and $x_{i-1}$ may lie outside their respective boundaries. For example, if $t = 0$ or $i \leq 1$ then the digits would be undefined. In those cases, the digits should respectively be replaced with a zero.

```
File: bn_mp_div.c
018    #ifdef BN_MP_DIV_SMALL
019
020    /* slower bit-bang division... also smaller */
021    int mp_div(mp_int * a, mp_int * b, mp_int * c, mp_int * d)
022    {
023       mp_int ta, tb, tq, q;
024       int   res, n, n2;
025
026       /* is divisor zero ? */
027       if (mp_iszero (b) == 1) {
028         return MP_VAL;
029       }
030
031       /* if a < b then q=0, r = a */
032       if (mp_cmp_mag (a, b) == MP_LT) {
033         if (d != NULL) {
034           res = mp_copy (a, d);
035         } else {
036           res = MP_OKAY;
037         }
```

---

[1]This is similar to the error introduced by optimizing Barrett reduction.

```
038        if (c != NULL) {
039          mp_zero (c);
040        }
041        return res;
042      }
043
044      /* init our temps */
045      if ((res = mp_init_multi(&ta, &tb, &tq, &q, NULL) != MP_OKAY)) {
046        return res;
047      }
048
049
050      mp_set(&tq, 1);
051      n = mp_count_bits(a) - mp_count_bits(b);
052      if (((res = mp_abs(a, &ta)) != MP_OKAY) ||
053         ((res = mp_abs(b, &tb)) != MP_OKAY) ||
054         ((res = mp_mul_2d(&tb, n, &tb)) != MP_OKAY) ||
055         ((res = mp_mul_2d(&tq, n, &tq)) != MP_OKAY)) {
056        goto LBL_ERR;
057      }
058
059      while (n-- >= 0) {
060        if (mp_cmp(&tb, &ta) != MP_GT) {
061          if (((res = mp_sub(&ta, &tb, &ta)) != MP_OKAY) ||
062             ((res = mp_add(&q, &tq, &q)) != MP_OKAY)) {
063            goto LBL_ERR;
064          }
065        }
066        if (((res = mp_div_2d(&tb, 1, &tb, NULL)) != MP_OKAY) ||
067           ((res = mp_div_2d(&tq, 1, &tq, NULL)) != MP_OKAY)) {
068            goto LBL_ERR;
069        }
070      }
071
072      /* now q == quotient and ta == remainder */
073      n  = a->sign;
074      n2 = (a->sign == b->sign ? MP_ZPOS : MP_NEG);
075      if (c != NULL) {
076        mp_exch(c, &q);
077        c->sign  = (mp_iszero(c) == MP_YES) ? MP_ZPOS : n2;
078      }
```

```
079    if (d != NULL) {
080       mp_exch(d, &ta);
081       d->sign = (mp_iszero(d) == MP_YES) ? MP_ZPOS : n;
082    }
083  LBL_ERR:
084    mp_clear_multi(&ta, &tb, &tq, &q, NULL);
085    return res;
086  }
087
088  #else
089
090  /* integer signed division.
091   * c*b + d == a [e.g. a/b, c=quotient, d=remainder]
092   * HAC pp.598 Algorithm 14.20
093   *
094   * Note that the description in HAC is horribly
095   * incomplete.  For example, it doesn't consider
096   * the case where digits are removed from 'x' in
097   * the inner loop.  It also doesn't consider the
098   * case that y has fewer than three digits, etc..
099   *
100   * The overall algorithm is as described as
101   * 14.20 from HAC but fixed to treat these cases.
102   */
103  int mp_div (mp_int * a, mp_int * b, mp_int * c, mp_int * d)
104  {
105    mp_int  q, x, y, t1, t2;
106    int     res, n, t, i, norm, neg;
107
108    /* is divisor zero ? */
109    if (mp_iszero (b) == 1) {
110      return MP_VAL;
111    }
112
113    /* if a < b then q=0, r = a */
114    if (mp_cmp_mag (a, b) == MP_LT) {
115      if (d != NULL) {
116        res = mp_copy (a, d);
117      } else {
118        res = MP_OKAY;
119      }
```

```
120          if (c != NULL) {
121            mp_zero (c);
122          }
123          return res;
124        }
125
126        if ((res = mp_init_size (&q, a->used + 2)) != MP_OKAY) {
127          return res;
128        }
129        q.used = a->used + 2;
130
131        if ((res = mp_init (&t1)) != MP_OKAY) {
132          goto LBL_Q;
133        }
134
135        if ((res = mp_init (&t2)) != MP_OKAY) {
136          goto LBL_T1;
137        }
138
139        if ((res = mp_init_copy (&x, a)) != MP_OKAY) {
140          goto LBL_T2;
141        }
142
143        if ((res = mp_init_copy (&y, b)) != MP_OKAY) {
144          goto LBL_X;
145        }
146
147        /* fix the sign */
148        neg = (a->sign == b->sign) ? MP_ZPOS : MP_NEG;
149        x.sign = y.sign = MP_ZPOS;
150
151        /* normalize both x and y, ensure that y >= b/2, [b == 2**DIGIT_BIT] */
152        norm = mp_count_bits(&y) % DIGIT_BIT;
153        if (norm < (int)(DIGIT_BIT-1)) {
154          norm = (DIGIT_BIT-1) - norm;
155          if ((res = mp_mul_2d (&x, norm, &x)) != MP_OKAY) {
156            goto LBL_Y;
157          }
158          if ((res = mp_mul_2d (&y, norm, &y)) != MP_OKAY) {
159            goto LBL_Y;
160          }
```

```
161    } else {
162       norm = 0;
163    }
164
165    /* note hac does 0 based, so if used==5 then its 0,1,2,3,4, e.g. use 4 */
166    n = x.used - 1;
167    t = y.used - 1;
168
169    /* while (x >= y*b**n-t) do { q[n-t] += 1; x -= y*b**{n-t} } */
170    if ((res = mp_lshd (&y, n - t)) != MP_OKAY) { /* y = y*b**{n-t} */
171      goto LBL_Y;
172    }
173
174    while (mp_cmp (&x, &y) != MP_LT) {
175      ++(q.dp[n - t]);
176      if ((res = mp_sub (&x, &y, &x)) != MP_OKAY) {
177        goto LBL_Y;
178      }
179    }
180
181    /* reset y by shifting it back down */
182    mp_rshd (&y, n - t);
183
184    /* step 3. for i from n down to (t + 1) */
185    for (i = n; i >= (t + 1); i--) {
186      if (i > x.used) {
187        continue;
188      }
189
190      /* step 3.1 if xi == yt then set q{i-t-1} to b-1,
191       * otherwise set q{i-t-1} to (xi*b + x{i-1})/yt */
192      if (x.dp[i] == y.dp[t]) {
193        q.dp[i - t - 1] = ((((mp_digit)1) << DIGIT_BIT) - 1);
194      } else {
195        mp_word tmp;
196        tmp = ((mp_word) x.dp[i]) << ((mp_word) DIGIT_BIT);
197        tmp |= ((mp_word) x.dp[i - 1]);
198        tmp /= ((mp_word) y.dp[t]);
199        if (tmp > (mp_word) MP_MASK)
200          tmp = MP_MASK;
201        q.dp[i - t - 1] = (mp_digit) (tmp & (mp_word) (MP_MASK));
```

```
202        }
203
204        /* while (q{i-t-1} * (yt * b + y{t-1})) >
205                 xi * b**2 + xi-1 * b + xi-2
206
207          do q{i-t-1} -= 1;
208        */
209        q.dp[i - t - 1] = (q.dp[i - t - 1] + 1) & MP_MASK;
210        do {
211          q.dp[i - t - 1] = (q.dp[i - t - 1] - 1) & MP_MASK;
212
213          /* find left hand */
214          mp_zero (&t1);
215          t1.dp[0] = (t - 1 < 0) ? 0 : y.dp[t - 1];
216          t1.dp[1] = y.dp[t];
217          t1.used = 2;
218          if ((res = mp_mul_d (&t1, q.dp[i - t - 1], &t1)) != MP_OKAY) {
219            goto LBL_Y;
220          }
221
222          /* find right hand */
223          t2.dp[0] = (i - 2 < 0) ? 0 : x.dp[i - 2];
224          t2.dp[1] = (i - 1 < 0) ? 0 : x.dp[i - 1];
225          t2.dp[2] = x.dp[i];
226          t2.used = 3;
227        } while (mp_cmp_mag(&t1, &t2) == MP_GT);
228
229        /* step 3.3 x = x - q{i-t-1} * y * b**{i-t-1} */
230        if ((res = mp_mul_d (&y, q.dp[i - t - 1], &t1)) != MP_OKAY) {
231          goto LBL_Y;
232        }
233
234        if ((res = mp_lshd (&t1, i - t - 1)) != MP_OKAY) {
235          goto LBL_Y;
236        }
237
238        if ((res = mp_sub (&x, &t1, &x)) != MP_OKAY) {
239          goto LBL_Y;
240        }
241
242        /* if x < 0 then { x = x + y*b**{i-t-1}; q{i-t-1} -= 1; } */
```

```
243      if (x.sign == MP_NEG) {
244        if ((res = mp_copy (&y, &t1)) != MP_OKAY) {
245          goto LBL_Y;
246        }
247        if ((res = mp_lshd (&t1, i - t - 1)) != MP_OKAY) {
248          goto LBL_Y;
249        }
250        if ((res = mp_add (&x, &t1, &x)) != MP_OKAY) {
251          goto LBL_Y;
252        }
253
254        q.dp[i - t - 1] = (q.dp[i - t - 1] - 1UL) & MP_MASK;
255      }
256    }
257
258    /* now q is the quotient and x is the remainder
259     * [which we have to normalize]
260     */
261
262    /* get sign before writing to c */
263    x.sign = x.used == 0 ? MP_ZPOS : a->sign;
264
265    if (c != NULL) {
266      mp_clamp (&q);
267      mp_exch (&q, c);
268      c->sign = neg;
269    }
270
271    if (d != NULL) {
272      mp_div_2d (&x, norm, &x, NULL);
273      mp_exch (&x, d);
274    }
275
276    res = MP_OKAY;
277
278  LBL_Y:mp_clear (&y);
279  LBL_X:mp_clear (&x);
280  LBL_T2:mp_clear (&t2);
281  LBL_T1:mp_clear (&t1);
282  LBL_Q:mp_clear (&q);
283    return res;
```

```
284     }
285
286     #endif
287
288
```

The implementation of this algorithm differs slightly from the pseudo–code presented previously. In this algorithm, either of the quotient $c$ or remainder $d$ may be passed as a **NULL** pointer, which indicates their value is not desired. For example, the C code to call the division algorithm with only the quotient is

```
mp_div(&a, &b, &c, NULL);   /* c = [a/b] */
```

Lines 109 and 113 handle the two trivial cases of inputs, which are division by zero and dividend smaller than the divisor, respectively. After the two trivial cases all of the temporary variables are initialized. Line 148 determines the sign of the quotient, and line 148 ensures that both $x$ and $y$ are positive.

The number of bits in the leading digit is calculated on line 151. Implicitly, an mp_int with $r$ digits will require $lg(\beta)(r-1) + k$ bits of precision that when reduced modulo $lg(\beta)$ produces the value of $k$. In this case, $k$ is the number of bits in the leading digit, which is exactly what is required. For the algorithm to operate, $k$ must equal $lg(\beta) - 1$, and when it does not, the inputs must be normalized by shifting them to the left by $lg(\beta) - 1 - k$ bits.

Throughout, the variables $n$ and $t$ will represent the highest digit of $x$ and $y$, respectively. These are first used to produce the leading digit of the quotient. The loop beginning on line 184 will produce the remainder of the quotient digits.

The conditional "continue" on line 187 is used to prevent the algorithm from reading past the leading edge of $x$, which can occur when the algorithm eliminates multiple non-zero digits in a single iteration. This ensures that $x_i$ is always non-zero since by definition the digits above the $i$'th position $x$ must be zero for the quotient to be precise[2].

Lines 215, 216, and 223 through 225 manually construct the high accuracy estimations by setting the digits of the two mp_int variables directly.

## 8.2 Single Digit Helpers

This section briefly describes a series of single digit helper algorithms that come in handy when working with small constants. All the helper functions assume the

---

[2]Precise as far as integer division is concerned.

single digit input is positive and will treat them as such.

## 8.2.1  Single Digit Addition and Subtraction

Both addition and subtraction are performed by "cheating" and using mp_set followed by the higher level addition or subtraction algorithms. As a result, these algorithms are substantially simpler with a slight cost in performance.

---

Algorithm **mp_add_d**.
**Input.** mp_int $a$ and a mp_digit $b$
**Output.** $c = a + b$

1. $t \leftarrow b$ ($mp\_set$)
2. $c \leftarrow a + t$
3. Return($MP\_OKAY$)

---

Figure 8.3: Algorithm mp_add_d

**Algorithm mp_add_d.** This algorithm initiates a temporary mp_int with the value of the single digit and uses algorithm mp_add to add the two values together (Figure 8.3).

```
File: bn_mp_add_d.c
018    /* single digit addition */
019    int
020    mp_add_d (mp_int * a, mp_digit b, mp_int * c)
021    {
022      int      res, ix, oldused;
023      mp_digit *tmpa, *tmpc, mu;
024
025      /* grow c as required */
026      if (c->alloc < a->used + 1) {
027        if ((res = mp_grow(c, a->used + 1)) != MP_OKAY) {
028          return res;
029        }
030      }
031
032      /* if a is negative and |a| >= b, call c = |a| - b */
033      if (a->sign == MP_NEG && (a->used > 1 || a->dp[0] >= b)) {
034        /* temporarily fix sign of a */
```

```
035          a->sign = MP_ZPOS;
036
037          /* c = |a| - b */
038          res = mp_sub_d(a, b, c);
039
040          /* fix sign  */
041          a->sign = c->sign = MP_NEG;
042
043          /* clamp */
044          mp_clamp(c);
045
046          return res;
047      }
048
049      /* old number of used digits in c */
050      oldused = c->used;
051
052      /* sign always positive */
053      c->sign = MP_ZPOS;
054
055      /* source alias */
056      tmpa    = a->dp;
057
058      /* destination alias */
059      tmpc    = c->dp;
060
061      /* if a is positive */
062      if (a->sign == MP_ZPOS) {
063          /* add digit, after this we're propagating
064           * the carry.
065           */
066          *tmpc   = *tmpa++ + b;
067          mu      = *tmpc >> DIGIT_BIT;
068          *tmpc++ &= MP_MASK;
069
070          /* now handle rest of the digits */
071          for (ix = 1; ix < a->used; ix++) {
072              *tmpc   = *tmpa++ + mu;
073              mu      = *tmpc >> DIGIT_BIT;
074              *tmpc++ &= MP_MASK;
075          }
```

```
076          /* set final carry */
077          ix++;
078          *tmpc++  = mu;
079
080          /* setup size */
081          c->used = a->used + 1;
082       } else {
083          /* a was negative and |a| < b */
084          c->used  = 1;
085
086          /* the result is a single digit */
087          if (a->used == 1) {
088             *tmpc++  =  b - a->dp[0];
089          } else {
090             *tmpc++  =  b;
091          }
092
093          /* setup count so the clearing of oldused
094           * can fall through correctly
095           */
096          ix       = 1;
097       }
098
099       /* now zero to oldused */
100       while (ix++ < oldused) {
101          *tmpc++ = 0;
102       }
103       mp_clamp(c);
104
105       return MP_OKAY;
106    }
107
108
```

Unlike the simple description in Figure 8.3, the implementation is more complicated. This is because we want to avoid the cost of building a new mp_int temporary variable just for a simple addition.

First, we handle the case of negative numbers (line 33). If the number is negative, and sufficiently large, then we subtract instead. After this point, we are going to add a single digit (line 66), and then propagate the carry upwards (lines 71 through 78).

**Subtraction**

The single digit subtraction algorithm mp_sub_d is essentially the same, except it uses mp_sub to subtract the digit from the mp_int.

## 8.2.2 Single Digit Multiplication

Single digit multiplication arises enough in division and radix conversion that it ought to be implemented as a special case of the baseline multiplication algorithm. Essentially, this algorithm is a modified version of algorithm s_mp_mul_digs where one of the multiplicands only has one digit.

---

Algorithm **mp_mul_d**.
**Input**. mp_int $a$ and a mp_digit $b$
**Output**. $c = ab$

---

1. $pa \leftarrow a.used$
2. Grow $c$ to at least $pa + 1$ digits.
3. $oldused \leftarrow c.used$
4. $c.used \leftarrow pa + 1$
5. $c.sign \leftarrow a.sign$
6. $\mu \leftarrow 0$
7. for $ix$ from 0 to $pa - 1$ do
   7.1 $\hat{r} \leftarrow \mu + a_{ix}b$
   7.2 $c_{ix} \leftarrow \hat{r} \pmod{\beta}$
   7.3 $\mu \leftarrow \lfloor \hat{r}/\beta \rfloor$
8. $c_{pa} \leftarrow \mu$
9. for $ix$ from $pa + 1$ to $oldused$ do
   9.1 $c_{ix} \leftarrow 0$
10. Clamp excess digits of $c$.
11. Return($MP\_OKAY$).

---

Figure 8.4: Algorithm mp_mul_d

**Algorithm mp_mul_d.** This algorithm quickly multiplies an mp_int by a small single digit value. It is specially tailored to the job and has minimal overhead. Unlike the full multiplication algorithms, this algorithm does not require any significant temporary storage or memory allocations (Figure 8.4).

```
File: bn_mp_mul_d.c
018   /* multiply by a digit */
019   int
020   mp_mul_d (mp_int * a, mp_digit b, mp_int * c)
021   {
022     mp_digit u, *tmpa, *tmpc;
023     mp_word  r;
024     int      ix, res, olduse;
025
026     /* make sure c is big enough to hold a*b */
027     if (c->alloc < a->used + 1) {
028       if ((res = mp_grow (c, a->used + 1)) != MP_OKAY) {
029         return res;
030       }
031     }
032
033     /* get the original destinations used count */
034     olduse = c->used;
035
036     /* set the sign */
037     c->sign = a->sign;
038
039     /* alias for a->dp [source] */
040     tmpa = a->dp;
041
042     /* alias for c->dp [dest] */
043     tmpc = c->dp;
044
045     /* zero carry */
046     u = 0;
047
048     /* compute columns */
049     for (ix = 0; ix < a->used; ix++) {
050       /* compute product and carry sum for this term */
051       r        = ((mp_word) u) + ((mp_word)*tmpa++) * ((mp_word)b);
052
053       /* mask off higher bits to get a single digit */
054       *tmpc++ = (mp_digit) (r & ((mp_word) MP_MASK));
055
056       /* send carry into next iteration */
057       u        = (mp_digit) (r >> ((mp_word) DIGIT_BIT));
```

```
058        }
059
060        /* store final carry [if any] and increment ix offset  */
061        *tmpc++ = u;
062        ++ix;
063
064        /* now zero digits above the top */
065        while (ix++ < olduse) {
066            *tmpc++ = 0;
067        }
068
069        /* set used count */
070        c->used = a->used + 1;
071        mp_clamp(c);
072
073        return MP_OKAY;
074    }
075
```

In this implementation, the destination $c$ may point to the same mp_int as the source $a$, since the result is written after the digit is read from the source. This function uses pointer aliases *tmpa* and *tmpc* for the digits of $a$ and $c$, respectively.

## 8.2.3  Single Digit Division

Like the single digit multiplication algorithm, single digit division is also a fairly common algorithm used in radix conversion. Since the divisor is only a single digit, a specialized variant of the division algorithm can be used to compute the quotient.

---

Algorithm **mp_div_d**.
**Input**. mp_int $a$ and a mp_digit $b$
**Output**. $c = \lfloor a/b \rfloor, d = a - cb$

---

1. If $b = 0$ then return($MP\_VAL$).
2. If $b = 3$ then use algorithm mp_div_3 instead.
3. Init $q$ to $a.used$ digits.
4. $q.used \leftarrow a.used$
5. $q.sign \leftarrow a.sign$
6. $\hat{w} \leftarrow 0$
7. for $ix$ from $a.used - 1$ down to 0 do
    7.1 $\hat{w} \leftarrow \hat{w}\beta + a_{ix}$
    7.2 If $\hat{w} \geq b$ then
        7.2.1 $t \leftarrow \lfloor \hat{w}/b \rfloor$
        7.2.2 $\hat{w} \leftarrow \hat{w} \pmod{b}$
    7.3 else
        7.3.1 $t \leftarrow 0$
    7.4 $q_{ix} \leftarrow t$
8. $d \leftarrow \hat{w}$
9. Clamp excess digits of $q$.
10. $c \leftarrow q$
11. Return($MP\_OKAY$).

---

Figure 8.5: Algorithm mp_div_d

**Algorithm mp_div_d.** This algorithm divides the mp_int $a$ by the single mp_digit $b$ using an optimized approach. Essentially, in every iteration of the algorithm another digit of the dividend is reduced and another digit of quotient produced. Provided $b < \beta$, the value of $\hat{w}$ after step 7.1 will be limited such that $0 \leq \lfloor \hat{w}/b \rfloor < \beta$ (Figure 8.5).

If the divisor $b$ is equal to three a variant of this algorithm is used, which is mp_div_3. It replaces the division by three with a multiplication by $\lfloor \beta/3 \rfloor$ and the appropriate shift and residual fixup. In essence, it is much like the Barrett reduction from Chapter 7.

```
File: bn_mp_div_d.c
018    static int s_is_power_of_two(mp_digit b, int *p)
019    {
020       int x;
021
```

```
022     for (x = 1; x < DIGIT_BIT; x++) {
023         if (b == (((mp_digit)1)<<x)) {
024             *p = x;
025             return 1;
026         }
027     }
028     return 0;
029 }
030
031 /* single digit division (based on routine from MPI) */
032 int mp_div_d (mp_int * a, mp_digit b, mp_int * c, mp_digit * d)
033 {
034     mp_int  q;
035     mp_word w;
036     mp_digit t;
037     int     res, ix;
038
039     /* cannot divide by zero */
040     if (b == 0) {
041         return MP_VAL;
042     }
043
044     /* quick outs */
045     if (b == 1 || mp_iszero(a) == 1) {
046         if (d != NULL) {
047             *d = 0;
048         }
049         if (c != NULL) {
050             return mp_copy(a, c);
051         }
052         return MP_OKAY;
053     }
054
055     /* power of two ? */
056     if (s_is_power_of_two(b, &ix) == 1) {
057         if (d != NULL) {
058             *d = a->dp[0] & ((((mp_digit)1)<<ix) - 1);
059         }
060         if (c != NULL) {
061             return mp_div_2d(a, ix, c, NULL);
062         }
```

```
063        return MP_OKAY;
064    }
065
066    #ifdef BN_MP_DIV_3_C
067      /* three? */
068      if (b == 3) {
069          return mp_div_3(a, c, d);
070      }
071    #endif
072
073      /* no easy answer [c'est la vie].  Just division */
074      if ((res = mp_init_size(&q, a->used)) != MP_OKAY) {
075          return res;
076      }
077
078      q.used = a->used;
079      q.sign = a->sign;
080      w = 0;
081      for (ix = a->used - 1; ix >= 0; ix--) {
082        w = (w << ((mp_word)DIGIT_BIT)) | ((mp_word)a->dp[ix]);
083
084        if (w >= b) {
085            t = (mp_digit)(w / b);
086            w -= ((mp_word)t) * ((mp_word)b);
087        } else {
088            t = 0;
089        }
090        q.dp[ix] = (mp_digit)t;
091      }
092
093      if (d != NULL) {
094          *d = (mp_digit)w;
095      }
096
097      if (c != NULL) {
098          mp_clamp(&q);
099          mp_exch(&q, c);
100      }
101      mp_clear(&q);
102
103      return res;
```

```
104     }
105
106
```

Like the implementation of algorithm mp_div, this algorithm allows either the quotient or remainder to be passed as a **NULL** pointer to indicate the respective value is not required. This allows a trivial single digit modular reduction algorithm, mp_mod_d, to be created.

The division and remainder on lines 85 and 86 can be replaced often by a single division on most processors. For example, the 32-bit x86 based processors can divide a 64-bit quantity by a 32-bit quantity and produce the quotient and remainder simultaneously. Unfortunately, the GCC compiler does not recognize that optimization and will actually produce two function calls to find the quotient and remainder, respectively.

### 8.2.4  Single Digit Root Extraction

Finding the $n$'th root of an integer is fairly easy as far as numerical analysis is concerned. Algorithms such as the Newton-Raphson approximation (8.6) series will converge very quickly to a root for any continuous function $f(x)$.

$$x_{i+1} = x_i - \frac{f(x_i)}{f'(x_i)} \tag{8.6}$$

In this case, the $n$'th root is desired and $f(x) = x^n - a$, where $a$ is the integer of which the root is desired. The derivative of $f(x)$ is simply $f'(x) = nx^{n-1}$. Of particular importance is that this algorithm will be used over the integers, not over a more continuous domain such as the real numbers. As a result, the root found can be above the true root by few and must be manually adjusted. Ideally, at the end of the algorithm the $n$'th root $b$ of an integer $a$ is desired such that $b^n \leq a$.

---

Algorithm **mp_n_root**.
**Input**. mp_int $a$ and a mp_digit $b$
**Output**. $c^b \leq a$

---

1. If $b$ is even and $a.sign = MP\_NEG$ return($MP\_VAL$).
2. $sign \leftarrow a.sign$
3. $a.sign \leftarrow MP\_ZPOS$
4. t2 $\leftarrow$ 2
5. Loop
   5.1 t1 $\leftarrow$ t2
   5.2 t3 $\leftarrow$ t1$^{b-1}$
   5.3 t2 $\leftarrow$ t3 $\cdot$ t1
   5.4 t2 $\leftarrow$ t2 $- a$
   5.5 t3 $\leftarrow$ t3 $\cdot b$
   5.6 t3 $\leftarrow \lfloor$t2/t3$\rfloor$
   5.7 t2 $\leftarrow$ t1$-$ t3
   5.8 If t1 $\neq$ t2 then goto step 5.
6. Loop
   6.1 t2 $\leftarrow$ t1$^b$
   6.2 If t2 $> a$ then
       6.2.1 t1 $\leftarrow$ t1 $- 1$
       6.2.2 Goto step 6.
7. $a.sign \leftarrow sign$
8. $c \leftarrow$ t1
9. $c.sign \leftarrow sign$
10. Return($MP\_OKAY$).

---

Figure 8.6: Algorithm mp_n_root

**Algorithm mp_n_root.** This algorithm finds the integer $n$'th root of an input using the Newton-Raphson approach. It is partially optimized based on the observation that the numerator of $\frac{f(x)}{f'(x)}$ can be derived from a partial denominator. That is, at first the denominator is calculated by finding $x^{b-1}$. This value can then be multiplied by $x$ and have $a$ subtracted from it to find the numerator. This saves a total of $b - 1$ multiplications by t1 inside the loop (Figure 8.6).

The initial value of the approximation is $t2 = 2$, which allows the algorithm to start with very small values and quickly converge on the root. Ideally, this algorithm is meant to find the $n$'th root of an input where $n$ is bounded by $2 \leq n \leq 5$.

```
File: bn_mp_n_root.c
018   /* find the n'th root of an integer
019    *
020    * Result found such that (c)**b <= a and (c+1)**b > a
021    *
022    * This algorithm uses Newton's approximation
023    * x[i+1] = x[i] - f(x[i])/f'(x[i])
024    * which will find the root in log(N) time where
025    * each step involves a fair bit.  This is not meant to
026    * find huge roots [square and cube, etc].
027    */
028   int mp_n_root (mp_int * a, mp_digit b, mp_int * c)
029   {
030     mp_int   t1, t2, t3;
031     int      res, neg;
032
033     /* input must be positive if b is even */
034     if ((b & 1) == 0 && a->sign == MP_NEG) {
035       return MP_VAL;
036     }
037
038     if ((res = mp_init (&t1)) != MP_OKAY) {
039       return res;
040     }
041
042     if ((res = mp_init (&t2)) != MP_OKAY) {
043       goto LBL_T1;
044     }
045
046     if ((res = mp_init (&t3)) != MP_OKAY) {
047       goto LBL_T2;
048     }
049
050     /* if a is negative fudge the sign but keep track */
051     neg     = a->sign;
052     a->sign = MP_ZPOS;
053
054     /* t2 = 2 */
055     mp_set (&t2, 2);
056
057     do {
```

```
058        /* t1 = t2 */
059        if ((res = mp_copy (&t2, &t1)) != MP_OKAY) {
060          goto LBL_T3;
061        }
062
063        /* t2 = t1 - ((t1**b - a) / (b * t1**(b-1))) */
064
065        /* t3 = t1**(b-1) */
066        if ((res = mp_expt_d (&t1, b - 1, &t3)) != MP_OKAY) {
067          goto LBL_T3;
068        }
069
070        /* numerator */
071        /* t2 = t1**b */
072        if ((res = mp_mul (&t3, &t1, &t2)) != MP_OKAY) {
073          goto LBL_T3;
074        }
075
076        /* t2 = t1**b - a */
077        if ((res = mp_sub (&t2, a, &t2)) != MP_OKAY) {
078          goto LBL_T3;
079        }
080
081        /* denominator */
082        /* t3 = t1**(b-1) * b  */
083        if ((res = mp_mul_d (&t3, b, &t3)) != MP_OKAY) {
084          goto LBL_T3;
085        }
086
087        /* t3 = (t1**b - a)/(b * t1**(b-1)) */
088        if ((res = mp_div (&t2, &t3, &t3, NULL)) != MP_OKAY) {
089          goto LBL_T3;
090        }
091
092        if ((res = mp_sub (&t1, &t3, &t2)) != MP_OKAY) {
093          goto LBL_T3;
094        }
095    }  while (mp_cmp (&t1, &t2) != MP_EQ);
096
097    /* result can be off by a few so check */
098    for (;;) {
```

```
099        if ((res = mp_expt_d (&t1, b, &t2)) != MP_OKAY) {
100          goto LBL_T3;
101        }
102
103        if (mp_cmp (&t2, a) == MP_GT) {
104          if ((res = mp_sub_d (&t1, 1, &t1)) != MP_OKAY) {
105            goto LBL_T3;
106          }
107        } else {
108          break;
109        }
110      }
111
112      /* reset the sign of a first */
113      a->sign = neg;
114
115      /* set the result */
116      mp_exch (&t1, c);
117
118      /* set the sign of the result */
119      c->sign = neg;
120
121      res = MP_OKAY;
122
123  LBL_T3:mp_clear (&t3);
124  LBL_T2:mp_clear (&t2);
125  LBL_T1:mp_clear (&t1);
126      return res;
127    }
128
```

# 8.3  Random Number Generation

Random numbers come up in a variety of activities, from public key cryptography to simple simulations and various randomized algorithms. Pollard-Rho factoring, for example, can make use of random values as starting points to find factors of a composite integer. In this case, the algorithm presented is solely for simulations and not intended for cryptographic use.

---

Algorithm **mp_rand**.
**Input**. An integer $b$
**Output**. A pseudo-random number of $b$ digits

---

1. $a \leftarrow 0$
2. If $b \leq 0$ return($MP\_OKAY$)
3. Pick a non-zero random digit $d$.
4. $a \leftarrow a + d$
5. for $ix$ from 1 to $d - 1$ do
   5.1 $a \leftarrow a \cdot \beta$
   5.2 Pick a random digit $d$.
   5.3 $a \leftarrow a + d$
6. Return($MP\_OKAY$).

---

Figure 8.7: Algorithm mp_rand

**Algorithm mp_rand.** This algorithm produces a pseudo-random integer of $b$ digits. By ensuring that the first digit is non-zero, the algorithm also guarantees that the result has at least $b$ digits. It relies heavily on a third-part random number generator, which should ideally generate uniformly all of the integers from 0 to $\beta - 1$ (Figure 8.7).

```
File: bn_mp_rand.c
018    /* makes a pseudo-random int of a given size */
019    int
020    mp_rand (mp_int * a, int digits)
021    {
022      int     res;
023      mp_digit d;
024
025      mp_zero (a);
026      if (digits <= 0) {
027        return MP_OKAY;
028      }
029
030      /* first place a random non-zero digit */
031      do {
032        d = ((mp_digit) abs (rand ())) & MP_MASK;
033      } while (d == 0);
034
```

```
035      if ((res = mp_add_d (a, d, a)) != MP_OKAY) {
036        return res;
037      }
038
039      while (--digits > 0) {
040        if ((res = mp_lshd (a, 1)) != MP_OKAY) {
041          return res;
042        }
043
044        if ((res = mp_add_d (a, ((mp_digit) abs (rand ())), a)) != MP_OKAY) {
045          return res;
046        }
047      }
048
049      return MP_OKAY;
050    }
051
```

## 8.4  Formatted Representations

The ability to emit a radix-$n$ textual representation of an integer is useful for interacting with human parties. For example, the ability to be given a string of characters such as "114585" and turn it into the radix-$\beta$ equivalent would make it easier to enter numbers into a program.

### 8.4.1  Reading Radix-n Input

For the purposes of this text we will assume that a simple lower ASCII map (Figure 8.8) is used for the values of from 0 to 63 to printable characters. For example, when the character "N" is read it represents the integer 23. The first 16 characters of the map are for the common representations up to hexadecimal. After that, they match the "base64" encoding scheme suitably chosen such that they are printable. While outputting as base64 may not be too helpful for human operators, it does allow communication via non–binary mediums.

| Value | Char | Value | Char | Value | Char | Value | Char |
|-------|------|-------|------|-------|------|-------|------|
| 0 | 0 | 1 | 1 | 2 | 2 | 3 | 3 |
| 4 | 4 | 5 | 5 | 6 | 6 | 7 | 7 |
| 8 | 8 | 9 | 9 | 10 | A | 11 | B |
| 12 | C | 13 | D | 14 | E | 15 | F |
| 16 | G | 17 | H | 18 | I | 19 | J |
| 20 | K | 21 | L | 22 | M | 23 | N |
| 24 | O | 25 | P | 26 | Q | 27 | R |
| 28 | S | 29 | T | 30 | U | 31 | V |
| 32 | W | 33 | X | 34 | Y | 35 | Z |
| 36 | a | 37 | b | 38 | c | 39 | d |
| 40 | e | 41 | f | 42 | g | 43 | h |
| 44 | i | 45 | j | 46 | k | 47 | l |
| 48 | m | 49 | n | 50 | o | 51 | p |
| 52 | q | 53 | r | 54 | s | 55 | t |
| 56 | u | 57 | v | 58 | w | 59 | x |
| 60 | y | 61 | z | 62 | + | 63 | / |

Figure 8.8: Lower ASCII Map

---

Algorithm **mp_read_radix**.
**Input**. A string *str* of length *sn* and radix *r*.
**Output**. The radix-$\beta$ equivalent mp_int.

---

1. If $r < 2$ or $r > 64$ return(*MP_VAL*).
2. $ix \leftarrow 0$
3. If $str_0 =$ "-" then do
   3.1 $ix \leftarrow ix + 1$
   3.2 $sign \leftarrow MP\_NEG$
4. else
   4.1 $sign \leftarrow MP\_ZPOS$
5. $a \leftarrow 0$
6. for $iy$ from $ix$ to $sn - 1$ do
   6.1 Let $y$ denote the position in the map of $str_{iy}$.
   6.2 If $str_{iy}$ is not in the map or $y \geq r$ then goto step 7.
   6.3 $a \leftarrow a \cdot r$
   6.4 $a \leftarrow a + y$
7. If $a \neq 0$ then $a.sign \leftarrow sign$
8. Return(*MP_OKAY*).

---

Figure 8.9: Algorithm mp_read_radix

**Algorithm mp_read_radix.** This algorithm will read an ASCII string and produce the radix-$\beta$ mp_int representation of the same integer. A minus symbol "-" may precede the string to indicate the value is negative; otherwise, it is assumed positive. The algorithm will read up to *sn* characters from the input and will stop when it reads a character it cannot map. The algorithm stops reading characters from the string, which allows numbers to be embedded as part of larger input without any significant problem (Figure 8.9).

```
File: bn_mp_read_radix.c
018    /* read a string [ASCII] in a given radix */
019    int mp_read_radix (mp_int * a, const char *str, int radix)
020    {
021      int      y, res, neg;
022      char     ch;
023
024      /* zero the digit bignum */
025      mp_zero(a);
026
```

```
027    /* make sure the radix is ok */
028    if (radix < 2 || radix > 64) {
029      return MP_VAL;
030    }
031
032    /* if the leading digit is a
033     * minus set the sign to negative.
034     */
035    if (*str == '-') {
036      ++str;
037      neg = MP_NEG;
038    } else {
039      neg = MP_ZPOS;
040    }
041
042    /* set the integer to the default of zero */
043    mp_zero (a);
044
045    /* process each digit of the string */
046    while (*str) {
047      /* if the radix < 36 the conversion is case insensitive
048       * this allows numbers like 1AB and 1ab to represent the same  value
049       * [e.g. in hex]
050       */
051      ch = (char) ((radix < 36) ? toupper (*str) : *str);
052      for (y = 0; y < 64; y++) {
053        if (ch == mp_s_rmap[y]) {
054          break;
055        }
056      }
057
058      /* if the char was found in the map
059       * and is less than the given radix add it
060       * to the number, otherwise exit the loop.
061       */
062      if (y < radix) {
063        if ((res = mp_mul_d (a, (mp_digit) radix, a)) != MP_OKAY) {
064          return res;
065        }
066        if ((res = mp_add_d (a, (mp_digit) y, a)) != MP_OKAY) {
067          return res;
```

```
068            }
069          } else {
070            break;
071          }
072          ++str;
073        }
074
075        /* set the sign only if a != 0 */
076        if (mp_iszero(a) != 1) {
077           a->sign = neg;
078        }
079        return MP_OKAY;
080      }
081
```

## 8.4.2   Generating Radix-$n$ Output

Generating radix-$n$ output is fairly trivial with a division and remainder algorithm.

---
Algorithm **mp_toradix**.
**Input**. A mp_int $a$ and an integer $r$
**Output**. The radix-$r$ representation of $a$

---

1. If $r < 2$ or $r > 64$ return($MP\_VAL$).
2. If $a = 0$ then $str = $ "0" and return($MP\_OKAY$).
3. $t \leftarrow a$
4. $str \leftarrow$ ""
5. if $t.sign = MP\_NEG$ then
   5.1 $str \leftarrow str+ $ "-"
   5.2 $t.sign = MP\_ZPOS$
6. While ($t \neq 0$) do
   6.1 $d \leftarrow t \pmod{r}$
   6.2 $t \leftarrow \lfloor t/r \rfloor$
   6.3 Look up $d$ in the map and store the equivalent character in $y$.
   6.4 $str \leftarrow str + y$
7. If $str_0 = $ "$-$" then
   7.1 Reverse the digits $str_1, str_2, \ldots str_n$.
8. Otherwise
   8.1 Reverse the digits $str_0, str_1, \ldots str_n$.
9. Return($MP\_OKAY$).

---

Figure 8.10: Algorithm mp_toradix

**Algorithm mp_toradix.** This algorithm computes the radix-$r$ representation of an mp_int $a$. The "digits" of the representation are extracted by reducing successive powers of $\lfloor a/r^k \rfloor$ the input modulo $r$ until $r^k > a$. Note that instead of actually dividing by $r^k$ in each iteration, the quotient $\lfloor a/r \rfloor$ is saved for the next iteration. As a result, a series of trivial $n \times 1$ divisions are required instead of a series of $n \times k$ divisions. One design flaw of this approach is that the digits are produced in the reverse order (see 8.11). To remedy this flaw, the digits must be swapped or simply "reversed" (Figure 8.10).

| Value of $a$ | Value of $d$ | Value of $str$ |
|:---:|:---:|:---:|
| 1234 | – | – |
| 123 | 4 | "4" |
| 12 | 3 | "43" |
| 1 | 2 | "432" |
| 0 | 1 | "4321" |

Figure 8.11: Example of Algorithm mp_toradix.

Figure 8.11 is an example of the values in algorithm mp_toradix at the various iterations.

```
File: bn_mp_toradix.c
018   /* stores a bignum as a ASCII string in a given radix (2..64) */
019   int mp_toradix (mp_int * a, char *str, int radix)
020   {
021     int     res, digs;
022     mp_int  t;
023     mp_digit d;
024     char    *_s = str;
025
026     /* check range of the radix */
027     if (radix < 2 || radix > 64) {
028       return MP_VAL;
029     }
030
031     /* quick out if its zero */
032     if (mp_iszero(a) == 1) {
033       *str++ = '0';
034       *str = '\0';
035       return MP_OKAY;
036     }
037
038     if ((res = mp_init_copy (&t, a)) != MP_OKAY) {
039       return res;
040     }
041
042     /* if it is negative output a - */
043     if (t.sign == MP_NEG) {
```

```
044        ++_s;
045        *str++ = '-';
046        t.sign = MP_ZPOS;
047      }
048
049      digs = 0;
050      while (mp_iszero (&t) == 0) {
051        if ((res = mp_div_d (&t, (mp_digit) radix, &t, &d)) != MP_OKAY) {
052          mp_clear (&t);
053          return res;
054        }
055        *str++ = mp_s_rmap[d];
056        ++digs;
057      }
058
059      /* reverse the digits of the string.  In this case _s points
060       * to the first digit [exluding the sign] of the number]
061       */
062      bn_reverse ((unsigned char *)_s, digs);
063
064      /* append a NULL so the string is properly terminated */
065      *str = '\0';
066
067      mp_clear (&t);
068      return MP_OKAY;
069    }
070
071
```

# Chapter 9

# Number Theoretic Algorithms

This chapter discusses several fundamental number theoretic algorithms such as the greatest common divisor, least common multiple, and Jacobi symbol computation. These algorithms arise as essential components in several key cryptographic algorithms such as the RSA public key algorithm and various sieve–based factoring algorithms.

## 9.1  Greatest Common Divisor

The greatest common divisor of two integers $a$ and $b$, often denoted as $(a, b)$, is the largest integer $k$ that is a proper divisor of both $a$ and $b$. That is, $k$ is the largest integer such that $0 \equiv a \pmod{k}$ and $0 \equiv b \pmod{k}$ occur simultaneously.

The most common approach [1, pp. 337] is to reduce one operand modulo the other operand. That is, if $a$ and $b$ are divisible by some integer $k$ and if $qa + r = b$, then $r$ is also divisible by $k$. The reduction pattern follows $\langle a, b \rangle \rightarrow \langle b, a \bmod b \rangle$.

---

Algorithm **Greatest Common Divisor (I)**.
**Input**. Two positive integers $a$ and $b$ greater than zero.
**Output**. The greatest common divisor $(a, b)$.

---

1. While $(b > 0)$ do
    1.1 $r \leftarrow a \pmod{b}$
    1.2 $a \leftarrow b$
    1.3 $b \leftarrow r$
2. Return($a$).

---

Figure 9.1: Algorithm Greatest Common Divisor (I)

This algorithm will quickly converge on the greatest common divisor since the residue $r$ tends to diminish rapidly (Figure 9.1). However, divisions are relatively expensive operations to perform and should ideally be avoided. There is another approach based on a similar relationship of greatest common divisors. The faster approach is based on the observation that if $k$ divides both $a$ and $b$, it will also divide $a - b$. In particular, we would like $a - b$ to decrease in magnitude, which implies that $b \geq a$.

---

Algorithm **Greatest Common Divisor (II)**.
**Input**. Two positive integers $a$ and $b$ greater than zero.
**Output**. The greatest common divisor $(a, b)$.

---

1. While $(b > 0)$ do
    1.1 Swap $a$ and $b$ such that $a$ is the smallest of the two.
    1.2 $b \leftarrow b - a$
2. Return($a$).

---

Figure 9.2: Algorithm Greatest Common Divisor (II)

**Theorem** *Algorithm 9.2 will return the greatest common divisor of $a$ and $b$.*
**Proof** The algorithm in Figure 9.2 will eventually terminate; since $b \geq a$ the subtraction in step 1.2 will be a value less than $b$. In other words, in every iteration that tuple $\langle a, b \rangle$, decrease in magnitude until eventually $a = b$. Since both $a$ and $b$ are always divisible by the greatest common divisor (*until the last iteration*) and in the last iteration of the algorithm $b = 0$, therefore, in the second to last iteration of the algorithm $b = a$ and clearly $(a, a) = a$, which concludes the proof.

**QED**

As a matter of practicality, algorithm 9.1 decreases far too slowly to be useful, especially if $b$ is much larger than $a$ such that $b - a$ is still very much larger than $a$. A simple addition to the algorithm is to divide $b - a$ by a power of some integer $p$ that does not divide the greatest common divisor but will divide $b - a$. In this case, $\frac{b-a}{p}$ is also an integer and still divisible by the greatest common divisor.

However, instead of factoring $b - a$ to find a suitable value of $p$, the powers of $p$ can be removed from $a$ and $b$ that are in common first. Then, inside the loop whenever $b - a$ is divisible by some power of $p$ it can be safely removed.

---

Algorithm **Greatest Common Divisor (III)**.
**Input**. Two positive integers $a$ and $b$ greater than zero.
**Output**. The greatest common divisor $(a, b)$.

---

1. $k \leftarrow 0$
2. While $a$ and $b$ are both divisible by $p$ do
   2.1 $a \leftarrow \lfloor a/p \rfloor$
   2.2 $b \leftarrow \lfloor b/p \rfloor$
   2.3 $k \leftarrow k + 1$
3. While $a$ is divisible by $p$ do
   3.1 $a \leftarrow \lfloor a/p \rfloor$
4. While $b$ is divisible by $p$ do
   4.1 $b \leftarrow \lfloor b/p \rfloor$
5. While $(b > 0)$ do
   5.1 Swap $a$ and $b$ such that $a$ is the smallest of the two.
   5.2 $b \leftarrow b - a$
   5.3 While $b$ is divisible by $p$ do
      5.3.1 $b \leftarrow \lfloor b/p \rfloor$
6. Return$(a \cdot p^k)$.

---

Figure 9.3: Algorithm Greatest Common Divisor (III)

This algorithm is based on the first, except it removes powers of $p$ first and inside the main loop to ensure the tuple $\langle a, b \rangle$ decreases more rapidly (Figure 9.3). The first loop in step 2 removes powers of $p$ that are in common. A count, $k$, is kept that will present a common divisor of $p^k$. After step 2 the remaining common divisor of $a$ and $b$ cannot be divisible by $p$. This means that $p$ can be safely divided out of the difference $b - a$ as long as the division leaves no remainder.

In particular, the value of $p$ should be chosen such that the division in step 5.3.1 occurs often. It also helps that division by $p$ be easy to compute. The ideal choice of $p$ is two since division by two amounts to a right logical shift. Another important observation is that by step 5 both $a$ and $b$ are odd. Therefore, the difference $b - a$ must be even, which means that each iteration removes one bit from the largest of the pair.

### 9.1.1   Complete Greatest Common Divisor

The algorithms presented so far cannot handle inputs that are zero or negative. The following algorithm can handle all input cases properly and will produce the greatest common divisor.

---

Algorithm **mp_gcd**.
**Input**. mp_int $a$ and $b$
**Output**. The greatest common divisor $c = (a, b)$.

---

1. If $a = 0$ then
    1.1 $c \leftarrow |b|$
    1.2 Return($MP\_OKAY$).
2. If $b = 0$ then
    2.1 $c \leftarrow |a|$
    2.2 Return($MP\_OKAY$).
3. $u \leftarrow |a|, v \leftarrow |b|$
4. $k \leftarrow 0$
5. While $u.used > 0$ and $v.used > 0$ and $u_0 \equiv v_0 \equiv 0 \pmod 2$
    5.1 $k \leftarrow k + 1$
    5.2 $u \leftarrow \lfloor u/2 \rfloor$
    5.3 $v \leftarrow \lfloor v/2 \rfloor$
6. While $u.used > 0$ and $u_0 \equiv 0 \pmod 2$
    6.1 $u \leftarrow \lfloor u/2 \rfloor$
7. While $v.used > 0$ and $v_0 \equiv 0 \pmod 2$
    7.1 $v \leftarrow \lfloor v/2 \rfloor$
8. While $v.used > 0$
    8.1 If $|u| > |v|$ then
        8.1.1 Swap $u$ and $v$.
    8.2 $v \leftarrow |v| - |u|$
    8.3 While $v.used > 0$ and $v_0 \equiv 0 \pmod 2$
        8.3.1 $v \leftarrow \lfloor v/2 \rfloor$
9. $c \leftarrow u \cdot 2^k$
10. Return($MP\_OKAY$).

---

Figure 9.4: Algorithm mp_gcd

**Algorithm mp_gcd.** This algorithm will produce the greatest common divisor of two mp_ints $a$ and $b$. It was originally based on Algorithm B, of Knuth [1, pp. 338] but has been modified to be simpler to explain. In theory, it achieves the same asymptotic working time as Algorithm B, and in practice, this appears to be true (Figure 9.4).

The first two steps handle the cases where either one or both inputs are zero. If either input is zero, the greatest common divisor is the largest input or zero if they are both zero. If the inputs are not trivial, $u$ and $v$ are assigned the absolute values of $a$ and $b$, respectively, and the algorithm will proceed to reduce the pair.

Step 5 will divide out any common factors of two and keep track of the count in the variable $k$. After this step, two is no longer a factor of the remaining greatest common divisor between $u$ and $v$ and can be safely evenly divided out of either whenever they are even. Steps 6 and 7 ensure that the $u$ and $v$, respectively, have no more factors of two. At most, only one of the while loops will iterate since they cannot both be even.

By step 8 both $u$ and $v$ are odd, which is required for the inner logic. First, the pair are swapped such that $v$ is equal to or greater than $u$. This ensures that the subtraction in step 8.2 will always produce a positive and even result. Step 8.3 removes any factors of two from the difference $u$ to ensure that in the next iteration of the loop both are again odd.

After $v = 0$ occurs the variable $u$ has the greatest common divisor of the pair $\langle u, v \rangle$ just after step 6. The result must be adjusted by multiplying by the common factors of two $(2^k)$ removed earlier.

```
File: bn_mp_gcd.c
018    /* Greatest Common Divisor using the binary method */
019    int mp_gcd (mp_int * a, mp_int * b, mp_int * c)
020    {
021      mp_int   u, v;
022      int      k, u_lsb, v_lsb, res;
023
024      /* either zero then gcd is the largest */
025      if (mp_iszero (a) == MP_YES) {
026        return mp_abs (b, c);
027      }
028      if (mp_iszero (b) == MP_YES) {
029        return mp_abs (a, c);
030      }
031
032      /* get copies of a and b we can modify */
033      if ((res = mp_init_copy (&u, a)) != MP_OKAY) {
034        return res;
035      }
036
037      if ((res = mp_init_copy (&v, b)) != MP_OKAY) {
038        goto LBL_U;
039      }
040
```

```
041     /* must be positive for the remainder of the algorithm */
042     u.sign = v.sign = MP_ZPOS;
043
044     /* B1.  Find the common power of two for u and v */
045     u_lsb = mp_cnt_lsb(&u);
046     v_lsb = mp_cnt_lsb(&v);
047     k     = MIN(u_lsb, v_lsb);
048
049     if (k > 0) {
050        /* divide the power of two out */
051        if ((res = mp_div_2d(&u, k, &u, NULL)) != MP_OKAY) {
052           goto LBL_V;
053        }
054
055        if ((res = mp_div_2d(&v, k, &v, NULL)) != MP_OKAY) {
056           goto LBL_V;
057        }
058     }
059
060     /* divide any remaining factors of two out */
061     if (u_lsb != k) {
062        if ((res = mp_div_2d(&u, u_lsb - k, &u, NULL)) != MP_OKAY) {
063           goto LBL_V;
064        }
065     }
066
067     if (v_lsb != k) {
068        if ((res = mp_div_2d(&v, v_lsb - k, &v, NULL)) != MP_OKAY) {
069           goto LBL_V;
070        }
071     }
072
073     while (mp_iszero(&v) == 0) {
074        /* make sure v is the largest */
075        if (mp_cmp_mag(&u, &v) == MP_GT) {
076           /* swap u and v to make sure v is >= u */
077           mp_exch(&u, &v);
078        }
079
080        /* subtract smallest from largest */
081        if ((res = s_mp_sub(&v, &u, &v)) != MP_OKAY) {
```

```
082             goto LBL_V;
083         }
084
085         /* Divide out all factors of two */
086         if ((res = mp_div_2d(&v, mp_cnt_lsb(&v), &v, NULL)) != MP_OKAY) {
087             goto LBL_V;
088         }
089     }
090
091     /* multiply by 2**k which we divided out at the beginning */
092     if ((res = mp_mul_2d (&u, k, c)) != MP_OKAY) {
093         goto LBL_V;
094     }
095     c->sign = MP_ZPOS;
096     res = MP_OKAY;
097 LBL_V:mp_clear (&u);
098 LBL_U:mp_clear (&v);
099     return res;
100 }
101
```

This function makes use of the macros mp_iszero and mp_iseven. The former evaluates to 1 if the input mp_int is equivalent to the integer zero; otherwise, it evaluates to 0. The latter evaluates to 1 if the input mp_int represents a non-zero even integer; otherwise, it evaluates to 0. Note that just because mp_iseven may evaluate to 0 does not mean the input is odd; it could also be zero. The three trivial cases of inputs are handled on lines 24 through 30. After those lines, the inputs are assumed non-zero.

Lines 32 and 37 make local copies $u$ and $v$ of the inputs $a$ and $b$ respectively. At this point, the common factors of two must be divided out of the two inputs. The block starting at line 44 removes common factors of two by first counting the number of trailing zero bits in both. The local integer $k$ is used to keep track of how many factors of 2 are pulled out of both values. It is assumed that the number of factors will not exceed the maximum value of a C "int" data type[1].

At this point, there are no more common factors of two in the two values. The divisions by a power of two on lines 62 and 68 remove any independent factors of two such that both $u$ and $v$ are guaranteed to be an odd integer before hitting the

---

[1]Strictly speaking, no array in C may have more than entries than are accessible by an "int" so this is not a limitation.

main body of the algorithm. The while loop on line 73 performs the reduction of the pair until $v$ is equal to zero. The unsigned comparison and subtraction algorithms are used in place of the full signed routines since both values are guaranteed to be positive and the result of the subtraction is guaranteed to be non-negative.

## 9.2   Least Common Multiple

The least common multiple of a pair of integers is their product divided by their greatest common divisor. For two integers $a$ and $b$ the least common multiple is normally denoted as $[a, b]$ and numerically equivalent to $\frac{ab}{(a,b)}$. For example, if $a = 2 \cdot 2 \cdot 3 = 12$ and $b = 2 \cdot 3 \cdot 3 \cdot 7 = 126$, the least common multiple is $\frac{126}{(12,126)} = \frac{126}{6} = 21$.

The least common multiple arises often in coding theory and number theory. If two functions have periods of $a$ and $b$, respectively, they will collide, that is be in synchronous states, after only $[a, b]$ iterations. This is why, for example, random number generators based on Linear Feedback Shift Registers (LFSR) tend to use registers with periods that are co-prime (*e.g., the greatest common divisor is 1.*). Similarly, in number theory if a composite $n$ has two prime factors $p$ and $q$, then maximal order of any unit of $\mathbb{Z}/n\mathbb{Z}$ will be $[p - 1, q - 1]$.

---

Algorithm **mp_lcm**.
**Input**. mp_int $a$ and $b$
**Output**. The least common multiple $c = [a, b]$.

1. $c \leftarrow (a, b)$
2. $t \leftarrow a \cdot b$
3. $c \leftarrow \lfloor t/c \rfloor$
4. Return($MP\_OKAY$).

---

Figure 9.5: Algorithm mp_lcm

**Algorithm mp_lcm.** This algorithm computes the least common multiple of two mp_int inputs $a$ and $b$. It computes the least common multiple directly by dividing the product of the two inputs by their greatest common divisor (Figure 9.5).

```
File: bn_mp_lcm.c
018   /* computes least common multiple as |a*b|/(a, b) */
019   int mp_lcm (mp_int * a, mp_int * b, mp_int * c)
020   {
021     int     res;
022     mp_int  t1, t2;
023
024
025     if ((res = mp_init_multi (&t1, &t2, NULL)) != MP_OKAY) {
026       return res;
027     }
028
029     /* t1 = get the GCD of the two inputs */
030     if ((res = mp_gcd (a, b, &t1)) != MP_OKAY) {
031       goto LBL_T;
032     }
033
034     /* divide the smallest by the GCD */
035     if (mp_cmp_mag(a, b) == MP_LT) {
036       /* store quotient in t2 such that t2 * b is the LCM */
037       if ((res = mp_div(a, &t1, &t2, NULL)) != MP_OKAY) {
038         goto LBL_T;
039       }
040       res = mp_mul(b, &t2, c);
041     } else {
042       /* store quotient in t2 such that t2 * a is the LCM */
043       if ((res = mp_div(b, &t1, &t2, NULL)) != MP_OKAY) {
044         goto LBL_T;
045       }
046       res = mp_mul(a, &t2, c);
047     }
048
049     /* fix the sign to positive */
050     c->sign = MP_ZPOS;
051
052   LBL_T:
053     mp_clear_multi (&t1, &t2, NULL);
054     return res;
055   }
056
```

## 9.3  Jacobi Symbol Computation

To explain the Jacobi Symbol we will first discuss the Legendre function off which the Jacobi symbol is defined. The Legendre function computes whether an integer $a$ is a quadratic residue modulo an odd prime $p$. Numerically it is equivalent to equation 9.1.

$$a^{(p-1)/2} \equiv \begin{array}{ll} -1 & \text{if } a \text{ is a quadratic non-residue.} \\ 0 & \text{if } a \text{ divides } p. \\ 1 & \text{if } a \text{ is a quadratic residue.} \end{array} \pmod{p} \qquad (9.1)$$

**Theorem.** *Equation 9.1 correctly identifies the residue status of an integer a modulo a prime p.*

**Proof.** Adapted from [21, pp. 68]. An integer $a$ is a quadratic residue if the following equation has a solution.

$$x^2 \equiv a \pmod{p} \qquad (9.2)$$

Consider the following equation.

$$0 \equiv x^{p-1} - 1 \equiv \left\{ \left(x^2\right)^{(p-1)/2} - a^{(p-1)/2} \right\} + \left( a^{(p-1)/2} - 1 \right) \pmod{p} \qquad (9.3)$$

Whether equation 9.2 has a solution or not, equation 9.3 is always true. If $a^{(p-1)/2} - 1 \equiv 0 \pmod{p}$, then the quantity in the braces must be zero. By reduction,

$$\left(x^2\right)^{(p-1)/2} - a^{(p-1)/2} \equiv 0$$
$$\left(x^2\right)^{(p-1)/2} \equiv a^{(p-1)/2}$$
$$x^2 \equiv a \pmod{p} \qquad (9.4)$$

As a result there must be a solution to the quadratic equation, and in turn, $a$ must be a quadratic residue. If $a$ does not divide $p$ and $a$ is not a quadratic residue, then the only other value $a^{(p-1)/2}$ may be congruent to is $-1$ since

$$0 \equiv a^{p-1} - 1 \equiv (a^{(p-1)/2} + 1)(a^{(p-1)/2} - 1) \pmod{p} \qquad (9.5)$$

One of the terms on the right-hand side must be zero.

**QED**

### 9.3.1 Jacobi Symbol

The Jacobi symbol is a generalization of the Legendre function for any odd non–prime moduli $p$ greater than 2. If $p = \prod_{i=0}^{n} p_i$, then the Jacobi symbol $\left(\frac{a}{p}\right)$ is equal to the following equation.

$$\left(\frac{a}{p}\right) = \left(\frac{a}{p_0}\right)\left(\frac{a}{p_1}\right)\cdots\left(\frac{a}{p_n}\right) \tag{9.6}$$

By inspection if $p$ is prime, the Jacobi symbol is equivalent to the Legendre function. The following facts[2] will be used to derive an efficient Jacobi symbol algorithm. Where $p$ is an odd integer greater than two and $a, b \in \mathbb{Z}$, the following are true.

1. $\left(\frac{a}{p}\right)$ equals $-1$, $0$ or $1$.

2. $\left(\frac{ab}{p}\right) = \left(\frac{a}{p}\right)\left(\frac{b}{p}\right)$.

3. If $a \equiv b$ then $\left(\frac{a}{p}\right) = \left(\frac{b}{p}\right)$.

4. $\left(\frac{2}{p}\right)$ equals 1 if $p \equiv 1$ or $7 \pmod 8$. Otherwise, it equals $-1$.

5. $\left(\frac{a}{p}\right) \equiv \left(\frac{p}{a}\right) \cdot (-1)^{(p-1)(a-1)/4}$. More specifically, $\left(\frac{a}{p}\right) = \left(\frac{p}{a}\right)$ if $p \equiv a \equiv 1 \pmod 4$.

Using these facts if $a = 2^k \cdot a'$ then

$$\left(\frac{a}{p}\right) = \left(\frac{2^k}{p}\right)\left(\frac{a'}{p}\right)$$
$$= \left(\frac{2}{p}\right)^k \left(\frac{a'}{p}\right) \tag{9.7}$$

By fact five,

---

[2]See HAC [2, pp. 72-74] for further details.

$$\left(\frac{a}{p}\right) = \left(\frac{p}{a}\right) \cdot (-1)^{(p-1)(a-1)/4} \tag{9.8}$$

Subsequently, by fact three since $p \equiv (p \bmod a) \pmod{a}$, then

$$\left(\frac{a}{p}\right) = \left(\frac{p \bmod a}{a}\right) \cdot (-1)^{(p-1)(a-1)/4} \tag{9.9}$$

By putting both observations into equation 9.7, the following simplified equation is formed.

$$\left(\frac{a}{p}\right) = \left(\frac{2}{p}\right)^k \left(\frac{p \bmod a'}{a'}\right) \cdot (-1)^{(p-1)(a'-1)/4} \tag{9.10}$$

The value of $\left(\frac{p \bmod a'}{a'}\right)$ can be found using the same equation recursively. The value of $\left(\frac{2}{p}\right)^k$ equals 1 if $k$ is even; otherwise, it equals $\left(\frac{2}{p}\right)$. Using this approach the factors of $p$ do not have to be known. Furthermore, if $(a, p) = 1$, then the algorithm will terminate when the recursion requests the Jacobi symbol computation of $\left(\frac{1}{a'}\right)$, which is simply 1.

---

Algorithm **mp_jacobi**.
**Input**. mp_int $a$ and $p$, $a \geq 0$, $p \geq 3$, $p \equiv 1 \pmod{2}$
**Output**. The Jacobi symbol $c = \left(\frac{a}{p}\right)$.

---

1. If $a = 0$ then
   1.1 $c \leftarrow 0$
   1.2 Return($MP\_OKAY$).
2. If $a = 1$ then
   2.1 $c \leftarrow 1$
   2.2 Return($MP\_OKAY$).
3. $a' \leftarrow a$
4. $k \leftarrow 0$
5. While $a'.used > 0$ and $a'_0 \equiv 0 \pmod{2}$
   5.1 $k \leftarrow k + 1$
   5.2 $a' \leftarrow \lfloor a'/2 \rfloor$
6. If $k \equiv 0 \pmod{2}$ then
   6.1 $s \leftarrow 1$
7. else
   7.1 $r \leftarrow p_0 \pmod{8}$
   7.2 If $r = 1$ or $r = 7$ then
      7.2.1 $s \leftarrow 1$
   7.3 else
      7.3.1 $s \leftarrow -1$
8. If $p_0 \equiv a'_0 \equiv 3 \pmod{4}$ then
   8.1 $s \leftarrow -s$
9. If $a' \neq 1$ then
   9.1 $p' \leftarrow p \pmod{a'}$
   9.2 $s \leftarrow s \cdot \text{mp\_jacobi}(p', a')$
10. $c \leftarrow s$
11. Return($MP\_OKAY$).

---

Figure 9.6: Algorithm mp_jacobi

**Algorithm mp_jacobi.** This algorithm computes the Jacobi symbol for an arbitrary positive integer $a$ with respect to an odd integer $p$ greater than three. The algorithm is based on algorithm 2.149 of HAC [2, pp. 73] (Figure 9.6).

Steps 1 and 2 handle the trivial cases of $a = 0$ and $a = 1$, respectively. Step 5 determines the number of two factors in the input $a$. If $k$ is even, the term $\left(\frac{2}{p}\right)^k$ must always evaluate to one. If $k$ is odd, the term evaluates to one if $p_0$ is congruent to one or seven modulo eight; otherwise, it evaluates to $-1$. After the $\left(\frac{2}{p}\right)^k$ term is handled, the $(-1)^{(p-1)(a'-1)/4}$ is computed and multiplied against the current product $s$. The latter term evaluates to one if both $p$ and $a'$ are congruent to one modulo four; otherwise, it evaluates to negative one.

By step 9 if $a'$ does not equal one a recursion is required. Step 9.1 computes $p' \equiv p \pmod{a'}$ and will recurse to compute $\left(\frac{p'}{a'}\right)$, which is multiplied against the current Jacobi product.

File: bn_mp_jacobi.c

```
018    /* computes the jacobi c = (a | n) (or Legendre if n is prime)
019     * HAC pp. 73 Algorithm 2.149
020     */
021    int mp_jacobi (mp_int * a, mp_int * p, int *c)
022    {
023      mp_int   a1, p1;
024      int      k, s, r, res;
025      mp_digit residue;
026
027      /* if p <= 0 return MP_VAL */
028      if (mp_cmp_d(p, 0) != MP_GT) {
029         return MP_VAL;
030      }
031
032      /* step 1.  if a == 0, return 0 */
033      if (mp_iszero (a) == 1) {
034        *c = 0;
035        return MP_OKAY;
036      }
037
038      /* step 2.  if a == 1, return 1 */
039      if (mp_cmp_d (a, 1) == MP_EQ) {
040        *c = 1;
041        return MP_OKAY;
042      }
043
044      /* default */
045      s = 0;
046
047      /* step 3.  write a = a1 * 2**k  */
048      if ((res = mp_init_copy (&a1, a)) != MP_OKAY) {
```

```
049        return res;
050      }
051
052      if ((res = mp_init (&p1)) != MP_OKAY) {
053        goto LBL_A1;
054      }
055
056      /* divide out larger power of two */
057      k = mp_cnt_lsb(&a1);
058      if ((res = mp_div_2d(&a1, k, &a1, NULL)) != MP_OKAY) {
059         goto LBL_P1;
060      }
061
062      /* step 4.  if e is even set s=1 */
063      if ((k & 1) == 0) {
064        s = 1;
065      } else {
066        /* else set s=1 if p = 1/7 (mod 8) or s=-1 if p = 3/5 (mod 8) */
067        residue = p->dp[0] & 7;
068
069        if (residue == 1 || residue == 7) {
070          s = 1;
071        } else if (residue == 3 || residue == 5) {
072          s = -1;
073        }
074      }
075
076      /* step 5.  if p == 3 (mod 4) *and* a1 == 3 (mod 4) then s = -s */
077      if ( ((p->dp[0] & 3) == 3) && ((a1.dp[0] & 3) == 3)) {
078        s = -s;
079      }
080
081      /* if a1 == 1 we're done */
082      if (mp_cmp_d (&a1, 1) == MP_EQ) {
083        *c = s;
084      } else {
085        /* n1 = n mod a1 */
086        if ((res = mp_mod (p, &a1, &p1)) != MP_OKAY) {
087          goto LBL_P1;
088        }
089        if ((res = mp_jacobi (&p1, &a1, &r)) != MP_OKAY) {
```

```
090              goto LBL_P1;
091         }
092         *c = s * r;
093       }
094
095       /* done */
096       res = MP_OKAY;
097   LBL_P1:mp_clear (&p1);
098   LBL_A1:mp_clear (&a1);
099       return res;
100   }
101
```

As a matter of practicality the variable $a'$ as per the pseudo-code is represented by the variable $a1$ since the $'$ symbol is not valid for a C variable name character.

The two simple cases of $a = 0$ and $a = 1$ are handled at the very beginning to simplify the algorithm. If the input is non-trivial, the algorithm has to proceed and compute the Jacobi. The variable $s$ is used to hold the current Jacobi product. Note that $s$ is merely a C "int" data type since the values it may obtain are merely $-1$, 0 and 1.

After a local copy of $a$ is made, all the factors of two are divided out and the total stored in $k$. Technically, only the least significant bit of $k$ is required; however, it makes the algorithm simpler to follow to perform an addition. In practice, an exclusive-or and addition have the same processor requirements, and neither is faster than the other.

Lines 62 through 73 determine the value of $\left(\frac{2}{p}\right)^k$. If the least significant bit of $k$ is zero, then $k$ is even and the value is one. Otherwise, the value of $s$ depends on which residue class $p$ belongs to modulo eight. The value of $(-1)^{(p-1)(a'-1)/4}$ is computed and multiplied against $s$ on lines 76 through 91.

Finally, if $a1$ does not equal one, the algorithm must recurse and compute $\left(\frac{p'}{a'}\right)$.

## 9.4 Modular Inverse

The modular inverse of a number refers to the modular multiplicative inverse. For any integer $a$ such that $(a, p) = 1$ there exists another integer $b$ such that $ab \equiv 1 \pmod{p}$. The integer $b$ is called the multiplicative inverse of $a$ which is denoted as $b = a^{-1}$. Modular inversion is a well–defined operation for any finite ring or field, not just for rings and fields of integers. However, the former will be the matter of discussion.

The simplest approach is to compute the algebraic inverse of the input; that is, to compute $b \equiv a^{\Phi(p)-1}$. If $\Phi(p)$ is the order of the multiplicative subgroup modulo $p$, then $b$ must be the multiplicative inverse of $a$–the proof of which is trivial.

$$ab \equiv a \left( a^{\Phi(p)-1} \right) \equiv a^{\Phi(p)} \equiv a^0 \equiv 1 \ (\mathrm{mod}\ p) \qquad (9.11)$$

However, as simple as this approach may be it has two serious flaws. It requires that the value of $\Phi(p)$ be known, which if $p$ is composite requires all of the prime factors. This approach also is very slow as the size of $p$ grows.

A simpler approach is based on the observation that solving for the multiplicative inverse is equivalent to solving the linear Diophantine[3] equation.

$$ab + pq = 1 \qquad (9.12)$$

Where $a$, $b$, $p$, and $q$ are all integers. If such a pair of integers $\langle b, q \rangle$ exists, $b$ is the multiplicative inverse of $a$ modulo $p$. The extended Euclidean algorithm (Knuth [1, pp. 342]) can be used to solve such equations provided $(a, p) = 1$. However, instead of using that algorithm directly, a variant known as the binary Extended Euclidean algorithm will be used in its place. The binary approach is very similar to the binary greatest common divisor algorithm, except it will produce a full solution to the Diophantine equation.

---

[3]See LeVeque [21, pp. 40-43] for more information.

## 9.4.1 General Case

---

Algorithm **mp_invmod**.
**Input.** mp_int $a$ and $b$, $(a,b) = 1$, $p \geq 2$, $0 < a < p$.
**Output.** The modular inverse $c \equiv a^{-1} \pmod{b}$.

---

1. If $b \leq 0$ then return($MP\_VAL$).
2. If $b_0 \equiv 1 \pmod{2}$ then use algorithm fast_mp_invmod.
3. $x \leftarrow |a|, y \leftarrow b$
4. If $x_0 \equiv y_0 \equiv 0 \pmod{2}$ then return($MP\_VAL$).
5. $B \leftarrow 0, C \leftarrow 0, A \leftarrow 1, D \leftarrow 1$
6. While $u.used > 0$ and $u_0 \equiv 0 \pmod{2}$
   6.1 $u \leftarrow \lfloor u/2 \rfloor$
   6.2 If $(A.used > 0$ and $A_0 \equiv 1 \pmod{2})$ or $(B.used > 0$ and $B_0 \equiv 1 \pmod{2})$ then
      6.2.1 $A \leftarrow A + y$
      6.2.2 $B \leftarrow B - x$
   6.3 $A \leftarrow \lfloor A/2 \rfloor$
   6.4 $B \leftarrow \lfloor B/2 \rfloor$
7. While $v.used > 0$ and $v_0 \equiv 0 \pmod{2}$
   7.1 $v \leftarrow \lfloor v/2 \rfloor$
   7.2 If $(C.used > 0$ and $C_0 \equiv 1 \pmod{2})$ or $(D.used > 0$ and $D_0 \equiv 1 \pmod{2})$ then
      7.2.1 $C \leftarrow C + y$
      7.2.2 $D \leftarrow D - x$
   7.3 $C \leftarrow \lfloor C/2 \rfloor$
   7.4 $D \leftarrow \lfloor D/2 \rfloor$
8. If $u \geq v$ then
   8.1 $u \leftarrow u - v$
   8.2 $A \leftarrow A - C$
   8.3 $B \leftarrow B - D$
9. else
   9.1 $v \leftarrow v - u$
   9.2 $C \leftarrow C - A$
   9.3 $D \leftarrow D - B$
Continued on the next page.

---

---

Algorithm **mp_invmod** (continued).
**Input**. mp_int $a$ and $b$, $(a, b) = 1$, $p \geq 2$, $0 < a < p$.
**Output**. The modular inverse $c \equiv a^{-1} \pmod{b}$.

---

10. If $u \neq 0$ goto step 6.
11. If $v \neq 1$ return($MP\_VAL$).
12. While $C \leq 0$ do
    12.1 $C \leftarrow C + b$
13. While $C \geq b$ do
    13.1 $C \leftarrow C - b$
14. $c \leftarrow C$
15. Return($MP\_OKAY$).

---

Figure 9.7: Algorithm mp_invmod

**Algorithm mp_invmod.** This algorithm computes the modular multiplicative inverse of an integer $a$ modulo an integer $b$. It is a variation of the extended binary Euclidean algorithm from HAC [2, pp. 608], and it has been modified to only compute the modular inverse and not a complete Diophantine solution (Figure 9.7).

If $b \leq 0$, the modulus is invalid and MP_VAL is returned. Similarly if both $a$ and $b$ are even, there cannot be a multiplicative inverse for $a$ and the error is reported.

The astute reader will observe that steps 7 through 9 are very similar to the binary greatest common divisor algorithm mp_gcd. In this case, the other variables to the Diophantine equation are solved. The algorithm terminates when $u = 0$, in which case the solution is

$$Ca + Db = v \qquad (9.13)$$

If $v$, the greatest common divisor of $a$ and $b$, is not equal to one, then the algorithm will report an error as no inverse exists. Otherwise, $C$ is the modular inverse of $a$. The actual value of $C$ is congruent to, but not necessarily equal to, the ideal modular inverse, which should lie within $1 \leq a^{-1} < b$. Steps 12 and 13 adjust the inverse until it is in range. If the original input $a$ is within $0 < a < p$, then only a couple of additions or subtractions will be required to adjust the inverse.

```
File: bn_mp_invmod.c
018    /* hac 14.61, pp608 */
019    int mp_invmod (mp_int * a, mp_int * b, mp_int * c)
020    {
021      /* b cannot be negative */
022      if (b->sign == MP_NEG || mp_iszero(b) == 1) {
023        return MP_VAL;
024      }
025
026    #ifdef BN_FAST_MP_INVMOD_C
027      /* if the modulus is odd we can use a faster routine instead */
028      if (mp_isodd (b) == 1) {
029        return fast_mp_invmod (a, b, c);
030      }
031    #endif
032
033    #ifdef BN_MP_INVMOD_SLOW_C
034      return mp_invmod_slow(a, b, c);
035    #endif
036
037      return MP_VAL;
038    }
039
```

## Odd Moduli

When the modulus $b$ is odd the variables $A$ and $C$ are fixed and are not required to compute the inverse. In particular, by attempting to solve the Diophantine $Cb + Da = 1$, only $B$ and $D$ are required to find the inverse of $a$.

The algorithm fast_mp_invmod is a direct adaptation of algorithm mp_invmod with all steps involving either $A$ or $C$ removed. This optimization will halve the time required to compute the modular inverse.

```
File: bn_fast_mp_invmod.c
018    /* computes the modular inverse via binary extended euclidean algorithm,
019     * that is c = 1/a mod b
020     *
021     * Based on slow invmod except this is optimized for the case where b is
022     * odd as per HAC Note 14.64 on pp. 610
023     */
024    int fast_mp_invmod (mp_int * a, mp_int * b, mp_int * c)
```

```
025   {
026     mp_int   x, y, u, v, B, D;
027     int      res, neg;
028
029     /* 2. [modified] b must be odd    */
030     if (mp_iseven (b) == 1) {
031       return MP_VAL;
032     }
033
034     /* init all our temps */
035     if ((res = mp_init_multi(&x, &y, &u, &v, &B, &D, NULL)) != MP_OKAY) {
036       return res;
037     }
038
039     /* x == modulus, y == value to invert */
040     if ((res = mp_copy (b, &x)) != MP_OKAY) {
041       goto LBL_ERR;
042     }
043
044     /* we need y = |a| */
045     if ((res = mp_mod (a, b, &y)) != MP_OKAY) {
046       goto LBL_ERR;
047     }
048
049     /* 3. u=x, v=y, A=1, B=0, C=0,D=1 */
050     if ((res = mp_copy (&x, &u)) != MP_OKAY) {
051       goto LBL_ERR;
052     }
053     if ((res = mp_copy (&y, &v)) != MP_OKAY) {
054       goto LBL_ERR;
055     }
056     mp_set (&D, 1);
057
058   top:
059     /* 4.  while u is even do */
060     while (mp_iseven (&u) == 1) {
061       /* 4.1 u = u/2 */
062       if ((res = mp_div_2 (&u, &u)) != MP_OKAY) {
063         goto LBL_ERR;
064       }
065       /* 4.2 if B is odd then */
```

```
066        if (mp_isodd (&B) == 1) {
067          if ((res = mp_sub (&B, &x, &B)) != MP_OKAY) {
068            goto LBL_ERR;
069          }
070        }
071        /* B = B/2 */
072        if ((res = mp_div_2 (&B, &B)) != MP_OKAY) {
073          goto LBL_ERR;
074        }
075      }
076
077      /* 5.  while v is even do */
078      while (mp_iseven (&v) == 1) {
079        /* 5.1 v = v/2 */
080        if ((res = mp_div_2 (&v, &v)) != MP_OKAY) {
081          goto LBL_ERR;
082        }
083        /* 5.2 if D is odd then */
084        if (mp_isodd (&D) == 1) {
085          /* D = (D-x)/2 */
086          if ((res = mp_sub (&D, &x, &D)) != MP_OKAY) {
087            goto LBL_ERR;
088          }
089        }
090        /* D = D/2 */
091        if ((res = mp_div_2 (&D, &D)) != MP_OKAY) {
092          goto LBL_ERR;
093        }
094      }
095
096      /* 6.  if u >= v then */
097      if (mp_cmp (&u, &v) != MP_LT) {
098        /* u = u - v, B = B - D */
099        if ((res = mp_sub (&u, &v, &u)) != MP_OKAY) {
100          goto LBL_ERR;
101        }
102
103        if ((res = mp_sub (&B, &D, &B)) != MP_OKAY) {
104          goto LBL_ERR;
105        }
106      } else {
```

```
107        /* v - v - u, D = D - B */
108        if ((res = mp_sub (&v, &u, &v)) != MP_OKAY) {
109          goto LBL_ERR;
110        }
111
112        if ((res = mp_sub (&D, &B, &D)) != MP_OKAY) {
113          goto LBL_ERR;
114        }
115      }
116
117      /* if not zero goto step 4 */
118      if (mp_iszero (&u) == 0) {
119        goto top;
120      }
121
122      /* now a = C, b = D, gcd == g*v */
123
124      /* if v != 1 then there is no inverse */
125      if (mp_cmp_d (&v, 1) != MP_EQ) {
126        res = MP_VAL;
127        goto LBL_ERR;
128      }
129
130      /* b is now the inverse */
131      neg = a->sign;
132      while (D.sign == MP_NEG) {
133        if ((res = mp_add (&D, b, &D)) != MP_OKAY) {
134          goto LBL_ERR;
135        }
136      }
137      mp_exch (&D, c);
138      c->sign = neg;
139      res = MP_OKAY;
140
141 LBL_ERR:mp_clear_multi (&x, &y, &u, &v, &B, &D, NULL);
142      return res;
143    }
144
```

# 9.5 Primality Tests

A non-zero integer $a$ is said to be prime if it is not divisible by any other integer excluding one and itself. For example, $a = 7$ is prime since the integers $2 \ldots 6$ do not evenly divide $a$. By contrast, $a = 6$ is not prime since $a = 6 = 2 \cdot 3$.

Prime numbers arise in cryptography considerably as they allow finite fields to be formed. The ability to determine whether an integer is prime quickly has been a viable subject in cryptography and number theory for considerable time. The algorithms that will be presented are all probabilistic algorithms in that when they report an integer is composite it must be composite. However, when the algorithms report an integer is prime the algorithm may be incorrect.

As will be discussed, it is possible to limit the probability of error so well that for practical purposes the probability of error might as well be zero. For the purposes of these discussions, let $n$ represent the candidate integer of which the primality is in question.

## 9.5.1 Trial Division

Trial division means to attempt to evenly divide a candidate integer by small prime integers. If the candidate can be evenly divided, it obviously cannot be prime. By dividing by all primes $1 < p \le \sqrt{n}$, this test can actually prove whether an integer is prime. However, such a test would require a prohibitive amount of time as $n$ grows.

Instead of dividing by every prime, a smaller, more manageable set of primes may be used instead. By performing trial division with only a subset of the primes less than $\sqrt{n} + 1$, the algorithm cannot prove if a candidate is prime. However, often it can prove a candidate is not prime.

The benefit of this test is that trial division by small values is fairly efficient, especially when compared to the other algorithms that will be discussed shortly. The probability that this approach correctly identifies a composite candidate when tested with all primes up to $q$ is given by $1 - \frac{1.12}{ln(q)}$.

At approximately $q = 30$ the gain of performing further tests diminishes fairly quickly. At $q = 90$, further testing is generally not going to be of any practical use. In the case of LibTomMath the default limit $q = 256$ was chosen since it is not too high and will eliminate approximately 80% of all candidate integers. The constant **PRIME_SIZE** is equal to the number of primes in the test base. The array __prime_tab is an array of the first **PRIME_SIZE** prime numbers.

---

Algorithm **mp_prime_is_divisible**.
**Input**. mp_int $a$
**Output**. $c = 1$ if $n$ is divisible by a small prime, otherwise $c = 0$.

1. for $ix$ from 0 to $PRIME\_SIZE$ do
   1.1 $d \leftarrow n \pmod{\_prime\_tab_{ix}}$
   1.2 If $d = 0$ then
      1.2.1 $c \leftarrow 1$
      1.2.2 Return($MP\_OKAY$).
2. $c \leftarrow 0$
3. Return($MP\_OKAY$).

---

Figure 9.8: Algorithm mp_prime_is_divisible

**Algorithm mp_prime_is_divisible.** This algorithm attempts to determine if a candidate integer $n$ is composite by performing trial divisions (Figure 9.8).

```
File: bn_mp_prime_is_divisible.c
018   /* determines if an integers is divisible by one
019    * of the first PRIME_SIZE primes or not
020    *
021    * sets result to 0 if not, 1 if yes
022    */
023   int mp_prime_is_divisible (mp_int * a, int *result)
024   {
025     int      err, ix;
026     mp_digit res;
027
028     /* default to not */
029     *result = MP_NO;
030
031     for (ix = 0; ix < PRIME_SIZE; ix++) {
032       /* what is a mod LBL_prime_tab[ix] */
033       if ((err = mp_mod_d (a, ltm_prime_tab[ix], &res)) != MP_OKAY) {
034         return err;
035       }
036
037       /* is the residue zero? */
038       if (res == 0) {
039         *result = MP_YES;
040         return MP_OKAY;
```

```
041            }
042        }
043
044        return MP_OKAY;
045    }
046
```

The algorithm defaults to a return of 0 in case an error occurs. The values in the prime table are all specified to be in the range of an mp_digit. The table _prime_tab is defined in the following file.

```
File: bn_prime_tab.c
017    const mp_digit ltm_prime_tab[] = {
018        0x0002, 0x0003, 0x0005, 0x0007, 0x000B, 0x000D, 0x0011, 0x0013,
019        0x0017, 0x001D, 0x001F, 0x0025, 0x0029, 0x002B, 0x002F, 0x0035,
020        0x003B, 0x003D, 0x0043, 0x0047, 0x0049, 0x004F, 0x0053, 0x0059,
021        0x0061, 0x0065, 0x0067, 0x006B, 0x006D, 0x0071, 0x007F,
022    #ifndef MP_8BIT
023        0x0083,
024        0x0089, 0x008B, 0x0095, 0x0097, 0x009D, 0x00A3, 0x00A7, 0x00AD,
025        0x00B3, 0x00B5, 0x00BF, 0x00C1, 0x00C5, 0x00C7, 0x00D3, 0x00DF,
026        0x00E3, 0x00E5, 0x00E9, 0x00EF, 0x00F1, 0x00FB, 0x0101, 0x0107,
027        0x010D, 0x010F, 0x0115, 0x0119, 0x011B, 0x0125, 0x0133, 0x0137,
028
029        0x0139, 0x013D, 0x014B, 0x0151, 0x015B, 0x015D, 0x0161, 0x0167,
030        0x016F, 0x0175, 0x017B, 0x017F, 0x0185, 0x018D, 0x0191, 0x0199,
031        0x01A3, 0x01A5, 0x01AF, 0x01B1, 0x01B7, 0x01BB, 0x01C1, 0x01C9,
032        0x01CD, 0x01CF, 0x01D3, 0x01DF, 0x01E7, 0x01EB, 0x01F3, 0x01F7,
033        0x01FD, 0x0209, 0x020B, 0x021D, 0x0223, 0x022D, 0x0233, 0x0239,
034        0x023B, 0x0241, 0x024B, 0x0251, 0x0257, 0x0259, 0x025F, 0x0265,
035        0x0269, 0x026B, 0x0277, 0x0281, 0x0283, 0x0287, 0x028D, 0x0293,
036        0x0295, 0x02A1, 0x02A5, 0x02AB, 0x02B3, 0x02BD, 0x02C5, 0x02CF,
037
038        0x02D7, 0x02DD, 0x02E3, 0x02E7, 0x02EF, 0x02F5, 0x02F9, 0x0301,
039        0x0305, 0x0313, 0x031D, 0x0329, 0x032B, 0x0335, 0x0337, 0x033B,
040        0x033D, 0x0347, 0x0355, 0x0359, 0x035B, 0x035F, 0x036D, 0x0371,
041        0x0373, 0x0377, 0x038B, 0x038F, 0x0397, 0x03A1, 0x03A9, 0x03AD,
042        0x03B3, 0x03B9, 0x03C7, 0x03CB, 0x03D1, 0x03D7, 0x03DF, 0x03E5,
043        0x03F1, 0x03F5, 0x03FB, 0x03FD, 0x0407, 0x0409, 0x040F, 0x0419,
044        0x041B, 0x0425, 0x0427, 0x042D, 0x043F, 0x0443, 0x0445, 0x0449,
045        0x044F, 0x0455, 0x045D, 0x0463, 0x0469, 0x047F, 0x0481, 0x048B,
```

```
046
047        0x0493, 0x049D, 0x04A3, 0x04A9, 0x04B1, 0x04BD, 0x04C1, 0x04C7,
048        0x04CD, 0x04CF, 0x04D5, 0x04E1, 0x04EB, 0x04FD, 0x04FF, 0x0503,
049        0x0509, 0x050B, 0x0511, 0x0515, 0x0517, 0x051B, 0x0527, 0x0529,
050        0x052F, 0x0551, 0x0557, 0x055D, 0x0565, 0x0577, 0x0581, 0x058F,
051        0x0593, 0x0595, 0x0599, 0x059F, 0x05A7, 0x05AB, 0x05AD, 0x05B3,
052        0x05BF, 0x05C9, 0x05CB, 0x05CF, 0x05D1, 0x05D5, 0x05DB, 0x05E7,
053        0x05F3, 0x05FB, 0x0607, 0x060D, 0x0611, 0x0617, 0x061F, 0x0623,
054        0x062B, 0x062F, 0x063D, 0x0641, 0x0647, 0x0649, 0x064D, 0x0653
055    #endif
056    };
057
```

Note that there are two possible tables. When an mp_digit is 7-bits long, only the primes up to 127 may be included; otherwise, the primes up to 1619 are used. Note that the value of **PRIME_SIZE** is a constant dependent on the size of a mp_digit.

## 9.5.2  The Fermat Test

The Fermat test is probably one the oldest tests to have a non-trivial probability of success. It is based on the fact that if $n$ is in fact prime, then $a^n \equiv a \pmod{n}$ for all $0 < a < n$. The reason being that if $n$ is prime, the order of the multiplicative subgroup is $n - 1$. Any base $a$ must have an order that divides $n - 1$, and as such, $a^n$ is equivalent to $a^1 = a$.

If $n$ is composite then any given base $a$ does not have to have a period that divides $n - 1$, in which case it is possible that $a^n \not\equiv a \pmod{n}$. However, this test is not absolute as it is possible that the order of a base will divide $n - 1$, which would then be reported as prime. Such a base yields what is known as a Fermat pseudo-prime. Several integers known as Carmichael numbers will be a pseudo-prime to all valid bases. Fortunately, such numbers are extremely rare as $n$ grows in size.

---

Algorithm **mp_prime_fermat**.
**Input.** mp_int $a$ and $b$, $a \geq 2$, $0 < b < a$.
**Output.** $c = 1$ if $b^a \equiv b \pmod{a}$, otherwise $c = 0$.

1. $t \leftarrow b^a \pmod{a}$
2. If $t = b$ then
   2.1 $c = 1$
3. else
   3.1 $c = 0$
4. Return($MP\_OKAY$).

---

Figure 9.9: Algorithm mp_prime_fermat

**Algorithm mp_prime_fermat.** This algorithm determines whether an mp_int $a$ is a Fermat prime to the base $b$ or not. It uses a single modular exponentiation to determine the result (Figure 9.9).

```
File: bn_mp_prime_fermat.c
018   /* performs one Fermat test.
019    *
020    * If "a" were prime then b**a == b (mod a) since the order of
021    * the multiplicative sub-group would be phi(a) = a-1.  That means
022    * it would be the same as b**(a mod (a-1)) == b**1 == b (mod a).
023    *
024    * Sets result to 1 if the congruence holds, or zero otherwise.
025    */
026   int mp_prime_fermat (mp_int * a, mp_int * b, int *result)
027   {
028     mp_int   t;
029     int      err;
030
031     /* default to composite  */
032     *result = MP_NO;
033
034     /* ensure b > 1 */
035     if (mp_cmp_d(b, 1) != MP_GT) {
036        return MP_VAL;
037     }
038
039     /* init t */
```

```
040      if ((err = mp_init (&t)) != MP_OKAY) {
041        return err;
042      }
043
044      /* compute t = b**a mod a */
045      if ((err = mp_exptmod (b, a, a, &t)) != MP_OKAY) {
046        goto LBL_T;
047      }
048
049      /* is it equal to b? */
050      if (mp_cmp (&t, b) == MP_EQ) {
051        *result = MP_YES;
052      }
053
054      err = MP_OKAY;
055    LBL_T:mp_clear (&t);
056      return err;
057    }
058
```

### 9.5.3   The Miller-Rabin Test

The Miller-Rabin test is another primality test that has tighter error bounds than the Fermat test specifically with sequentially chosen candidate integers. The algorithm is based on the observation that if $n - 1 = 2^k r$ and if $b^r \not\equiv \pm 1$, then after up to $k - 1$ squarings the value must be equal to $-1$. The squarings are stopped as soon as $-1$ is observed. If the value of 1 is observed first, it means that some value not congruent to $\pm 1$ when squared equals one, which cannot occur if $n$ is prime.

---

Algorithm **mp_prime_miller_rabin**.
**Input.** mp_int $a$ and $b$, $a \geq 2$, $0 < b < a$.
**Output.** $c = 1$ if $a$ is a Miller-Rabin prime to the base $a$, otherwise $c = 0$.

---

1. $a' \leftarrow a - 1$
2. $r \leftarrow n1$
3. $c \leftarrow 0, s \leftarrow 0$
4. While $r.used > 0$ and $r_0 \equiv 0 \pmod 2$
   4.1 $s \leftarrow s + 1$
   4.2 $r \leftarrow \lfloor r/2 \rfloor$
5. $y \leftarrow b^r \pmod a$
6. If $y \not\equiv \pm 1$ then
   6.1 $j \leftarrow 1$
   6.2 While $j \leq (s - 1)$ and $y \not\equiv a'$
      6.2.1 $y \leftarrow y^2 \pmod a$
      6.2.2 If $y = 1$ then goto step 8.
      6.2.3 $j \leftarrow j + 1$
   6.3 If $y \not\equiv a'$ goto step 8.
7. $c \leftarrow 1$
8. Return($MP\_OKAY$).

---

Figure 9.10: Algorithm mp_prime_miller_rabin

**Algorithm mp_prime_miller_rabin.** This algorithm performs one trial round of the Miller-Rabin algorithm to the base $b$. It will set $c = 1$ if the algorithm cannot determine if $b$ is composite or $c = 0$ if $b$ is provably composite. The values of $s$ and $r$ are computed such that $a' = a - 1 = 2^s r$ (Figure 9.10).

If the value $y \equiv b^r$ is congruent to $\pm 1$, then the algorithm cannot prove if $a$ is composite or not. Otherwise, the algorithm will square $y$ up to $s - 1$ times stopping only when $y \equiv -1$. If $y^2 \equiv 1$ and $y \not\equiv \pm 1$, then the algorithm can report that $a$ is provably composite. If the algorithm performs $s - 1$ squarings and $y \not\equiv -1$, then $a$ is provably composite. If $a$ is not provably composite, then it is *probably* prime.

File: bn_mp_prime_miller_rabin.c

```
018    /* Miller-Rabin test of "a" to the base of "b" as described in
019     * HAC pp. 139 Algorithm 4.24
020     *
021     * Sets result to 0 if definitely composite or 1 if probably prime.
022     * Randomly the chance of error is no more than 1/4 and often
023     * very much lower.
```

```
024     */
025     int mp_prime_miller_rabin (mp_int * a, mp_int * b, int *result)
026     {
027       mp_int   n1, y, r;
028       int      s, j, err;
029
030       /* default */
031       *result = MP_NO;
032
033       /* ensure b > 1 */
034       if (mp_cmp_d(b, 1) != MP_GT) {
035          return MP_VAL;
036       }
037
038       /* get n1 = a - 1 */
039       if ((err = mp_init_copy (&n1, a)) != MP_OKAY) {
040         return err;
041       }
042       if ((err = mp_sub_d (&n1, 1, &n1)) != MP_OKAY) {
043         goto LBL_N1;
044       }
045
046       /* set 2**s * r = n1 */
047       if ((err = mp_init_copy (&r, &n1)) != MP_OKAY) {
048         goto LBL_N1;
049       }
050
051       /* count the number of least significant bits
052        * which are zero
053        */
054       s = mp_cnt_lsb(&r);
055
056       /* now divide n - 1 by 2**s */
057       if ((err = mp_div_2d (&r, s, &r, NULL)) != MP_OKAY) {
058         goto LBL_R;
059       }
060
061       /* compute y = b**r mod a */
062       if ((err = mp_init (&y)) != MP_OKAY) {
063         goto LBL_R;
064       }
```

```
065     if ((err = mp_exptmod (b, &r, a, &y)) != MP_OKAY) {
066       goto LBL_Y;
067     }
068
069     /* if y != 1 and y != n1 do */
070     if (mp_cmp_d (&y, 1) != MP_EQ && mp_cmp (&y, &n1) != MP_EQ) {
071       j = 1;
072       /* while j <= s-1 and y != n1 */
073       while ((j <= (s - 1)) && mp_cmp (&y, &n1) != MP_EQ) {
074         if ((err = mp_sqrmod (&y, a, &y)) != MP_OKAY) {
075           goto LBL_Y;
076         }
077
078         /* if y == 1 then composite */
079         if (mp_cmp_d (&y, 1) == MP_EQ) {
080           goto LBL_Y;
081         }
082
083         ++j;
084       }
085
086       /* if y != n1 then composite */
087       if (mp_cmp (&y, &n1) != MP_EQ) {
088         goto LBL_Y;
089       }
090     }
091
092     /* probably prime now */
093     *result = MP_YES;
094   LBL_Y:mp_clear (&y);
095   LBL_R:mp_clear (&r);
096   LBL_N1:mp_clear (&n1);
097     return err;
098   }
099
```

# Exercises

[3]    Devise and implement a method of computing the modular inverse of multiple numbers at once, by using a single inversion.

[2]    Look up and implement the "Almost Inverse" algorithm for integers. (Hint: Look in the IACR Crypto'95 proceedings.)

[4]    Devise and implement a method of generating random primes that avoids the need for trial division.

[4]    Devise and implement a method of generating large primes which are provably prime. Hint: Use a constructive approach to avoid the need for primality proof algorithms such as ECCP or AKS.

# Bibliography

[1]    Donald Knuth, *The Art of Computer Programming*, Third Edition, Volume Two, Seminumerical Algorithms, Addison-Wesley, 1998.

[2]    A. Menezes, P. van Oorschot, S. Vanstone, *Handbook of Applied Cryptography*, CRC Press, 1996.

[3]    Michael Rosing, *Implementing Elliptic Curve Cryptography*, Manning Publications, 1999.

[4]    Paul G. Comba, *Exponentiation Cryptosystems on the IBM PC*. IBM Systems Journal 29(4): 526-538, 1990.

[5]    Andre Weimerskirch and Christof Paar, *Generalizations of the Karatsuba Algorithm for Polynomial Multiplication*, Submitted to Design, Codes and Cryptography, March 2002.

[6]    Paul Barrett, *Implementing the Rivest Shamir and Adleman Public Key Encryption Algorithm on a Standard Digital Signal Processor*, Advances in Cryptology, Crypto '86, Springer-Verlag.

[7]    P. L. Montgomery. *Modular multiplication without trial division*. Mathematics of Computation, 44(170):519-521, April 1985.

[8]    Chae Hoon Lim and Pil Joong Lee, *Generating Efficient Primes for Discrete Log Cryptosystems*, POSTECH Information Research Laboratories.

[9]    J. Daemen and R. Govaerts and J. Vandewalle, *Block ciphers based on Modular Arithmetic*, State and Progress in the Research of Cryptography, 1993, pp. 80-89.

[10]     R.L. Rivest, A. Shamir, L. Adleman, *A Method for Obtaining Digital Signatures and Public-Key Cryptosystems.*

[11]     Whitfield Diffie, Martin E. Hellman, *New Directions in Cryptography*, IEEE Transactions on Information Theory, 1976.

[12]     IEEE Standard for Binary Floating-Point Arithmetic (ANSI/IEEE Std 754-1985).

[13]     GNU Multiple Precision (GMP), www.swox.com/gmp/.

[14]     Multiple Precision Integer Library (MPI), Michael Fromberger, http://thayer.dartmouth.edu/~sting/mpi/.

[15]     OpenSSL Cryptographic Toolkit, http://openssl.org.

[16]     Large Integer Package, http://home.hetnet.nl/~ecstr/LIP.zip.

[17]     JTC1/SC22/WG14, ISO/IEC 9899:1999, "A draft rationale for the C99 standard."

[18]     The Sun Java Website, http://java.sun.com/.

[19]     Doklady Akad. Nauk SSSR 145, 1962, pp. 293–294, Reference due to Donald Knuth, The Art of Computer Programming, Volume Two, Third Edition, p.295.

[20]     Captured from Wikipedia, May 18th 2006, http://en.wikipedia.org/wiki/Polynomial_interpolation.

[21]     William J. LeVeque, Fundamentals of Number Theory, 1977, Dover Publication, New York.

# Index

$k$-ary exponentiation, 195

Absolute value, 42
Addition, 54
    single digit, 232
Algorithm fast_mp_montgomery_reduce,
    168
Algorithm fast_mult, 105
Algorithm fast_s_mp_mul_digs, 100
Algorithm fast_s_mp_sqr, 134
Algorithm mp_2expt, 214
Algorithm mp_abs, 42
Algorithm mp_add, 64
Algorithm mp_add_d, 232
Algorithm mp_clamp, 31
Algorithm mp_clear, 22
Algorithm mp_cmp, 50
Algorithm mp_cmp_mag, 48
Algorithm mp_copy, 36
Algorithm mp_div(), 221
Algorithm mp_div_2, 73
Algorithm mp_div_2d, 85
Algorithm mp_div_d, 238
Algorithm mp_dr_is_modulus, 183
Algorithm mp_dr_reduce, 179
Algorithm mp_dr_setup, 182
Algorithm mp_expt_d, 194
Algorithm mp_exptmod, 199
Algorithm mp_gcd, 259

Algorithm mp_grow, 25
Algorithm mp_init, 20
Algorithm mp_init_copy, 40
Algorithm mp_init_multi, 29
Algorithm mp_init_size, 27
Algorithm mp_invmod, 273
Algorithm mp_jacobi, 268
Algorithm mp_karasuba_mul, 111
Algorithm mp_karatsuba_sqr, 139
Algorithm mp_lcm, 263
Algorithm mp_lshd, 76
Algorithm mp_mod_2d, 88
Algorithm mp_montgomery_reduce, 163
Algorithm mp_montgomery_setup, 174
Algorithm mp_mul, 126
Algorithm mp_mul_2, 70
Algorithm mp_mul_2d, 82
Algorithm mp_mul_d, 235
Algorithm mp_n_root, 242
Algorithm mp_prime_fermat, 283
Algorithm mp_prime_is_divisible, 280
Algorithm mp_prime_miller_rabin, 285
Algorithm mp_rand, 246
Algorithm mp_read_radix, 249
Algorithm mp_reduce, 153
Algorithm mp_reduce_2k, 184
Algorithm mp_reduce_2k_setup, 186
Algorithm mp_reduce_is_2k, 188
Algorithm mp_reduce_setup, 157

Algorithm mp_rshd, 79

Algorithm mp_set, 45

Algorithm mp_set_int, 46

Algorithm mp_sqr, 144

Algorithm mp_sub, 67

Algorithm mp_toom_mul, 117

Algorithm mp_toradix, 252

Algorithm mp_zero, 41

Algorithm s_mp_add, 55

Algorithm s_mp_exptmod, 203

Algorithm s_mp_mul_digs, 93

Algorithm s_mp_sqr, 130

Algorithm s_mp_sub, 60

Algorithms

    calling convention, *see* Argument
        passing

    inputs and outputs, 6

    reduction, 147

    single digit helpers, 231

Aliases, *see* pointer aliases

Angled brackets <>, 53

Argument passing, 17–18

Arithmetic, 53

    addition and subtraction, 54

    bit shifting, 69

    by powers of two, 81

    digit shifting, 69

    division by $2^b$, 85

    division by $x$, 78

    division by two, 72

    fixed point, 148

    high level addition, 63

    high level subtraction, 66

    low level addition, 54

    low level subtraction, 59

    multiplication by $2^b$, 82

    multiplication by $x$, 75

    multiplication by two, 69

    polynomial operations, 75

    Remainder of division by $2^b$, 88

Arithmetic on polynomials, 3

ASCII map

    lower, 248

Asymptotic Running Time of Polyno-
    mial Basis Multiplication, 108

Barrett algorithm, 153

Barrett modular exponentiation, 203

Barrett reduction, 2, 148, 189

    choosing a radix point, 150

    setup, 156

    trimming the quotient, 151

    trimming the residue, 152

Barrett, Paul, 97

big-Oh, 7

Bignum math, 2

Bit shifting, 53

bn_mp_lshd(), 76

Brackets

    in mathematical expressions, 6

C programming language

    Data types, 2

Carmichael numbers, 282

Code, *see* Source code

Code Base, 10–11

Comba method, 94

    fixup algorithm, 98

    multiplication with, 97

    squaring with, 133

Comba, Paul, 97

Comparing

    modular reduction algorithms, 189

    signed comparisons, 50

    unsigned comparisons, 47

Comparisons, *see* Comparing

Constants, 44
  setting large, 46
  setting small, 44
Cryptography
  public key, 148, 191, 245

Data types
  definition, 13
  high precision floating point, 2
  precision notation, 6
Destinations
  allowing arguments sources to be, 18
Diffie-Hellman, 2, 148
Digit shifting, 53
Diminished radix algorithm, 175, 189
Division
  by power of two, 85
  integer, with remainder, 217
  normalized integers, 220
  quotient estimation, 219
  radix-$\beta$ with remainder, 221
  remainder of division by power of two, 88
  single digit, 237
Downloading
  LibTomMath library, 12

ECC, *see* Elliptic Curve Cryptography
Elliptic curve cryptography, 3
Errors
  trapping runtime, 18
Exponentiation, 203
  $k$-ary, 195
  Barrett modular, 203
  modular, 198
  overview, 191
  power of two, 214

  single digit, 193
  sliding window, 197
Expressions
  precision notation, 6

Fast multiplication, 105
fast_mp_invmod(), 275
fast_mp_montgomery_reduce(), 169
fast_s_mp_mul_digs(), 101
fast_s_mp_sqr(), 135
Fixed point arithmetic, 148
Floating point math, *see* high precision floating point
Formatted Representations, 247

GCC
  pointer arithmetic, 39
GMP library, 10, 11
GNU C Compiler, 9
Goals
  of LibTomMath, 9–12
Greatest common divisor, 255, 256

Handbook of Applied Cryptography, 4
Header files, 13
Horner's method, 108

Integer
  comparing signed, 50
  comparing unsigned, 47
  division, 218
  division with remainder, 217
  greatest common divisor, 255
  Jacobi symbol, 265
  least common multiple, 263
  modular inverse, 271
  negation, 43

Jacobi symbol computation, 265

Karatsuba
    multiplication, 91, 109
    squaring, 138

Least common multiple, 263
Left to Right Exponentiation, 192
Legendre function, 265
Libraries
    writing useful source code, 13
LibTom, xv
    Public Domain, xv
LibTomMath, 9
LibTomMath library, 4
Linear feedback shift register, 263
LIP library, 10, 11, 17

Maintenance Algorithms, 24
Measuring
    algorithms' efficiency, 7
Memory management
    algorithms, 15
        multiple precision algorithm over-
        head, 3
Miller-Rabin test, 284
Mirror points, 108
Modular exponentiation, 198
Modular inversion, 271
Modular reduction
    algorithm compared, 189
    Barrett algorithm, 153
    Barrett reduction, 148
    diminished radix algorithm, 175
    Montgomery reduction, 158
    overview, 147
Modular residue, 147
Modularity of projects, 13
Montgomery reduction, 158, 189
    baseline, 162

digit based, 160
    Faster "Comba", 167
mp_2expt(), 214
mp_abs(), 42
mp_add(), 65
mp_add_d(), 232
mp_clamp(), 32
mp_clear(), 23
mp_cmp(), 51
mp_cmp_mag(), 49
mp_copy(), 36
mp_digit, 6
mp_div(), 224
mp_div_2(), 73
mp_div_2d(), 85
mp_div_d(), 238
mp_dr_is_modulus(), 183
mp_dr_reduce(), 180
mp_dr_setup(), 182
mp_expt_d(), 194
mp_exptmod(), 14, 199
mp_gcd(), 260
mp_grow(), 25
mp_init(), 21
mp_init_copy(), 40
mp_init_multi(), 29
mp_init_size(), 27
mp_int, 5, 16
mp_int structure, 15–17
    assigning value, 35
    augmenting precision, 24
    clamping, 31
    clearing, 22
    copying, 35
    creating a clone (copy), 39
    initializing, 19
    initializing variable precision, 27
    zeroing, 41

mp_invmod(), 275
mp_jacobi(), 269
mp_karatsuba_mul(), 112
mp_karatsuba_sqr(), 140
mp_lcm(), 264
MP_MEM, 18
mp_mod_2d(), 88
mp_montgomery_reduce(), 164
mp_montgomery_setup(), 174
mp_mul(), 127
mp_mul_2(), 71
mp_mul_2d(), 83
mp_mul_d(), 236
mp_n_root(), 242
MP_NEG, 16
mp_neg(), 44
MP_OKAY, 18
mp_prime_fermat(), 283
mp_prime_is_divisible(), 280
mp_prime_miller_rabin(), 285
mp_rand(), 246
mp_read_radix(), 249
mp_reduce(), 154
mp_reduce_2k(), 184
mp_reduce_2k_setup(), 186
mp_reduce_is_2k(), 188
mp_reduce_setup(), 157
mp_rshd(), 79
mp_set(), 45
mp_set_int(), 46
mp_sqr(), 144
mp_sub(), 68
mp_toom_mul(), 119
mp_toradix(), 253
MP_VAL, 18
mp_word, 6
mp_zero(), 41
MP_ZPOS, 16

MPI library, 10, 11
MSVC
    pointer arithmetic, 39
Multiple integer
    initialization and clearing, 29
Multiple Precision Arithmetic
    Initialization and clearing, 19
    notation, 5–7
    overview, 1–4
Multiple precision integers, 14–17
Multiplication
    baseline multiplication, 92
    by power of two, 82
    Comba method, 97
    Karatsuba, 91, 109
    polynomial basis, 107
    polynomial basis squaring, 138
    signed, 126
    single digit, 235
    squaring, 128
    the multipliers, 91
    Toom-Cook Algorithm, 116
Multiplication algorithm mp_mul(), 9

Nested statements, 39
Newton-Raphson approximation, 241

Open source
    LibTom Projects, xv
OpenSSL library, 10
Optimizations, 11–12

Pointer aliases, 38
Pointer arithmetic, 39
Polynomial basis, 3
    multiplication, 107
    squaring, 138
Portability, 12

Power of two, 214
precision, 3
Primality tests, 279
    Fermat test, 282
    Miller-Rabin test, 284
    trial division, 279
Prime numbers
    tests, 279
pseudo–code, 4
Public key cryptography, 2

Radix Point, 111
Radix-n input
    reading, 247
Random number generation, 245
Representations
    formatted, 247
Return values, 18
Rose, Greg, xviii
RSA Algorithm, 2
RSA algorithm, 148, 191
Runtime errors, 18

s_mp_add(), 56
s_mp_exptmod(), 207
s_mp_mul_digs(), 95
s_mp_sqr(), 131
s_mp_sub(), 61
Scoring system
    book's exercises, 8
Sign manipulation, 42
Signed addition, *see* High level addition
Signed comparisons, 50
Signed subtraction, *see* High level sub-
    traction
Single digit
    division, 237
    exponentiation, 193

multiplication, 235
    root extraction, 241
Sliding Window Exponentiation, 198
source, *see* Source code
Source code
    header files, 13
    LibTomMath, xv, 10
    modular design, 13
    precision data types in, 6
    return values, 18
    writing useful libraries, 13
Speed
    measuring algorithms', 7
Squaring
    Comba method, 133
    high level, 144
    Karatsuba, 138
    polynomial basis, 138
St Denis, Tom, xvii, 10
Stability, 12
Subtraction, 54
    single digit, 232

TomsFastMath project, 12
Toom-Cook
    multiplication, 116
    squaring, 143

Variables
    algorithm inputs and outputs, 6

XFREE, 24
XMALLOC, 21
XREALLOC, 26

CPSIA information can be obtained at www.ICGtesting.com
Printed in the USA
BVOW09s2011160614

356541BV00009B/109/P